Era of Faith

by Kurt Koppetsch

Era of Faith

BY THE POWER OF THE HOLY SPIRIT
– FAITH FOR QUALITY OF LIFE
– HOPE FOR A NEW BEGINNING
– LOVE FOR GOD AND PEOPLE

– Kurt Koppetsch

Prayer for Unity

Praise the Lord.
Praise the Lord, people of God.
Nations of the world, proclaim the Word:
The Lord is God. The Lord is One.

We are one with the Lord in freedom,
We are one with the Lord in truth,
We are one with the Lord in justice,
We are one with the Lord in peace.

Praise the Lord.
Praise the Lord, people of God.
Nations of the world, proclaim the Word:
The Lord is God. The Lord is One.

– Amen.

Era of Faith

by Kurt Koppetsch

SHEPHERD NEWS TRUST, INC.
WEST BOYLSTON, MASSACHUSETTS 01583

Library of Congress Control Number: 2004090751

Subject identification recommended by author:
1. Religion. 2. Spirituality. 3. Meditation. 4. Contemplation.

ISBN 0-933663-01-3   Printed in the United States of America

To Tante

Her life of giving and caring made God's love real.

Preface

The Era of Faith is the story of mission and goals according to God's plan for human life. The mission is to fill spiritual needs by means of the connection with God. The goal is to experience the presence of God in all that we do.

Once spiritual needs are met, the physical needs will also be met. God is out in the world. Christ says: "Come and see!" (John 1:39) He wants us to see God in him. And God wants us to experience the spiritual connection as the permanent bond with the Creator of all that is and in whom we have our true being. The Era of Faith is God's gift of hope for a new beginning to make our life spiritually complete.

To know God as our Father in Heaven is to love, honor, and respect him on Earth with the same intensity and commitment that Jesus Christ demonstrated during his earthly life. Jesus gave the world a foretaste of spiritual things to come when he told the Samaritan woman: "God is Spirit, and those who worship him must worship in spirit and truth." (John 4:24) Within this context of spirituality, the Holy Spirit widens our horizons for the purpose of seeing God, whom we now love, honor, and respect.

God is providing ample time for reflection and study of all the aspects of our relationship with him. We search his will. We examine the purpose of our creation. And we plan our behavior around the purpose for our creation: As children of God we are his voice and his hands in the world. God initiates this process of learning about him by setting the stage for a new beginning. The Era of Faith is the new beginning. It is absolute reality in which God supports our lives with his presence. This new beginning is his permanent gift by the power of the Holy Spirit for all generations to come. We all have now the opportunity to see God. This was precisely what Job experienced about 3,500 years ago when God came to him personally. An awestruck Job experienced eternal truth as the presence of the all-powerful Creator: "I heard of thee by the hearing of the ear, but now my eye sees thee." (Job 42:5) God was speaking with Job face to face!

This demonstrates that God calls each of us in person. He personally invites us to represent him and be "the salt of the Earth" and his "light of the world." Our light therefore must "so shine before men, that they may see your good works and give glory to your Father who is in Heaven." (Matthew 5:16) Faithful believers heed his call and summarily yield to the authority of God and submit to his guidance. God subsequently empowers the faithful by the power of the Holy Spirit with faith, hope, and love. Together we then build fortresses of truth from which the light of God in Christ shines piercingly bright and penetrates even the farthest corners in the world of doubt and disbelief. The Era of Faith is God's way of helping us to make the world a better place. God invites us to work with him "to take back what is his own" by witnessing to the world that the transformation of life from imperfection to perfection is by grace in faith! The Word of God defines the "perfect life" as the spiritual life in union with God.

In this book, Pilgrim T. Homosapien is modern man. He is God's prophet to all people in the Era of Faith. He represents humanity in the universe as the creative energy of God. Pilgrim is constantly moving about to make things perfect. He helps people appreciate the Word of God as the most powerful resource in solving personal and social problems.

Pilgrim T. Homosapien follows the role model of Jesus Christ for trust in God and trust in relationships with people. Pilgrim loves God. He likes people. He submerges all selfish desires in the Will of God.

Pilgrim is a faithful steward of the love of God. He lives to the glory of God. His mission in life is to help people. His happiness is the happiness of the other person. His presence inspires and transforms the lives of the people around him. Chaos vanishes and order prevails. Hatred loses its sting. Ignorance turns into determination to excel in learning all the truth about God.

Pilgrim lives by the motto that there is always room to improve. His top agenda is *corrective action*. And *change* is second nature to him when relationships are threatened.

Kurt Koppetsch

West Boylston, Massachusetts, USA
Anno Domini 2003

Introduction

Faith, hope, and love are gifts from God. They are manifestations of excellence, goodness, and power. Faith, hope, and love are spiritual, miraculous, and timeless.

Faith, hope, and love personify spiritual energy. These divine virtues are heavenly food for thought.

Faith, hope, and love are precious gifts because God is letting us draw from his reservoir of power all the necessary spiritual resources to overcome the stress and pressure in an uncertain world. Indeed, God is blessing every pilgrim to make spiritual life *the* story of success in the modern world.

In the context of a successful spiritual life,

Faith is a timeless relationship of trust with the living God—God is with us.

Hope is the lens to see God in all that we do.

Love is life with God by the power of the Holy Spirit.

Faith, hope, and love are reliable gifts. They are true friends in our pilgrimage. Life, happiness, and peace are contingent on these virtues.

Let us now celebrate life in the light of faith, hope, and love as ordained by God for the Era of Faith.

We thank God for his precious gifts!

Acknowledgment

The Era of Faith is the work of God by the power of the Holy Spirit. The Holy Spirit is implementing the Word of God as the new Covenant of Christian Love. God is commanding change in human attitudes and behavior toward love for God and neighbor. And the Covenant of Christian Love is his way for installing the Era of Faith. The drama of human salvation unfolds in three divine acts.

God sees no need to amend the workings of creation; he sees a definite need for people to change and align human behavior with his will and purpose.

For 2,000 years God has been forbearing as people have debated and argued about his entering the world in the person of Jesus Christ to help his human creation with life in his presence. Much of God's effort, however, went for naught during this time. Generations of people in the last 2,000 years have discussed God without making a commitment of faith to live according to God's Way. Our ancestors overruled God by telling him what their expectations were. We too are so slow in learning to faithfully accept his will. We too fail to carry out his purpose in these critical times of worldly disarray.

Now God is speaking again in these modern times by the power of the Holy Spirit. God is giving us another chance to accept his Word as the sole authority above all human intelligence, deliberations, and actions. I have been fortunate to be an instrument of the Holy Spirit in preparing this writing on the Era of Faith and speaking the Word of God as his servant in these crucial times. God has provided me a generous assortment of people. Some have conveyed their opinions more vociferously than others. This only strengthens my conviction that life on Earth is a continuous struggle.

But I have also found answers for persevering by doing what we believe is right and what others accept as just. The Golden

Rule prevailed in times of conflict and controversy. I have seen that severe tests in life are blessings that refine the hidden and inner qualities of true life. Overpowering all manner of hardships are friends ready and willing to help. In all these experiences I have also met people in desperate need of hope. I have seen people of all walks of life struggle to cope in their specific life situations—some suffering more than others. Their needs must become our concern. We pray for them to know God, and we pray for them to find security in the presence of God as the only relationship of value.

To family and friends who helped me write *Era of Faith* I say, "Thank you for support and encouragement." A separate word of appreciation is indeed appropriate to my editor, Mr. Darrell Turner.

Kurt Koppetsch

Anno Domini 2006

Editor's Preface

Kurt Koppetsch is a man with ideas, and he wants to share them with the rest of the world. His seven decades of experience, both in postwar Germany and the United States, have provoked him to think about how God works in the modern world. It has also saddened him to see how people, including many Christians, stubbornly ignore the promptings of the Holy Spirit to live God's way.

"Era of Faith" describes Mr. Koppetsch's pilgrimage to see God's activities behind such phenomena as economic competition, war, religious strife, and tensions in family life. In each situation, he finds biblical parallels that show how humanity hasn't changed fundamentally over the centuries. At the same time, he brings a message of hope as he shares his perspectives on how God is acting in what Mr. Koppetsch describes as the modern Era of Faith.

Mr. Koppetsch's style of communication may seem a bit challenging at times, but I encourage the reader to press on. The writings of people such as Soren Kierkegaard and Blaise Pascal and even the Apostle Paul can be challenging at times, but they yield many treasures for the discerning reader.

My hope, and the writer's hope, is that this book will inspire you to see how God may be working in your own life in the modern Era of Faith.

Darrell Turner

Anno Domini 2006

Table of Contents

Invocation v
Preface xi
Introduction xv
Acknowledgment xvii
Editor's Preface xix
Table of Contents xxi
Key Words xxxi

PROLOGUE

Chapter 1
The Word of God

– The creation of the universe 3
– The creation of life 5
– The creation of human spirituality 8
– The creation of covenants 10
– The creation of a new world order 13
– The creation of the Christian Covenant
   of Love 17
– The creation of the Era of Faith 19
Grace 28

ACT I
THE GIFT OF FAITH

Chapter 2

The new faith versus old faith presumptions 31
– Background 31
– The relation of the new faith to the old 36
– Comparative reality 38
– The manifestation of the new faith 44
The spiritual connection in the new faith 46

ACT II
THE CONFLICT OF THE NEW FAITH WITH THE OLD

Chapter 3

Conflict over "faith promise"... 53
Confrontation over "Jesus Christ the Supreme Revelation
of God".. 57

ACT III
THE NEW REALITY

Chapter 4

The Holy Spirit

  – Background.. 61
  – The Holy Spirit is God revealed in Jesus Christ...... 63
  – The Holy Spirit saves us from evil........................... 63
  – The Holy Spirit is God's sole source for the
    spiritual connection... 66
  – The Holy Spirit is the presiding authority on faith
    relationships 70
  – The Holy Spirit is the presiding authority
    on history 73
  – The Holy Spirit is God's teacher on truth and
    history 77
  – The Holy Spirit leads us to God for every need...... 79
  – The Holy Spirit and Sundays 85
  – Baptism with the Holy Spirit 92
  – The Holy Spirit in everyday life 94
  – The Holy Spirit works the transformation of life...... 97
  – The Holy Spirit helps us become God's friends...... 99
  – The Holy Spirit is freedom 102
  – The Holy Spirit is our future of promise...................102

Christianity
  – Key words 103
  – Prelude.. 104
  – The call 106
  – The mission 111
  – The action... 119
  – The forum 122
  – The finale 128
The Era of Faith
  – Key words.. 128
  – Background 129
  – The historic "from" in the Era of Faith.......................... 129
  – The prelude to the Era of Faith — the initial gift
    of faith.. 131
  – God wants us, and we need God.................................... 132
  – The unity of God and people.. 133
  – Opposition to the Era of Faith.. 133
  – Our love for God and people makes love the
    common ground 134
  – Jesus Christ reveals spiritual truth for the
    Era of Faith.. 134
  – Jesus Christ tells us about his Father........................... 135
The From/to method for spiritual fulfillment
  – The method 135
  – The process... 136
  – The action.. 140
  – Illustration I: Social reform 140
  – Illustration II: Literature reform 141
  – The result 145
  – Who benefits from the From/to method for
    spiritual fulfillment?.. 145

ACT III
DIVERSITY

Chapter 5

Key ingredient in the melting pot for faith,
hope, and love 148
One God, one word, one voice 150
Diversity perspectives 152
Storm clouds on the horizon 153
Unity through diversity 154
Diversity of world religions 155
Current diversity assessment 155

ACT III
FOCUS ON THE NEW REALITY

Chapter 6

Family

 – God's contributions to families are faith,
   hope, and love 157
 – The human response to God's contributions 169

Family and work—the spiritual perspective

 – Assessment of everyday situations 171
 – Spiritual blindness 174
 – Priorities 176
 – Goals in life 178
 – At the crossroads of life 181
 – Divine truth versus human ambition 184
 – The grand finale: cosmic victory 187

Economics

 – Preface 188
 – The spiritual perspective on the economy and
   economics 189

   – Modern economics 191
   – Global economics 196
   – The human side of economics 199
   – The renaissance of manufacturing in America 206
Education
   – God's contributions to education are truth and
       spiritual values 210
   – The human response to God's contributions 213
Relationships
   – God's contributions to relationships are
       trust and respect 216
   – The human response to God's contributions 218

ACT III
AMERICA IS GOD'S COUNTRY

Chapter 7
America And Americans 221
A modern phenomenon 221
Spiritual versus secular conflicts 222
The ever-present God 223
God's faithful remnant 224
Unity through diversity II 225

ACT III
ILLUSTRATIONS OF SPIRITUAL REALITIES

Chapter 8
God is out in the world 227
Pilgrim T. Homosapien 228
   – Pilgrim salutes America 228
   – In service to God and people 229

    – Pilgrim's mission to America 229

    – The Word of God in action 231

    – Editorial tribute to Pilgrim T. Homosapien 233

Trust 235

Inspiration 235

    – Background 235

    – Inspiration and quality of life 235

    – Inspired for service 236

    – Food for thought 236

Chief doctrine of Christianity 237

Christian covenant of love 238

Fear and stress 238

    – Background 238

    – Searching for answers 238

    – Freedom from fear and stress 241

    – God's victory over fear and stress is our
       freedom in Christ 241

Drug abuse 242

I.D. Crisis 243

Do we exist in an identity crisis? 247

War and peace 252

    – The crucial issue 252

    – The conflict in man as the source of war 256

    – Theology of the sword 261

    – The horror of war 266

ACT III
THE HISTORIC 'FROM' IN FROM/TO

Chapter 9

Source for reflections 275

    – Reflections and healing 277

Springboard for meditations 278

   – Meditations build bridges... 278
Baseline for change.. 279
   – The quagmire of doubt and confusion 279
Illustrations of "from" scenes 281
   – Transformation Scene 1 281
   – Transformation Scene 2 282
   – Transformation Scene 3 284
What history tells us 286

EPILOGUE
FROM EDEN TO ETERNITY VIA THE SERENE EXPANSE

Chapter 10
   "Islands of hope".. 289

INDEXES

Index to scripture passages... 320-322

Subject Index 323-329

POETRY ADDENDUM

The Celebration Of Life _____ 290

INTRODUCTION _____ 290

Era of Faith _____ 291
Truth _____ 292
Reality _____ 293
By the power of the Holy Spirit _____ 293
The call _____ 294
Faith in action _____ 295
Grace _____ 295
Trust in God _____ 296
True happiness _____ 296
Stress _____ 297
God is with us _____ 297
Wholeness of life _____ 298
Miracles _____ 299
Family _____ 300-301
Bridges _____ 302
God is calling for change _____ 302
Assurance _____ 303
Unity _____ 303
America _____ 304
Come, Holy Spirit _____ 304
Seeds of faith _____ 305
Sunday _____ 306
Faith and reason _____ 306
Melody of life _____ 306
A ceaseless prayer _____ 307
Quality of life _____ 307
A hobo with class _____ 308-309
Paradise _____ 309

The serene expanse _____ 310-311
Eternal value _____ 311
Freedom of the press _____ 312
My tribute to God _____ 313
A silly numbers game _____ 314-315
Puppy _____ 316-317
Rays of hope and freedom _____ 317
A national prayer _____ 318-319

Key Words

AMERICA. America is more than just a nation. America is people. America is the land of pilgrims. America is God's fortress of faith, hope, and love in the world to demonstrate unity through diversity. America is an immense sea of diverse and faithful pilgrims working the rule of God. The American pilgrim stands tall as champion of truth, justice, and equality. "America is God's country" is the spiritual connection of God and pilgrims. God connects each pilgrim by the power of the Holy Spirit to fill the spiritual needs of family, friend, neighbor, the community, and people throughout the world.

ASPIRATION. Aspiration is a goal-oriented thought process. Aspirations are mental exercises in search of human greatness. They are driven by ambition. Hence we *aspire* to honor. We *aspire* to superiority. We *aspire* to recognition. We *aspire* to success. Aspirations for self-esteem without consideration for the common good are egocentric wishes. They are boorish endeavors to succeed at any cost. Human aspirations are limited in scope, inasmuch as the human mind has limits. Individuals possessed by greed and lust for power will resort to extremes in behavior to have their desires come true. For example, Cain killed Abel. Aspirations prompted by the power of the Holy Spirit are blessings ordained by God.

CHIEF DOCTRINE OF CHRISTIANITY. The chief doctrine of Christianity is the divine declaration on the fellowship of love documented in Holy Writ: "He who has my commandments and keeps them, he it is who loves me; and he who loves me will be loved by my Father, and I will love him and manifest myself to him." (John 14:21) The believer's relationship with the resurrected Christ is contingent on love. Of the three theological virtues—faith, hope, and love—love is the greatest. Divine love is Jesus Christ alive in believers: Love unites people with God. Love keeps believers faithful; love has more power than any decree of law. Commitments based on love draw believers together in a permanent bond. Love embraces; love forgives; love never threatens, denies, or rejects. The love of God for people is the supreme example of Christianity's chief doctrine.

CHRISTIAN COVENANT OF LOVE. The Christian covenant of love is supreme reality for modern man. Its authority is God. Its sole source of power is the Word of God. Its purpose is to bond God and people in fellowship for eternity. The Christian covenant of love has ancient roots. Jeremiah first prophesied its future around 600 B.C. as an inward and personal relationship with God based on love. Jesus Christ formulated the new covenant about 2,000 years ago into the two Great Commandments in the relationship of God and people: Love for God and love for neighbor. The Christian Covenant of Love supplants the ancient order of rituals and of laws.

ERA OF FAITH. The Era of Faith is an act of God. (1) It is the state of reality in its purest spiritual form. By divine decree the beginning of time is not defined. And the end of time remains the secret in the hands of God the Almighty Creator of all that is, and all that ever will be. Securely nestled between the beginning and end of creation, the Era of Faith is the time for performance in real-life situations. Real-life drama unfolds as relationships. The Era of Faith is the proving ground for humanity as spiritual beings in the image of God. Spirituality and relationships define the era. Justice and peace are its manifestations. (2) The Era of Faith in time and place is an inspirational forum on relationships, faith, hope, love, equality, justice, peace, trust, and truth.

FAITH. Faith is a timeless relationship of trust with the living

God. The duly inspired confession of faith is the Lord's Prayer.

GOD. God is supreme, absolute, and sole reality. God is the creator of all that is and all that ever will be. God is known also as Our Father in Heaven, Jesus Christ, and Holy Spirit. The God of the Bible is the God of revelation.

HOPE. Hope is looking forward to what is good and beautiful by trusting God and relying on his promise that he will take care of us.

HUMAN EQUATION. (1) In its secular meaning, the human equation is the sum total of inspiration plus aspirations in proper balance for yielding quality of life. The human equation is the story of humanity in all its forms and relationships to make the world a better place. (2) In its spiritual sense, the human equation is the realization of the Lord's Prayer in support of spiritual life. Quality of life for the whole being is a ceaseless prayer. The human equation as a spiritual tool is so immense in scope that it defies all simple definitions of progress, evolution, and growth.

I.D. CRISIS. (1) I.D. Crisis is a spiritual and personal conflict in modern man of devastating magnitude. Confusion about the past and uncertainty about personal status in the present prevent us from knowing our true nature. As a direct consequence of such confusion, visions of the future are clouded. Some of the diversions that prevent people from realizing their true identity as children of God are philosophies, politics, economics, and false religions. The solution is remembering that human beings are dependent creatures of God. (2) Title of a book dealing with the spiritual, intellectual, and social conflict in man. The writing details the impact of the Christian faith on everyday life as theology in the workplace. It presents the Holy Spirit as

God's guide for leading us out of the maze of confusion to the truth of God.

INSPIRATIONS. Inspirations apply to life in the presence of God. Inspirations are means of grace. God attends to faithful believers by the power of the Holy Spirit with comfort, guidance, and direction. Inspirations are the limitless activities of the Holy Spirit in support of the human spirit. Inspired persons are servants of God who live in the world by divine grace and work according to the will and purpose of God. They are God's people for transforming human lives from chaos to harmony. The goal in inspirations is to advance the common good in the world.

PEACE OF GOD. The peace of God is the secure knowledge that our life is not wasted and useless but a fulfillment of the will and purpose of God. In our total submission to the Holy Spirit, we know God as Creator and share a mutual relationship of love through our life in union with Christ our Redeemer.

PILGRIM. Pilgrims are servants of God sojourning in a hostile world for 70 years, more or less. Pilgrim T. Homosapien is God's role model in this writing.

QUALITY OF LIFE. God as the source of life, liberty, and happiness ordains quality of life by the power of the Holy Spirit. The prerequisite for this blessing is reverence for life, liberty, and happiness for all members in God's creation. In this blessed state of existence, the human spirit is at peace with itself, at peace with God, and at peace with other people in a wide-open world of uncharted space to allow for the expansion of tolerance, compassion, and unconditional submission to God for taking care of us. Quality of life requires discipline and respect for God and people.

RELATIONSHIP. (1) Relationships are real-life dramas. (1a) Each relationship is a personal statement of belief and trust. (1b) Relationships are spiritual engagements and personal encounters in three dimensions: the believer's relation to God, the believer's relation to other people, and the believer's relation to the world. (2) In our spiritual relationship with God, we know God as Father, and God meets us face to face in our daily encounters. In our relationship with nature, we protect God's creation, and nature makes our environment a mighty fortress. (3) In our relationships with family, friends, and neighbors our happiness is the happiness of the other person, and we share eternal bliss. (4) In our relationships with the community and the world, our helping hand satisfies the other person's needs, and our resources will prove inexhaustible. (5) Relationships are dynamic and creative but subject to evolution and change. Wholesome attitudes and discerning behavior are fertile soil for growth in relationships. (6) Servants of God experience relationships as the stewardship of time, talents, and resources. In every encounter, faithful stewards are responsible partners of the love of God.

REVELATION. Revelations are spiritual events. In the world of spiritual fulfillment, disciples know God as Father. God speaks. Faithful people listen. God says, "You are my child," and obedient followers are assured of lasting spiritual relationships. Revelations are God's promises of his presence in faithful believers. God gives. All creation receives and gives thanks. Revelations are the wondrous gifts of divine love as new horizons are opened with each revelation.

SEE. To see is to receive God's revelations and then experience them as daily routine. Receptive attitudes towards the Word of God make room for new faith to develop. What we already see is old faith realized and applied, and old faith turns into belief and trust. New faith is hope vigorously at work to help us see the things to come.

SERVANT. Servant of God is the noblest position in a pilgrim's relationship with God. In this privileged status, God is choosing disciples to do his work in the world. Life in union with Jesus Christ makes disciples children of God who can rightfully boast about a working relationship with God as Father. In the Old Testament, God singles out Job as "my servant Job." In The New Testament, however, Christ elevates the servant role to friend, pointing to intimacy in working with God. Love for God, nature, and people are high priorities for friends of God. By the power of the Holy Spirit, friends of God promote justice and peace in the world and foster harmony in a universe of relationships.

THEOLOGY. Theology is to know God as ultimate reality. Knowledge of God is to understand his will for creation and acting accordingly. This implies that human desires are submerged in the purpose ordained by God for all humanity. The two Great Commandments—love for God and neighbor—detail the practical aspects of theology.

THREE BLESSINGS. God ordains the three blessings as life, liberty, and happiness for every person in the world. The time-honored American Declaration of Independence [1776] focuses on life, liberty, and happiness as inalienable rights granted by God.

TRUST. Trust is the essence of relationships. Trust in God is the nucleus of faith. Trust builds bridges of friendships. Trust is the glue that connects people and God for a lasting and fruitful spiritual life in the world. Plain communication and clear understanding are paramount in maintaining trust. The time-honored adage "Say what you mean, and mean what you say" is key to trust and relationships. Mutual trust makes relationships a blessing.

WHOLE BEING. The whole being combines life, liberty, and happiness as an integrated body of mind and spirit. The whole being is friend of God and his light in the world. Dedicated to do the good works of God in the world, friends of God are disciples who live for the glorification of God as the father of mankind. The godly model of a whole being for Christians is the resurrected Christ.

WORKPLACE. The workplace is a universal description of the environment where people live, worship, serve, and work to earn a living. The workplace for human beings is God's laboratory for human performance. On the grand scale, the workplace is nature as the habitat of all that is living. The human function in the workplace is caring. For example, humanity is charged by God to care for nature, societies, communities, the economy, government, and places of employment. Humanity is further charged to work for equality, justice, harmony, and peace in all domains. Within the realm of caring individuals, the workplace is family, neighbor, friend, and the co-worker in need of help and support. The grand master of the workplace, of course, is Jesus Christ.

PROLOGUE

The Word Of God
Grace

Chapter 1

The Word Of God.

God speaks to us always in his Word but sometimes also in events that seem far removed from ecclesiastical religion. God sees our needs, and he hastens to help us. The Word of God is sufficient for spiritual wholeness of life. By the power of the Holy Spirit God heals us in body, mind, and spirit. We cry out to God when in distress, and God soothes the pain of stress. God comforts us in our sorrows, and he weeps with us as Jesus did over the death of his friend Lazarus. And God fights with us when evil attacks us. God calls his work on our behalf the right thing to do. We call the mighty acts of God miracles.

The Word of God is creative, and all the miraculous events in the universe show it to be true. God speaks the Word, and nature is full of wondrous surprises. We now enjoy pastures, woodlands, lakes, rivers, and wide-open fields. God speaks, and with wide-open eyes we see his miracles unfold right before us. God speaks the Word, and he blesses us in multiple and inexplicable ways to enjoy life with him. He blesses us with faith. He listens to our prayers. He is with us when we cry for help. We are humbled to behold the powerful Word of God as the glorious wonders of majestic love. We experience the over-whelming power of his love as life in the presence of God. He sustains us. He cares for us. He strengthens our faith. The Word of God encourages us to be bold in trusting God as we

1

greet his certain sunrise each morning in an uncertain world.

God speaks the Word. There is nothing on Earth that can match the experience or the majesty of the Word of God. The Lord of Creation assures us by the power of the Holy Spirit that everything we see physically in the world with our eyes is but a replica of the true spiritual form in Heaven. God makes us feel at home on Earth with heavenly surroundings. And God speaks to us in words we can easily understand. We have no choice but to tell the world about his immense love for us. We readily share with all of God's children his indelible message of faith, hope, and love. We are his living testament in the world. We give witness to all his miraculous deeds as we see God in the universe, nature, and ourselves. God speaks by the power of the Holy Spirit, and things happen in our lives.

We carefully listen to what our heavenly Father has to say. When God speaks, something important is always taking place. We see the world change for the better. We sense our knowledge of God increasing. We feel inspired by new revelations of truth, and we respond to God's requests to remove barriers of entrenched human traditions that do not make spiritual sense. Indeed, God our Father lives among us and does what he believes is best for us. By his speaking directly to us, we now see what friends of God have been trying to tell us all along— that God speaks to us face to face. God was directly involved in Job's life, and God is directly involved in our lives. Our God, indeed, speaks in language we can understand. His encouragements, his admonitions—and even his scolding—are tailored for our personal use. God speaks as any loving father speaks to the children he cares about. One thing is certain in the modern world: God is at all times telling us about faith, hope, and love.

His words speak truth. God speaks in precise language

about our needs and our concerns, and all the while he wipes away our fears and tears. His words are comfort and strength. God wants us to enjoy our life in his presence without feeling intimidated by his awe-inspiring love. God assures us: "You are my child." Indeed, God made us more than just ordinary children. We are God's friends for all eternity! His love now dwells in our soul. Though we test God over and over again, God never tempts us needlessly. Above all, God speaks to us to educate us. Our education is a priority for him. He wants to make sure that we are smarter than foxes in the world. God teaches truth plainly. We appreciate eternal truth in its simplest form. God is now using us to teach his Word to family, friend, and neighbor.

The Era of Faith is all about God speaking. By the power of the Holy Spirit God speaks through us, and the world hears the Word of God in the Era of Faith; in all this we are wordless to describe the mighty acts of God—so we let God speak. Now let us see and learn all we can about the omnipotent Word of God in action.

The creation of the universe

"In the beginning was the Word,
And the Word was with God,
And the Word was God.
He was in the beginning with God;
All things were made through him,
And without him was not anything made that was made.
In him was life,
And the life was the light of men.
The light shines in the darkness,
And the darkness has not overcome it."
(John 1:1-5)

Christ spoke the Word of God 10 to 20 billion years ago, and the universe was formed from utter chaos into perfect order. God spoke. Events happened. We now see the sky, the sun, the moon, and the stars appearing in clockwork precision day and night. The creation event recorded in Holy Writ has two differing versions, Genesis 1:1-2:4a and Genesis 2:4b-3:24. The spiritual account of creation, of course, is the Gospel of John 1:1-5. In all three recordings God is speaking. And the Word of God at the present is offering for our use great teachings about divine power at work. It is up to us now to understand the event of the creation of the universe in contemporary language.

Christians rely on the Holy Spirit for the truth about the creation event. The Holy Spirit is teacher and guide for revealing what God has done. God speaks, the Holy Spirit reveals, and we listen to what God has to say. God has blessed us with discerning minds to comprehend complex context stories, such as the creation of the universe. We may not get it all at once. In due time, however, the Holy Spirit will reveal the whole picture of God's wondrous works of creation. This may not be in our time, but surely future humanity will see the whole truth before the end of time.

In the meantime, let us carefully listen, examine, and learn; we must learn all we can about the subject of God speaking and judiciously discriminate. Speculative promoters will without fail promote their theories about the creation of the universe and declare them as fact. God leaves it up to us to use critical scholarship in sorting truth from fiction. But human knowledge is in constant flux. It is always on the move in the search for truth. New discoveries are new revelations. The sooner we accept our predicament, the faster we will arrive at seeing the true picture.

Thus we revert to the beginning of this section and the poetic version of the creation story of the universe in the Gospel of John. Christ spoke the Word of God 10 to 20 billion years ago, and things happened. The poetic style of any story, like the creation account in the Gospel according to John, is best suited for expansion and correction. Poetry is inspirational and creative at the same time. The poetic license is a liberal tool in this investigation. We can readily accept John's version of the creation story. It is open-ended. As we look at the pictures taken by the Hubble telescope of galaxies previously beyond the imagination of mankind we see majestic splendor and surmise God's hand in it.

The only certainty about the origin of the universe is the truth that the Word of God is active and alive in creation and always will be. In evidence of God's creative hand in the formation of the universe, the heavenly bodies keep their prescribed course with atomic clock precision according to the divine plan.

The universe is not the only creation manifestation of the Word of God. As we travel the road of creation mysteries let us now stop at the next station and learn all we can about the creation of life. This stop is more intriguing than what we learned about the universe. The story of life touches us very intimately. We are an integral part of this earth-shaking event. God speaks, and we have our being!

The creation of life

Thus says the Lord: "Life is because I AM. I speak the Word, and life is. I speak the Word, and my love abides in your life."

God as the author of life has no interest in competing with human speculation about the origin of life. His focus is on love as the major component in life. God says: "My love is your life!" In God's formulation of life, life and love are intimately tied together. One is not without the other. Love is the principal spiritual wonder in the mysteries of the creation of life. Belief in

Jesus Christ secures the love of God. Believers in Jesus Christ are for certain children of God: "All who received him, who believed in his name, he gave power to become children of God; who where born, not of blood nor of the will of the flesh nor of the will of man, but of God." (John 1:12-13) A child is the issue of love. Love is so overwhelming that even the most hardened skeptics eventually succumb to God's tender love. Love, indeed, is central in the Gospel. Love is God's mission on behalf of people! Having thus demonstrated that life and love make up a continuous chain of events with a definite beginning but no end in sight, the life story quickly advances to the mission of human life on Earth. The human mission in the world resembles more closely a simple story of love rather than the complex treatise of what life on Earth should be.

What is my mission in life?

This question is purposely stated in the first person singular to show our direct involvement in the mystery of life on Earth. The answer to this vital question starts with the premise that our mission for God is motivated by love. This premise is grounded in the divine revelation by Jesus Christ that we are children of a loving God. Christ's Father is also our loving Father and a mighty God. His nature is pure grace. In our life of union with God we are free in the Spirit to fulfill our obligations freely. We are free to love God and neighbor, as this is our mission from birth to the end of our lives. For this purpose, God has set us free from the fears that bring certain death to secular people. We trust God for our salvation. God is always looking after us to protect our lives now on Earth and, ultimately, in Heaven. Therefore, we are free in the Spirit to work God's purpose in the world as a mission of love to fill the spiritual needs of people according to God's plan.

Now, then, what is this mission in life that we call love?

Jesus Christ confirms: "You are the light of the world." (Matthew 5:14) Our performance in this task of enlightening the world with the Gospel of Christ is recorded in the Book of Life, where the central theme is also love. Life, then, generates light as a beacon for others to also see God and enjoy with him a rewarding relationship of love. The success stories in the Book of Life are detailed accounts about life, light, and love. Life is a central experience in the universe, and life is a prerequisite for love. Each story of life is a drama of love acted out individually but with ample help from the Holy Spirit.

Life is light in Christ. We live in his light.
We are Christ's light in the world!

God made it so. His radiant love glorifies life and light. And God sustains life on Earth by means of procreation until the day he decides to end it all. As we listen to the Word of God creating life, we see God as chemist, physicist, electrical engineer, and mechanical genius. To be sure, the essence of life is the breath of the living God. But our God is also a practical God of perfection who puts each one of us together according to a plan of perfection that he alone can appreciate. God balances the elements of life in perfect proportions for top performance. He structures them to make them operational. He energizes this delicate biological wonder with electrical power to make life functional. He then bundles chemistry and physics into a mechanical masterpiece we best know as a human body. In the end, he gives it his own breath. Lo and behold, the breath of God makes us then spiritually living beings. And if there is even the slightest miss in perfection, God compensates for it with an overabundance of his miraculous love.

To be sure, procreation and birth are the criterion of physical

life on Earth. As human beings, God is not only giving us physical life, but he is giving us full control over our destiny; however, physical life on Earth always terminates in death in due season. But that is not the end of the story. God unites our spiritual life with his life in Heaven.

The human life experience on Earth is a mystery founded in
divine promise. The life forever in the peace of God for human
beings is the realized spiritual experience of life on Earth
according to God's precious gifts of faith, hope, and love for
every person who believes and trusts in God. The important link
in the continuity of life after death is the spiritual connection.
God enters our life on Earth so that we easily can find our life
in him and continue living with him in Heaven. The human life
story is tied to the miracle of all miracles in creation: the Word
of God creating human spirituality. Great wonders are in store
as we continue reading about the creation of human spirituality.

The creation of human spirituality

Life without the Spirit of God is an empty earthly vessel aimlessly adrift on turbulent waters in a stormy sea. Meaning in life
is found in the presence of God and his spiritual connection.
After an indeterminate amount of time in human evolution, God
endowed humanity with the gift of faith. Faith is a timeless relationship of trust with the living God.

This gift makes it possible for believers in God to share his
life. Human spirituality is a form of relationship we know in the
world as family. In the spiritual context, we are God's family. We
are his children. We know God as our Father in Heaven. We
live in a relationship with God according to the divine precepts
of faith, hope, and love.

When God crowned the man Abram from the city of Ur in

ancient southern Mesopotamia some 3,900 years ago with the gift of faith, low-level civilizations were already in bloom in many places on Earth. Egypt, for example, was an empire expanding its rule at the expense of neighbors near and far. Slavery, too, was routine practice. The poorest citizens of Egypt were enslaved. Hagar, the concubine of Abram, was an Egyptian slave girl. We know her as the mother of Ishmael—Abraham's first son—and the ancestress of the Muslim religion.

Biblical Writ tells us of her and her child's inhumane treatment by the first family of faith on Earth. Abraham and his wife Sarah colluded to get rid of Hagar and Ishmael. Sarah's jealousy could not stand to have Isaac, her child of God's promise, share his life with Ishmael, his half-brother. Sarah caused Abraham to drive mother and child into the desert to die. God rescued both. In his compassion, God set the stage for a future version of a monotheistic faith system based on Ishmael, son of Abraham and Hagar, his slave girl from Egypt.

We see human spirituality taking hold following the death of Abraham when Ishmael and Isaac jointly bury their father. Human spirituality had a rocky start. Yet God accepted Abraham because he believed in God (Genesis 15:6). There is a definite need in the modern world to differentiate belief in God and a living relationship of trust with God. Many people believe in God without having a living relationship of trust with him. At many dark moments in his life, for example, Abraham too would qualify as a man of the flesh, yet believing in God. He was the first great manipulator of God's trust in man. This only proves that God's love for the spiritual wellbeing of his children is beyond human folly.

With his blessing of human spirituality, God is setting human life apart from the rest of life for mainly one purpose: Love.

God blesses us with love so that we can love him. God

secures his love in the world through us so that we can love our neighbor.

We are his children on Earth to do his will and fulfill his purpose in the dispensation of the love of God. When all is said and done, however, God will welcome home his faithful children to live with him forever in Heaven as we have welcomed God on Earth into our hearts. Human spirituality is a gift we grow into. This divine attribute takes hold of us. It keeps on growing and growing within us until we are one with God. When we speak about spiritual rebirth—as mentioned in Nicodemus' encounter with Jesus—Christ is telling us that the only way this can happen is through change: We must change. We must believe the Word of God. To see God in all that we do in his name is the only true experience for illustrating human spirituality.

Life and human spirituality are great wonders of creation. Let us continue on the road of creation mysteries to our next stop and see how God preserves these creation wonders through covenants.

The creation of covenants

In divine language, a covenant signals the beginning of an important event in which God is totally in charge. The something new in covenants can be dramatically important, such as the beginning of a new age on the eternal timeline; or it can be more subtle, such as God calling for moral and ethical reform. In all situations of covenants, God is the covenant giver and the absolute authority in the covenant relationship of people and God.

In covenant relationships, God binds himself through promise to a supporting role with his covenant people according to the precepts revealed in the promise through revelation by the Holy Spirit. The divine intent in a covenant governs the relationship of people and God. God relates to people as a matter of grace while he expects faithfulness in return as a matter of obedience.

God says: "I promise to give you freely, but you must obey without question. Mine is the promise; yours is the obligation."

A divine covenant, therefore, is a two-way commitment of trust. We trust God because God trusted us in issuing the covenant in the first place.

The number of old covenants are many. Each new effort by God to teach the children of Abraham the way of God was short lived and ultimately ended in failure. The chosen people preferred their ways of living to the way of God as prescribed in the covenants.

According to God's Way, Jesus Christ is the living Word of God, and in every occurrence Christ is the covenant giver as well as the absolute authority. When the Jews denied Jesus' authority by claiming a privileged status with God as Abraham's children, Christ set the record straight by telling them bluntly: "Before Abraham was, I AM." (John 8:58)

In the fierce debate (John 8:37-57) over Christ's declaration that he existed before Abraham was born, the Son of God reviled the arrogance of the Jews and their clamor to a free ride on the coattails of Abraham's belief in God. The Word of God spoken by Christ provoked such great anger among the Jews that they tried to kill him. Christ was threatened because he spoke the truth. This must have been especially painful to God because he is the God of truth. The absolute authority of the covenant with Abraham was denounced; Christ was ridiculed, branded a liar, and threatened with death. Abraham's children cursed God in Christ although God had blessed Abraham. But empty words in fierce debate do not deter God.

As the God of action in the lives of his children, God raises the issue of covenants to the highest level. In an edifying disclosure on the mountaintop, Christ appears with Moses and Elijah in the Transfiguration scene. It was God's way to show the world a new covenant and a new age.

God signaled from the mountaintop the new Christian covenant of love. And he endorsed the new covenant at the mountaintop for the entire world to hear and see: "This is my Son, my beloved; listen to him!" (Luke 9:35) God made himself part of the Christian covenant of love when he declared his Son as the Messiah!

But the world of Jesus' time would not listen to God or his Son. Yet not all was lost. No time has been wasted. Time is important to God, and he uses every breath of life to make it count to the benefit of his children. What once was lost is now our gain.

We have now in the modern world over 2,000 years of valuable experience on Christian love. The lessons teach us about good and evil. God teaches about indifferent attitudes toward himself and people. God points to good and bad behavior to help us choose the high road of his righteousness. By the power of the Holy Spirit, God encourages us to nourish our spiritual relationship with him. The Holy Spirit further helps us build bridges of Christian love with friend and neighbor. When God's prophet Jeremiah foretold the covenant of Christian love around 600 B.C., God was considering the welfare of his children in modern times. We now share the results of God's direct involvement with people in the past.

God mourned the failure of Abraham's children to accept his covenants. But now the master creator of covenants rejoices as he celebrates with us our Christian life in union with him. Indeed, Heaven rejoices with all creation as we celebrate with each sunrise the renewal of God's everlasting covenant.

Mourning is turned into joy. The Christian covenant of love is among God's greatest gifts for us!

As we continue on the road of creation mysteries our next stop is the creation of a new world order. Let us now venture into the exciting times of creation and attentively listen to the Word of God about a new world order. God has a lot to tell us.

The creation of a new world order

About 2,000 years ago God decided that a new world order was needed. Things just had not been going right in the previous 1,900 years since he had blessed Abraham with the gift of faith. The future looked grim. The children of Abraham chose to promote personal aspirations over God's inspirations and revelations. God wanted inclusiveness of faith for all people, but this did not happen. He could not see this ever taking place without his intervention. God had provided faith as a precious gift for everyone to make the ancient world of Abraham's children a better place for all people, but it was going nowhere.

So God decided to take full charge of a new world order. The Son of God entered the world to live with his people. Jesus Christ came as an innocent child. But the reception he got was anything but a hearty welcome.

The missing fundamental in all modern historical and religious deliberations is the important fact that God came into a hostile world as a helpless child, using the trough of animals for a cradle. Animals shared what human beings denied. Lonely shepherds received the initial news as God's angelic message of hope, and animal instinct was the means of grace by which animals saw in the child God incarnate.

God had chosen to withhold the revelation of his entry into

the world from established rulers, the secular privileged among the Jews, and the educated religious authorities of Israel. God delivered his first Gospel message of hope to unknown shepherds in the field, to the animals in a manger, and to foreign Wise Men. The birth of the Son of God in a manger, with animals as the only witnesses, is just one of many divine mysteries and miracles. Our belief, and our acceptance of this truth, is trust beyond human understanding. God's human birth in a manger is the greatest mystery of all mysteries. Its historical value is the human angle in the Christ event. Human arrogance made it happen in a manger.

God is calling for change, and therefore, the story has a deeper meaning. God is demonstrating love as pure grace for humans. The story of God's human birth in the home of animals is the most sacred story in recorded history. Sheep and oxen accepted the birth of Jesus Christ with child-like trust. They accepted God as a human being without hesitation. Undoubtedly, their trust in God as a new-born child was inherent instinct. But God goes beyond instincts. The birth of the Christ child in a manger proves once and for all that God wanted to experience personally what human desperation in the world is all about. Consequently, he understands the pain of rejection, and he knows best how to help the homeless. He will save despised souls from their deep despair of human rejection.

What does this story really tells us?

A new world order has been created. God wanted to experience for himself human hardships under oppressive rule. And God received more than he bargained for.   Mary's birth pangs in a manger were real agony for God. Thereafter God in Christ was ridiculed, rejected, and condemned to death. God in Christ went to hell. By the power of the Holy Spirit, God is forcing a change in attitudes and behavior. He wants to keep from innocent children the pain and death that God in Christ had to endure.

The new world order established by God is equality, justice, and peace under God's universal decree of love. In the new world order, the resurrected Christ knows suffering, agony, and pain caused by man's inhumanity to man. Hence Christ is qualified as humanity's friend to save God's children from death and hell. In the new world order, the resurrected Christ shares his glorious life with us.

This is God's Gospel message for the new world order: "Christ is the Savior of mankind." The condemned one now teaches, heals, and redeems the children of God throughout the entire world. He blesses each of us with his living Word. He transforms our lives from despair to holiness in his presence. Christ is our model of the godly life. We now share his love, truth, and justice. He makes us perfect, as God is perfect.

Christ has risen in the eyes of the world from being a derelict during his sojourn on Earth to now being welcomed as the Lord of mankind. God has raised Christ as the head of a new world order, and he is raising us to a newness of life that the world before had never experienced. The birth of the Son of God in a manger, his life saddened by open rebellion against God, his agony of suffering, and his death as a common criminal authenticate the new world order. Christianity is secured with God's seal of approval—the Cross of Christ—as a permanent imprint in human history. The new world order is one of the most astounding of cosmic events. We live in a new world order in which Christ has fought and won our battle for a glorious life in the here and now—and freed us from Satan and death. His victory is now our cosmic glory in the presence of God.

The historical background of the Christ event is important in our deliberations today on the new world order for faith, religion, ethics, and the healing of mankind. It helps us to better understand who and whose we are. And we are not afraid of the future, for we know for certain where Christ is leading us! History points to the simple truth that God always reveals himself for our benefit in ways we would least expect. It happened in the Christ event. God is telling us that he is not interested in traditions and the teaching of religion according to doctrines and dogma. Neither is God involved in academic speculations about his nature. Human ideas about humanity's salvation are foreign to him.

By entering the world as a child, God confirmed the value of faith and trust in him. God has lifted the teaching of faith to new standards. Our faith is based on his righteousness alone. Therefore, God scorns human wisdom and prized human methods in teaching the world's view about God and truth. God entered the world as a child, and he invites all children in the world to his classroom of faith. Christ confirms the divine invitation: "Truly, I say to you, whoever does not receive the Kingdom of God like a child shall not enter it." (Mark 10:15) Let us enter God's classroom of faith in faith. Let us listen to the Word of God with child-like trust. Let us accept the truth about God in faith as children of the living God in Jesus Christ our Lord.

As children of God, we trust Christ to enrich our lives with very exciting realities about life in union with God. The Holy Spirit reveals spiritual realities that secular teaching methods cannot envision. In the new world order the Word of God prevails by means of revelation. Our mission is to earnestly learn the truth about God and then do what God always wanted us to do: to love God and neighbor.

The truly exciting feature in the new world order is the Christian covenant of love. Let's continue on the road of creation mysteries to the next stop, where Christ is teaching all we need to know about the Christian covenant of love.

The creation of the Christian covenant of love

Love is like the wind: It blows where it wills, and we experience the effect. We do not know where love comes from. Nor do we know where it is going. Love is like a thousand eyes watching over us, and ten thousand hands touching us in healing and protection. What is love? Where does it come from? We do not know. But God knows. Love is. And God is all love.

The Christian covenant of love is God telling us over and over again, "I love you!" He has written the Christian covenant of love in our hearts, but there are no words to prove it. Love is like the toothache. We feel it. We experience it. We know it is there. And we don't need to see the evidence to accept it. This we know for certain: Love is a powerful Spirit.

Love is the inexhaustible theme of the Gospel. God loves us so much as to sacrifice himself to draw us closer to him because we are his children. God's love for us fills our spiritual needs, and at the same time our physical needs are also met. The Christian covenant of love is God's way to let us mature in faith by the power of the Holy Spirit. We grow and we grow; yet God always sees the child in us. God wants it that way. He wants our love in return as the love of a child.

But there is more to the story of the Christian covenant of love.

The modern interpretation of the Christian covenant of love is trusting God. We trust God, and God trusts us to live in peace and harmony with all his children in the modern world as our brothers and sisters. God provides the Christian covenant of love as a "relationship bridge" for trust and respect. We honor God as we follow Christ's lead by the power of the Holy Spirit in loving our neighbors as brothers and sisters. We are then complete and whole as God's family in the world. As a united family we love and trust each other as we all trust God, our Father in Heaven.

In the Christian covenant of love, God and Christ are making their home with us. Theologians may want to continue their speculation about God being both distant and near *ad infinitum.* Let it be their work. Let them write all the stories they want. Our love for God dictates that God is living in us as a matter of faith. In the Christian covenant of love, we demonstrate on Earth the divine mysteries of God's love with child-like trust.

This shift in understanding from abstract theology to an active relationship based on love and trust is God's way of saving a faltering humanity. God is transforming theological precepts from a complex academic view limited to the birth, life, suffering, and death of Jesus Christ to a simple theology of love and trust in which everyone has the opportunity to excel in the love of God. This new understanding, furthermore, signals spiritual truth of far greater importance than ever before envisioned: God is living with ordinary people. God is like us. God is a living God. God is a God of the living. By the power of the Holy Spirit, we are one with God through Christ. Christ has full authority over our lives to make sure that all the children of the world are secure in God's care!

Certainly, we should accept the birth, life, suffering, and death of Jesus Christ. This is historical truth. These events continue to be the foundation of Christian theology. But we evermore hold dearly above all theological precepts Christ's demonstration of lifeline opportunities of love and trust offered by God. The life-giving process starts with our baptism. Baptism is a spiritual event. Our pilgrimage on Earth henceforth is a chain of spiritual events initiated by God. These specific spiritual events conclude when God welcomes us home to Heaven at the rainbow bridge of grace after the temporary journey on Earth ends. The Christian covenant of love contains all the details from baptism on Earth to our transformation of eternal life in Heaven. The Christian covenant of love is theology at its best, for it tells the world what God in Christ has done for us. At the same time, it also contains God's expectations of us. We are in full compliance as covenant people of God when our love for God is the Word of God in our hearts according to Christ's teaching and his demonstration of God's Way for life on Earth.

The Christian covenant of love is God's oasis of hope in seemingly hopeless surroundings. It is God's healing center in an uncertain world. We enter confused, stressed out, and burdened with unnecessary guilt. We leave cleansed, refreshed, and focused on the Word of God.

We are now on the final stretch on the road of creation mysteries. Our ultimate destination is the mountaintop where Christ will teach us practical piety for the Era of Faith. We have successfully passed all the milestones as the Holy Spirit journeyed with us. And now we are at the mountaintop with Jesus Christ ready to learn all about life in the Era of Faith.

The creation of the Era of Faith

God says: "You are my light and my life in the world!"

The Era of Faith is based on God's premise that the essence of life is spiritual. The spiritual life is full of joy, for we live in the panoramic splendor of divine glory, the glory that God now shares with us. God shares with us the sky, the sun, the moon, the stars, and nature with all its beauty—mountains, lakes, rivers, and wide, open fields. Our Father is generous in sharing his possessions. He makes his creation our environment and gives us the most prominent role in divine revelations on Earth. God says: "You are my light and my life in the world!" Therefore, Christ tells us: "Let your light so shine before men, that they may see your good works and give glory to your Father, who is in Heaven." (Matthew 5:16) In the Era of Faith the Kingdom of God is within us; our life is God's home on Earth.

Henceforth our life on Earth is the center of joy. We experience this joy as spiritual fulfillment. The premise of joy in the presence of God is breathtaking in two different ways. Certainly God formalizes his blessing in this new experience of spiritual wellbeing in the Era of Faith, but God also calls for our total submission to his will and his purpose for our creation. God defines his expectations in the Era of Faith as faithfulness and obedience to his will. The premise shuns freedom of choice as a human alternative to God's will; the Era of Faith is free of human manipulation. We must obey the Word of God and accept his premise of glorious life in his presence based on God's righteousness alone or reject God and subsist in sin. Sin, of course, is the stressful state of secular life in which God is not the powerful source of joy.

As we take our first steps in the Era of Faith, God reveals his divine majesty in the panoramic splendor of the universe. In four explanatory discourses God tells us everything we need to know about the Era of Faith: He reveals his majesty; he describes his role as a servant; he answers our concern about the era's reality; he gives us the unconditional assurance of his protection.

God's majesty in the panoramic splendor of the universe

We now see the majestic wonders of God's handiwork.

A single entry on the timeline in creation, like the Era of Faith, is best understood in light of the whole picture of the universe. Since we have an active part in it, our role in the Era of Faith is an important component in this consideration. We are told that the universe belongs to God and us! Yes, God makes us his partners. When we see God in the totality of his majesty as the master creator of all that is, only then can we fully appreciate the importance of single details to the whole. The Era of Faith as a single entity in time and place has an important role because human behavior, especially our treatment of nature, will influence the successful operation of the whole according to God's plan. For example, when we pollute the atmosphere we cause changes. "Holes" in the ozone layer leak excessive ultraviolet radiation; this creates global warming that alters God's plan for temperature stability on Earth and can have dire consequences for every living being. We truly understand the Era of Faith when we fully appreciate our total involvement in the ongoing process of the universe with all that is therein; but let us especially focus on our involvements that force changes in God's plan of creation. The role of man—though an infinitesimal detail—is as important to the function of the whole as the universe is in its totality to cosmic harmony. It behooves us, therefore, to look again at the universe to find ourselves on that portion of the eternal timeline that we now call the Era of Faith. In the Era of Faith each sunrise signals a new creation in which God displays the glory of his majesty. The birds of the air see it. We see it. The birds open each new day with a new song about the marvelous things that God is doing; let us too praise him with a new song in our hearts and greet God with thanksgiving as we rise each morning.

At the time of creation of the universe some 10-20 billion years ago, God envisioned perfection and harmony within his system of absolute reality. Christ spoke the Word, and cosmic order replaced a gaseous chaos. Cosmic order is the spiritual force behind the perfection of the universe. What God has wrought in totality we now see through the details of our lives.

We now see the majestic wonders of God's handiwork. His marvelous things of creation, as viewed with modern eyes, are beyond the imagination of ancient philosophers and the multitude of wise men. They could only imagine what we now see. We are blessed with hard copies from manned space explorations and the Hubble telescope. These new revelations solidify our modern vision of the universe as a complex but very delicate system. Our perceptions now are beyond the wildest of dreams of thinkers in past ages. Before us is absolute reality of the majesty of God.

Absolute reality according to divine decree is prescribing the paths of celestial bodies never before imagined by man. God is in control of the forces holding gigantic galaxies in place as they move freely in space according to divine plan. In this greatness of creation, we experience God's protection of small planet Earth and us, his fragile children on Earth. We see falling stars and wonder in fright. God protects us from vaporizing meteorites as well as excessive cosmic rays. Absolute reality says God is in charge in protecting his children.

Certainly, God protects us in big ways. Yet God mourns when we inflict harm on nature, innocent others, and ourselves. Too often we are rebellious toward God and offensive to nature, family, and neighbor. We conceive wars that are more harmful to the human soul than the giant craters from the impact of meteorites. In this great human conflict, God seeks us out to protect our spirits from self-destruction, and he saves our souls from annihilation. We see the fruit of God's labor in his love for a frail humanity. God is our active partner in the Era of Faith.

Let us now learn more about our partnership with God and especially his miraculous saving acts through his role as servant to all.

The majestic God in the role of a humble servant

A loving father never abandons his children.

We have delved into the true significance of the Era of Faith when we have seen the majestic Creator of the universe humble himself to serve his children. But before we proceed further on this most important homage in spiritual bliss, let us seriously ask a soul-searching question of great spiritual consequence: Are we truly worthy of such massive honor from Almighty God? God as our servant? We are not worthy of even the slightest consideration from Almighty God, for time and again we need his rescue because of our rebellious attitudes toward him. What is behind this story of God serving us? The answer is simple: God created us. And he created the Era of Faith. What God ordains he also sustains. But above all, God loves us!

The answers to these questions and a multitude of similar questions are straightforward. First of all, God loves us. And it is entirely his decision to look after us. We are his children. Despite our arrogance God welcomes us into his Kingdom. When we suffer, God suffers with us. We are his children made in our Father's spiritual likeness. A loving father never abandons his children. God is that loving father! God is speaking the Word, and we are spiritually connected with him. This is the divine plan! This is God's Way of doing things in the Era of Faith.

Certainly, we are the children of his creation, but we are rebellious children. We are rebellious when it comes to living in the peace of God with one another. We are rebellious when it comes to the care of the environment and nature. We are rebellious toward the Word of God when we pollute it with our own ideas about self-righteousness, equality, and justice. We are rebellious when we carry on wars that are motivated by greed and lust for power. We claim to be God's special creation, yet we allow the evil of human nature to overpower us. In this quagmire of human insolence, God speaks to us as a servant to help us see that our God is a caring God. God sheds the mantle of majesty and in plain language assures us: "I will help you. Your troubles are now my problem. Be of good cheer!" This type of language is the talk of a servant who is ready and willing to die for us. God serves us because every human life is sacred and precious to him. Is this truly for real? Are we fools in believing it? God says: "My love for you is grace. No one can earn it. It is my gift to you." So let us continue with the reality check.

How real is the Era of Faith?

What God ordains, God also sustains.

In a dramatic reversal of roles, the Almighty God from high Heaven humbled himself, and he entered our troubled world 2,000 years ago to become a servant to mankind in the person of Jesus Christ. God was all the while hoping that people would welcome his incarnate Word, open their hearts to Christ, correct their behavior, and joyfully follow the model of the godly life of the Son of God who also is the anointed Messiah. It was a great gamble for God. God took a chance. And the divine plan failed. God had done his part. It failed because human arrogance wanted it to fail. The people of Jesus' time opposed it. The Jews in Jesus' day did not welcome God's offer of a new life in the Spirit. They scorned God. The heir of the vineyard was rejected. And the mob killed the Son of God. Have we changed? Are we any different from the Jews in Jesus' time? Yes and no. Some people have experienced God as servants and changed; others have not. And a great number of people today offer only lip service and continue in their merry old ways. Are things really different today to make the Era of Faith real?

The answer is "yes," but it is conditional by divine decree. The Word of God is among us now by the power of the Holy Spirit. Though we are not much different when it comes to poor attitudes about life and living it to the glory of God than people in previous generations, God is more eager now than ever before to help us. We experience the spiritual connection of people and God. The Holy Spirit assures us today—and every day—that this is so. Skeptics in Jesus' time uttered vicious threats to wipe the Word of God from the face of the Earth. Modern people also harbor ill feelings toward the heir of the vineyard when his spiritual way of living interferes with evil mortal desires. This is all the evidence needed to indict our poor behavior in modern times. But this also prompts God to act aggressively on our behalf and make the world a better place. Our role is that we are in the world but not a part of it. We are heavenly beings temporarily assigned to the desert of sin.

Therefore, to correct the great modern evil of insolence in the sight of God, the Holy Spirit moves freely among us as grace. He freely offers faith, hope, and love for all of God's children in the world—even the most disheartened among the hopeless— and invites them to change. Faithful believers in God now have a renewed opportunity in this movement of grace to also become servants of Christ's Gospel. We are the living reality of the Era of Faith. We are servants of God inviting everyone to work with us and make the world a better place. God's focus is on the children of the world. God is counting on the young people to work with the Holy Spirit and make their forthcoming world a better place. God inspires hope in the young people of the world.

Will the world change? How real is the Era of Faith? We ask the question over and over again. God gives us his answer.

God says: "The Era of Faith is as real as I am! I believe in my young people. I count on them to work with me as servants together. This makes the Era of Faith as real as I can describe it!"

What God ordains, God also sustains. The future of the children is in the hands of God! God challenges his children in the world to build their future on faith, hope, and love. God is very serious about it. He speaks the Word, and the Era of Faith is as real as our participation in it.

Now that we know that the Era of Faith is real, the follow-up question concerns our security in it. God takes full charge of our security and deals with all aspects of it.

How secure is the Era of Faith?

The only certainty in uncertain times is the presence of God.

The children of God in the modern world inherited baggage they never bargained for. They are burdened to correct the wrongs of ages past. They must change the curse of the past into the blessing for a promising future. Among the curses of worldly inheritance are brutal colonization schemes. Colonial powers have conjured up great evils to exploit innocent people and their resources, and the records are written in blood in most cases. Increasingly brutal curses that burden the young people of the modern world have been two world wars and the atomic cataclysm at the end of World War II. The ongoing curse to this very day continues in merciless suffering and death in localized skirmishes, the terror of religious fanatics, the insanity of suicide bombers, and unjust wars initiated by great powers saying, "The world must be made safe for democracy." History recorded the first installment of this now rather common battle cry in the annals of the American Congress on April 2, 1917. America's young people must now sort out issues and facts and make truth the only sound criterion for their future of hope and promise. The search for truth is an act of faith for our young people.

The children of God in the modern world must now work extra hard to extinguish the wildfires of greed, lust for power, and the economic instability created by evil men, deceit, and deficit spending. God is supportive. God says: "The only certainty in uncertain times is my presence."

We are not alone when bombs are falling and when manipulated economies collapse. God is with us when human madness is the evil of the day. God stands in front of us to absorb the hurt of the explosions directed at innocent people when wars rage according to human plans and without consideration that all human lives are sacred in the eyes of God. When enemy forces attack other people, they attack the Almighty Creator of all that is, and they hope to get away with it. They never have. And they never will.

God's will is to make the Era of Faith secure and universal through diversity. God's plan is a united front of believers to make the Word of God succeed in giving hope to all people. Hope is the eternal flame of divine power for the cleansing of human souls. By the power of the Holy Spirit, faith, hope, and love overpower past, present, and future evils. And the world will be a better place—and, by the Grace of God, it will be a secure world.

To prevent future conflicts in the family of God, God has made faith all-inclusive for all people and assigned for this universal faith a new era. The Era of Faith is God's way for a new beginning. God acted to improve the human condition.

By divine decree the era is destined to last to the end of time. The Holy Spirit makes it all-inclusive for every person. By the power of the Holy Spirit the Era of Faith is supreme spiritual reality and is beyond the reach of human interference. God has taken the cosmic revelations of billions of years to shape the faith of children in the modern world.

God speaks by the power of the Holy Spirit, and faith for all people in God's family is a new beginning. Let the children of the whole world rejoice and be thankful for the Era of Faith! Let us now follow up in our deliberations by taking a very close look at grace as the divine force that presides over security in the Era of Faith.

Grace

> Thus says the Lord: *"The true meaning of Grace is my love for people."*

Our God is a God of grace. Grace transforms lives by the power of the Holy Spirit as we advance in faith from seeing to experiencing to living in grace through faith. Grace is as old as creation, some 10-20 billions of years at best estimation. Grace is the first revelation of God in creation. Grace is the inherent nature of God. God showered humanity with grace upon grace as he entered the world some 2,000 years ago.

The grace of God is truly active and alive in the modern world. Grace, indeed, is the sole creative force at all times. We live today and have our true being by grace through faith. The Holy Spirit reveals grace and teaches all we need to know about faith. By the power of the Holy Spirit God heals and comforts us as a matter of grace. Grace leads the modern world into the spiritual realities of the here and now.

Grace in the here and now is the single outstanding feature in the Era of Faith. Grace is a major component in the new Christian covenant of love. Grace is revelation theology at its best. By the grace of God we live and have our being in God.

Grace and faith bond God and people in unity for common goals and objectives. Grace is a powerful force in relationships, family structures, and educational prowess. God says: "My grace is sufficient for you. I always act in due time and in due season. In the meantime, all you have to do is practice your faith. Do not question my love for you; all I am expecting of you is to be obedient to my will and faithful to my singular purpose for your creation. Accept grace, and again I say, accept grace and believe in me. Put all your trust in me, and believe. The true meaning of grace is my love for people. I AM the LORD!" Our common response, "The Lord is God," completes the unity of people and God.

By grace, Christ the living Word of God lived among us. And the resurrected Christ affirms eternal truth in the working of grace: "I am with you always, to the close of the age." (Matthew 28:20)

As we now submerge all worldly desires in the will of God, our life on Earth is by the grace of God. According to the rule of grace, we do God's work on Earth with a contrite heart and a humble spirit. We do not add to it our judgment. We do not tarnish the quality of grace with prejudice or pride.

Grace keeps us from harm. It is the power of God against "evil thoughts, fornication, theft, murder, adultery, coveting, wickedness, deceit, licentiousness, envy, slander, pride, and foolishness." (Mark 7:21)

We experience the spiritual connection of grace as the fruit of the Spirit. "The fruit of the Spirit is love, joy, peace, patience, kindness, goodness, faithfulness, gentleness, self-control." (Galatians 5:22) These gifts we cannot buy or work for. God showers us with his love, and we know it as living in the grace of God. And the peace of God is our protective umbrella in a stormy world.

When all is said and done, grace secures our entry into the Kingdom of God. Our loving Father waits at the rainbow bridge of divine grace, where he welcomes home his faithful pilgrims. Henceforth we will live in the presence of God forever. Life in the presence of God is now *fait accompli* for the Era of Faith. The Era of Faith is God's time of grace!

ACT I
THE GIFT OF FAITH

The new faith versus old faith presumptions
The spiritual connection in the new faith

Chapter 2

The new faith versus old faith presumptions

Background

"Before Abraham was, I am."

Jesus Christ is firm about his divine existence since the beginning of time. The Son of God emphatically declared the truth of the Word of God to the Jews of his day: "Before Abraham was, I am." (John 8:58) Jesus reiterates that he was present when God called Abram from the fertile crescent of southern Mesopotamia (now modern Iraq) and offered him the covenant of faith to live in Palestine. Jesus Christ indeed had an active role in God's call that went to the very prosperous city of Ur in Mesopotamia and singled out Abram. And the Son of God received Abram's response to God's call. He knew that Abram would have to leave all known comforts behind when God told him to venture into the wide-open unknowns, not knowing anybody where he was going save God. Abraham did not have any roadmap, and he relied totally on God to guide him. In his move to Palestine the Son of God was Abraham's manager.

We now introduce a brief departure from the main theme to help us truly appreciate the fundamental nature of Abraham's call and its implication for today in the context of life in modern Palestine. Abraham was a pilgrim, like many of the pilgrims to modern America. But unlike the unity through diversity that unites the heirs of a diversity of pilgrims in modern America, Abraham's sole journey to the land of Canaan (now Palestine) was driven by the single motive to possess the land. Abraham manipulated his world toward this end. His self-imposed isolation to reach this goal has become the source of violent conflicts in modern Palestine. Abraham maintained his identity with the family he had left behind. This we see in his selection of a wife for his son Isaac. Abraham never considered integration with the native population. Ethnicity was his pride.

In contrast, when pilgrims arrived in modern America, they shed the past of ethnicity and all other baggage that were burdens, and they became Americans as fast as they could. They kept the faith traditions they brought with them, but they united as a nation. They started a new life as Americans in the hope that God would provide. Faith in God was not only part of their lives, it was life for them. To be American means new life within a diversity of faith convictions that every American honors and respects. The American pilgrims relied on the Holy Spirit for guidance and support. "Come, Holy Spirit" is the constant prayer of a majority of American pilgrims today. The subsequent strength of political unity in America is the very essence of diverse beliefs in God.

This has never been the case in Palestine. Modern Palestine is a land of claims and counterclaims. Unless all parties in Palestine heed, honor, and respect God, as the God who ordained diversity, it will never be a land under God. Furthermore, at the core of the modern conflict in Palestine is a claim that is of equal importance to the major groups of people living there, Jews and Muslims alike: Who are the true children of faith? If Abraham is truly the father of faith for the three monotheistic religions, then the entire ruckus is a family fight.

Family fights are commonly known as the most vicious, as we indeed see it in Palestine today. But things are not quite that simple.

There are secular undertones in today's family struggle between Jews and Palestinians. The ultimate conflict is not only the inheritance of Abraham's faith. That would be too simple an issue to resolve. The modern conflict in Palestine deals with two opposing realities. On the one hand, of course, are the distractions in faith convictions. As far as diversity in faith convictions is concerned, God loves diversity. But we are not seeing a fight about faith diversity. Jews and Palestinians alike must resolve with equality, honor, and respect the greater secular problem of land with water. The hard-core issues are secular interests whose sole concern is the possession of the land *and* the water—independent of faith in God on the part of Jews and Muslims.

Jews and Muslims kill each other today for the possession of the land *and* the water. Water is more than the religious symbol of purification and baptism in modern Palestine. Water means physical survival. Clean water is scarce in Palestine as clean water is slowly but surely becoming scarce all over the world. Clean water is essential for the survival of life on Earth. The need for clean and potable water is becoming more important in the future of modern man than the human need for oil.

The outside world has been misled into believing that the troubles in modern Palestine are faith issues alone. Faith is an issue in Palestine insofar as it affects the drive to secure secular interests. Jews and Muslims alike abuse the issue of faith to challenge each other about land and water. Abraham knew the importance of water, as did his nephew Lot when he chose the green and fertile valley to live in, and we all know that land without water is useless.

The controversy in modern Palestine resembles a two-pronged fork. Hence the conflict has two battlefronts: control of religious sites for securing secular interests in tourism and possession of land with water for maintaining the good life. The issue of faith inheritance in these modern times is primarily used to cover up the main problem of possession of the land with water. Even the ownership of land alone is just a hypothetical concern. The crux of the problem is to own the land with the water in it. Let us now return to the main text of New Faith versus Old Faith discussions.

What then sparked the confrontations between Jesus and the Jews?

The Jews were afraid of losing religious clout in the rest of the world. They felt threatened by Jesus as the Messiah, the anointed one of God, the Christ. How real is the issue of Abraham as the father of faith in light of the new reality where the Messiah, the anointed one of God, is ruler of all that is? We can bring the inheritance conflict to a quick conclusion by asking the soul-searching question about the pertinence of Abraham's faith example in the relationship of God and people in today's world. If our true concern in the modern world is love for God as the Father of all mankind, Abraham is just one of many ancient examples in the evolution of modern faith. Nonetheless Jesus deemed the Abraham issue appropriate to the full appreciation of faith, and he decided to confront the Jews about faith in light of the messianic reality. Though Jesus never claimed the title, all signs pointed to him as God's Messiah.

Hence Christ resolved the ancient conflict by revealing the future for all the people in the world once and for all: "God is the Father of faith for all mankind."

If the Jews want to continue fighting about the faith of

Abraham and its hold on humanity today, it is solely for the purpose of maintaining a privileged status as children of Abraham while the children of God in the world are being held hostage. This family feud about the fatherhood of faith—God versus Abraham—is a conflict in faith perception. Nonetheless the faith issue needs to be resolved if peace on Earth is to be the rule of God.

As Christ called Abraham in ancient times, so Christ is calling us today. He is looking for our positive response to serve him. Christ is the living Word of God since the beginning of time and, therefore, the authority on divine calls and covenants. This truth is contingent on faith and is authenticated by our faith and trust in God. But we also know that a spiritual connection with God is essential to make faith real. Relationships with the living God are faith commitments contingent on the spiritual connection. Abraham enjoyed that spiritual connection with God when he ventured to Palestine, but the Jews in Jesus' time had never experienced a spiritual bond with God—if they had they would never have opposed Jesus' claim to be God's Son. For this very reason of faith perception, the wrangles with the Jews exploded into a raw conflict between Jesus and his opponents.

Certainly Christ has resolved the issue of Messiah for Christians. And Christians are generous in sharing their faith convictions and trust in God with the rest of the world in the context of the Christian covenant of love. In this covenant, Christians accept Jews and Muslims as spiritual brothers and sisters as a matter of faith. We believe that for this very purpose Jesus Christ issued a new covenant, the covenant of Christian love, to bring all people of the world into fellowship and communion with God according to the Gospel. The Gospel's theme is sharing the love of God. Christ tells the children of the world: "By your faith in God you are children of God." The ancient conflict about old covenant claims has lost its sting for Christians.

From a strictly humanitarian point of view, killing each other about who are God's true children of faith makes no sense at all. It makes no sense to any persons with strictly secular outlooks on life that people who claim faith in God destroy each other in the name of God to prove a claim to Abraham's faith inheritance for which theological arguments are clouded and truth is sparse. The Abraham faith issue, therefore, remains contentious at best in the modern world.

Moreover, Palestine is beset by other problems. In these modern times the Jewish faith is plagued by problems from within. Zionism has surfaced to give the Jewish faith a different twist. Though a relatively new phenomenon, Zionism has gained world influence since 1917. Unfortunately, in the current times, the political arrogance of Zionism surpasses the Jewish aggressiveness from the religious parties of the Sadducees and Pharisees in Jesus' time. World politics is challenged. But even more so, God is put to the test as never before. Zionism has turned the religious conflict into a political battlefield in which barrages on the traditional faith of Abraham, Isaac, and Jacob are as common as the everyday attacks against Palestinian Muslims by the political state of Israel. Religious arrogance in modern Palestine, and throughout the world, is the root cause of terrorism.

The relation of the new faith to the old

Christ says:
*"I am the way, and the truth, and the life;
no one comes to the Father, but by me."*

What is the relation of the new faith to the old?

This is a complex question because of faith diversity. For the proper answer to this intricate question, we look to each faith tradition to speak for itself. In the Christian tradition, Jesus Christ is the Son of God. He is the Messiah. He supplanted the Law of Moses with his Gospel of faith, hope, and love. Christians believe that Christ is the living Word of God, and he was with God since the beginning of time.

Therefore, Christians have a timeless relationship of trust with the living God. Our access to God is solely through Jesus Christ. Our knowledge of God is Christ's revelations in word and deeds. His Word opens the eyes of believers to see God. Christ says: "I am the way, and the truth, and the life; no one comes to the Father but by me." (John 14:6) His deeds are his works of teaching and healing in the name of God; within this context, God is the Father of faith for all people. Furthermore, Christians believe in the Holy Spirit as God living among us.

The Gospel writer John states that Jesus Christ came to his own people, the Jews, but they rejected him: "He came to his own home, and his own people received him not. But to all who received him, who believed in his name, he gave power to become children of God; who were born, not of blood nor of the will of the flesh nor of the will of man, but of God." (John 1:11-13)

Henceforth God claims all who believe in Jesus Christ as his children. Christians, therefore, are free forever from the burden of worldly controversies about faith, and we are not touched by worldly claims as to who are the true heirs of Abraham. As disciples of Christ we categorically state that Christians, Jews, Muslims, as well as all other peace-loving people from the diversity of religions in the world who believe in God as the supreme reality are his children. All children of the world therefore are children of God, the believers, the seekers, the agnostics, and all others who are spiritually connected with God. All humanity is one family in which God Almighty is our Father.

Comparative reality

By the power of the Holy Spirit, God forever sealed
human destiny in the Christian covenant of love.

The Holy Spirit gained status in Old Testament times in the
prophecies of Isaiah. Isaiah pointed to a new beginning in the
relationship of people and God. The prophet projected a future
hitherto unknown. Isaiah prophesied about the spiritual connection by the power of the Holy Spirit. He implied the eventual
transition of life from the law given to Moses to freedom in the
Spirit. Following Isaiah's initial prophecies, spiritual life gained
substance in messianic prophecies. The people of Israel from
742 to 687 B.C. were given a foretaste of spiritual realities and
life in the presence of God through prophecies.

The prophet Isaiah succinctly projected the true life as life in
the Spirit of the Lord. The Spirit of the Lord is the life-giving and
life-sustaining authority of creation. Isaiah unfolds the new spiritual life as the rule of God's Son: "And the Spirit of the Lord
shall rest upon him, the spirit of wisdom and understanding, the
spirit of counsel and might, the spirit of knowledge and the fear
of the Lord. And his delight shall be in the fear of the Lord. He
shall not judge by what his eyes see, or decide by what his ears
hear, but with righteousness he shall judge the poor, and
decide with equity for the meek of the Earth; and he shall smite
the Earth with the rod of his mouth, and with the breath of his
lips he shall slay the wicked. Righteousness shall be the girdle
of his waist and faithfulness the girdle of his loins." (Isaiah 11:2-
5)

Additionally, the prophet Jeremiah gave the people of Israel
a foretaste of the Christian covenant of love before to the downfall of Judah. Through his prophet, God addressed the inhabitants of Jerusalem in their darkest hour. God spoke about a
new covenant written in the hearts of men: "Behold, the days

are coming, says the Lord, when I will make a new covenant with the house of Israel and the house of Judah, not like the covenant which I made with their fathers when I took them by the hand to bring them out of the land of Egypt, my covenant which they broke, though I was their husband, says the Lord. But this is the covenant which I will make with the house of Israel after those days, says the Lord: I will put my law within them, and I will write it upon their hearts; and I will be their God, and they shall be my people. And no longer shall each man teach his neighbor and each his brother, saying, 'Know the Lord,' for they shall all know me, from the least of them to the greatest, says the Lord; for I will forgive their iniquity, and I will remember their sin no more." (Jeremiah 31:31-34) The inevitable then happened.

The destruction of Solomon's Temple followed, and the prominent citizens of Judah faced a very uncertain future. Abraham's children were at the mercy of Nebuchadrezzar, the Chaldean king of Babylon. Eventually he deported the prominent citizens of Judah to Babylon. And the Diaspora—the dispersion of the Jewish people into foreign lands—set the stage for the persecution of Jewish people ever since.

Though the foundation for spiritual fulfillment is now history because of what God through Christ has done, persecutions of people because of their religious faith continue to this very day. Christ shares his resurrected life with all believers. By the power of the Holy Spirit, Christ blesses all who believe in him with his spiritual qualities. What then is all the fighting about? The answer is human obstinacy. We want all the benefits from God, but we want them according to our way.

Certainly the spiritual connection is a gift from God. We have the potential as children of God to excel in everything we do according to our Father's will. What becomes of it is entirely up to us. That does not seem good enough for many people. Christ has fulfilled both Isaiah's and Jeremiah's prophesies for the three monotheistic faith religions of Judaism, Christianity, and Islam. By the power of the Holy Spirit, God forever sealed human destiny in the Christian covenant of love. God is generous for sure, but we complain that our inputs don't count. We feel slighted because God is ignoring our personal wishes.

Life with the resurrected Christ and baptism
with the Holy Spirit is the future.

Little is known about the spiritual nature of relationships between people and God in ancient Israel before the coming of Christ. Temple rituals were prominent, but they ceased with the destruction of Solomon's Temple circa 586 B.C. The land of previously glorious temple rituals is a spiritual unknown following the Diaspora. Prophecies declined. Spiritual life with the living God never blossomed into meaningful relationships before the Christian era. The promise of God in the land of promise never flourished to the full extent of God's intent. The record is spotty at best. Life with the resurrected Christ and baptism with the Holy Spirit was the future. It was yet to come.

The ancient land of promise and its Jewish inhabitants passed through several hands in the seven centuries before Jesus Christ, which adds to the uncertainties. Assyrians, Babylonians, Persians, Greeks, and Romans desired a piece of God in action, but all the conquering was to no avail. God cannot be captured like the property of nations. God is God! God is Spirit, and where the Spirit of God is there is ultimate freedom and absolute reality. Can anyone enslave the author of freedom with the power of the sword? No! No one can threaten God and expect to survive. Can conquerors intimidate God and gain his favor? No! God is God! If spiritual gain is the prize of battle, the sword of the world cannot overpower the Sword of the Spirit. Freedom is how people use God's spiritual gift of faith. Freedom is life in the presence of God by the power of the Holy

Spirit!

God has remained elusive to the heroes of the world. From his throne in high Heaven, God watches and wonders what the world will do next. And God laughs as he joins the heavenly host to see his people in the world squirming, wheeling, and dealing. God says: "What do my earthlings aspire? What are they up to now?" In this confusion, God says: "People try to reach up to me. But they will never come near me. Henceforth I will provide the solution to the spiritual needs of my children. I will come down to Earth and meet my children face to face." The once distant God of temple rituals is now near in Jesus Christ. Life by the power of the Holy Spirit is daily routine! Spiritual life is now absolute reality in the Christian covenant of love! God will baptize his children of faith with the Holy Spirit.

People fight and kill in defiance of God's wishes for cosmic peace and universal harmony.

In retrospect, let us take a quick look at ancient history in the land of promise. A good portion of this history is about wars. Let us learn from the past and review past shortcomings in light of the present. Let us then build a better future. The immediate threat facing people in ancient times was war. What are people always fighting for? Why do individuals and nations conquer the lands and fortunes of neighbors? History in the ancient land of promise proves an uncompromising and frightening state of human insolence because of wars.

People fight and kill in defiance of God's wishes for cosmic peace and universal harmony. No one in God's creation is exempt from the rule of God. However, people claim special privileges and dispensations and then act in defiance of world order. The only certainty of uncertain history in the Holy Land is that there was little or no peace in Palestine ever since Joshua led the people of Israel into the Promised Land.

Greed reaps profits at the expense of culture and heritage.

The people of Israel also experienced the problems associated with greed that plagued her neighbors. Greed fostered reliance on material riches. Wealth became a formidable ideological force in Palestine during the reign of Solomon. Trade and making money continue today to be of greater interest to the diverse Jews and Palestinians in the region than a working relationship with the living God and peace among men. All the gains of material riches have been, and continue to be, hard fought at the expense of faith.

Greed always shoves faith aside. History has shown this to have been so in Israel 2,000 years ago. History is witness to the workings of old-fashioned greed in Palestine in modern times. But all the money of the world—and all the power and might of nations—cannot buy faith. Money cannot buy love. Money cannot buy respect. Money cannot secure peace. Money cannot buy God.

The divine lesson by the power of the Holy Spirit in all this turbulence in modern events is that human greed has no respect for God and people. Greed wants immediate rewards. Greed reaps profits at the expense of culture and heritage. The greed in human aspirations operates without past or future. Greed fights in the present and destroys the future.

The truth about God is a constant revelation
by the Holy Spirit.

The Holy Spirit is God's sole teacher of historical truth and its contribution to values in the present. The Holy Spirit points out all the pitfalls in life. Powerful armies cannot create harmony and peace. Materialism is short-lived. Greed and lust for power die with people. But the Holy Spirit brings salvation by the Word of God. The Holy Spirit tells us that we are children of God.

The aforementioned is only part of the problem. Let us beware! There is a greater evil than greed. Where armies and greed fail, ideologies succeed. The real threat to the relationship of people and God in ancient Palestine and in the modern world is not conquering armies but ideologies. Ideologies work on the mind to force a change of commitment in the heart. Ideologies never acknowledge the powerful God of creation or his presence in the world. Ideologies press forward by the drive of personal ambition. Ideologies are the creations of fanatics. Religious and political fanatics in modern times gun down the innocent to gain the upper hand in controlling peace-loving people by force.

In this ongoing battle instigated by human ideologies, God supports his faithful people as spiritual beings to live in faith, by faith, and for faith. A commitment in faith alone can free us from the slavery of human ideologies. The truth about God is a constant revelation by the Holy Spirit. The Holy Spirit does not compromise with philosophy. As philosophy has no room for inspiration, inspiration has no room for philosophy. God speaks by the power of the Holy Spirit. And the Word of God is guide and support for all human needs in every situation that might confront us.

By the power of the Holy Spirit God addresses all our concerns. So we press on with our questions. What about undocumented history and the scars left open for which there is no closure? God has turned the loss of historic documentation into our greatest personal gain by making us totally dependent on the Holy Spirit. The Holy Spirit inspires us with truth that is eternal—this truth knows neither beginning nor ending. The Holy Spirit soothes and heals the wounds inflicted by evil, and all we have to do is ask for God's help.

Jesus Christ is the living Word of God among us. Jesus Christ is eternal truth. The Holy Spirit reveals the truth. Truth transforms comparative reality into absolute reality of life in union with God. Before us is the manifestation of the New Faith. Let us read on.

The manifestation of the new faith

Jesus Christ is a bountiful source of faith, hope, and love.

The Christian faith is a timeless relationship of trust with the living God. The seeds of faith are plenteous. Jesus Christ is a bountiful source for faith, hope, and love. The Holy Spirit guides us on the path of faith based on the righteousness of God. Faith is God's power active in our lives. Faith makes things happen. Foremost among the examples is the healing power of faith. Faith is God's medicine in healing body, mind, and spirit. He prescribes it for every person in the world in need of perseverance in trusting him. Faith creates spiritual health and maintains physical well being. God says: "Call your faith into action, and I come running!"

A tiny seed of faith always in due time grows into a giant shade tree. The shade of faith trees keeps us safe from the burning rays of discord and hate. Faith trees are oases of rest for weary souls traveling in the desert of confusion and hate.

For the sojourner in the spiritual desert, faith trees are the last source of hope when confusion and doubt tell wretched souls that there is really nothing to live for. Our souls will see and experience the healing balm of God's saving waters from the well of life. The Holy Spirit is with us at faith stations drawing the water of life to quench the spiritual thirst.

Rescue from harm's way is possible in the desert of confusion and doubt because God is planting the seeds of faith in the path of experiences. All we have to do is conscientiously care for our own faith tree in God's forest of faith. With faith comes abundant life. God blesses us with the Word of God so that faith can mature and bear fruit. The fruits of faith are spiritual gifts and love.

Spiritual gifts of love foster creative environments. And Christians are giant pillars of love in the chaos of their respective communities. America is strong, for example, because the faith-love commitment of her people is beyond reproach. An abundance of human talents adds to America's faith blessings. Our faith and talents are powerful engines to move all manner of stress and pressures facing us in an uncertain world. By the power of the Holy Spirit, God provides all the necessary energy of love to conquer every uncertainty of confusion and doubt with love. Our faith initiatives transform failures into opportunities, and love sustains these opportunities.

God makes us victorious over every kind of stress and pressure in the world. His love for people of faith is self-evident in the activities of everyday life. Christian conduct is living the Golden Rule (Matthew 7:12) even beyond the minimum of God's expectations in practical piety. God is the author of spiritual bliss. To be sure, he is the sole author of our inner strength. But God is also with us in our weakest moments. God is with us in our trials and temptations. When we need love, God strengthens us with ever-increasing amounts of faith.

God never gives up his search to find the weak in faith who are on the verge of folding under pressure. God is our most trusted friend. He constantly looks for the wavering in faith until he finds the disheartened. God then makes sure that we are secure in his care. God is always working overtime when we are in trouble because of lack of faith. He strengthens our faith. He works our spiritual renewal until we are safely out of harm's way. In the presence of God, all worldly concerns about the future are trivial. The Era of Faith is God's assurance that this indeed is true. Truly, faith is a timeless relationship of trust with the living God. Let us keep going on the trail of faith and love and learn all about the spiritual connection with God.

The spiritual connection in the new faith

The spiritual connection is the divine process of salvation by grace through faith in Jesus Christ.

When God speaks by the power of the Holy Spirit and saves us, the Holy Spirit spiritually connects us with God. The spiritual connection, therefore, is God's way of supporting the Christian bond of love while we are still pilgrims on Earth. At the same time, the Holy Spirit fortifies the very same bond in preparation for the transformation of our lives in union with God in Heaven when the earthly pilgrimage comes to its certain end.

To help us better comprehend the importance of the spiritual connection let us compare the spiritual connection to a lifeline and look at the new faith as salvation—i.e., God's deliverance from circumstances—by grace through faith in Jesus Christ. A lifeline is the means of saving people from peril. Like lifelines in the physical world, the lifeline in the spiritual connection also is tied to a solid foundation and will hold its ground against the forces of danger facing the person in peril. As in physical life, there too is someone in the spiritual connection throwing the lifeline for eternal life to the person in danger of perishing.

The lifeline in the spiritual connection is grace, the pure love of God for his people. The Holy Spirit is the means of grace giving the lifeline to people in peril. And the Word of God is the solid ground to which the lifeline is anchored. In the modern world, the Holy Spirit connects us spiritually with God through inspired writings on faith. Most prominent among inspired writings is the Bible.

Even though the events in Holy Writ happened ages ago, the events and the recorded stories are as valid today as they were thousands of years ago. Because God is the source of the events, and the authority behind these writings, the Word of God is the same today as it was yesterday and will be tomorrow. In all inspired writings, we are but instruments of the Word of God in bringing a timeless message of hope to people in need of salvation.

For instance, Saint Paul's letters to Christian communities are historic examples illustrating how God works the spiritual connection. Saint Paul's letters started around 50 A.D., roughly 20 years after the resurrection of Jesus Christ. The letter to the Church at Galatia—"the Magna Carta of Christian liberty"—was probably written in A.D. 52. The very influential Christian teachings in Romans were perhaps composed in A.D. 56. Specific dates in holy writings do not matter. The important point in life is our spiritual connection with God by the power of the Holy Spirit.

Following Saint Paul's letters, the Gospels have even later dates in recording. The Gospel stories concerning the life, death, and resurrection of Jesus Christ were collected perhaps as late as A.D. 70 for the Gospel of Mark, and even later— maybe around A.D. 90 to A.D. 110—for the Gospel of John. Specific dates have little meaning in Gospel stories because God's Word is timeless. And the Holy Spirit teaches the truth of the timeless Word of God when we are deemed ready to absorb it all properly.

Clearly, God chose to withhold the Gospel stories in John for over 60 years with no detriment to truth. For the Holy Spirit reveals the truth—and its value for current needs—whenever facts are missing. Let us, therefore, listen to the Holy Spirit as the agent of God in making spiritual connections. The Holy Spirit will always connect us with God in our daily needs. Christ says, "He is the Counselor, the Holy Spirit, whom the Father will send in my name, he will teach you all things, and bring to your remembrance all that I have said to you." (John 14:26) Christ has given his disciples assurances beyond all human expectations in the only sermon of consequence ever preached in

human history: "I am with you always, to the close of the age."
(Matthew 28:20)

All we have to do is accept the Word of God as revealed by
the Holy Spirit. The Holy Spirit connects Christians and God
spiritually for realizing absolute reality.

Concerning the importance of the spiritual connection

Let us ponder the situation of indifference toward the authority of the Holy Spirit of God in making the spiritual connection.
Let us review the consequences of spiritual neglect in light of
the faith of earlier saints and martyrs. This assuredly will help
us to appreciate the contribution of the spiritual connection in
times of trials and temptations.

Had the first followers of Christ treated the blessing of God's
Holy Spirit with less vigor than we actually find recorded, salvation by grace through faith could easily have ended up just as
another religious curiosity. But God did not allow this to happen.

The Pentecost celebration formalized the foundation of the
Christian church. The banner message was "Christ is risen."
And the joyous cry, "He is risen indeed," reverberates God's
message for all generations of Christians. The witness by
saints confirms the Pentecost celebration as an event in human
history. History in the spiritual connection is an agent of God.

But the Holy Spirit is also the catalyst for making the spiritual connection real in people. Saint Paul has given a human
touch to the spiritual connection: "No one can say 'Jesus is
Lord' except by the Holy Spirit." (1 Corinthians 12:3) God has
spoken. Christ has followed through. And now the Holy Spirit
encourages us to do the same and help people with the spiritual connection.

The personal sacrifice of Stephen to witness to the risen
Christ launched the apostleship of Saul of Tarsus. Stephen

offered himself as a living sacrifice. He was not timid in his witness to the new life in the Spirit. We have written testimony that
he had received the full comfort of God's Holy Spirit. Stephen
had submitted to the Will of God in total obedience. He allowed
the Holy Spirit to expose and denounce the rebellious behavior
of the resurrected Christ's persecutors.

The inspiration we get today from reading these early
accounts about the activity of the Holy Spirit is an integral part
of spiritual truth in the modern world. We reap immense benefits from the faith of saints and martyrs. These testimonies to
Christ nourish spiritual growth. Servants of the Gospel make up
the victorious assembly of saints to help us appreciate grace,
truth, and salvation.

Many saints and martyrs throughout history, like Stephen in
earlier times, have suffered agonizing pain. They have given of
themselves to build the foundation for Christ's church.
Salvation by grace through faith is the spiritual foundation for us
today.

Stephen, indeed, is God's model for Christian conduct under
trying circumstances. He demonstrated what it means to give
up one's life in doing the work of God. His effort is bearing fruit
in the world for all generations of Christians to come.

Stephen's death by stoning propelled Saul of Tarsus to be
among the greatest of Christ's teachers. He preached the Word
of God about salvation through grace and faith with perseverance. He gave up all the comforts of secular life so that we may
live in full spiritual knowledge that our salvation is assured by
grace through faith.

The specifics of Saul's conversion story show how Saint Paul
proclaimed Jesus as the Christ, saying: "He is the Son of God."
(Acts 9:20) Paul was able to proclaim this message boldly
because he was "filled with the Holy Spirit." (Acts 13:9)

Stephen, indeed, was God's pillar of grace in the manifestation of the new covenant. The Christian covenant of love now

rules the souls of men. His death at the hands of a defiant world means life for us now.

The instant Saul was baptized by God with the Holy Spirit, God's message of salvation and hope began to spread like wildfire in the ancient world. We now have a glorious future in a life of union with Christ. Stephen's commitment has, indeed, produced bounteous results for spiritual connections with God ever since.

The Good News of the Gospel of Christ traveled near and far. Jews and Gentiles became believers. Saint Paul's work was inspired by the power of the Holy Spirit. Saint Paul recognized his blessing to be a teacher of the Word of God. And he took advantage in bringing the Word of God to the Gentiles in building their spiritual connections with God.

Let us, therefore, search our hearts and thoroughly comprehend God's blessing of the spiritual connection in the new faith. God wants us to be an effective witness to his Christian covenant of love. God's salvation story is a love story. God has given us a powerful message. We now plow the fields, and the Holy Spirit spreads the seeds of faith. And faith grows. God does the rest. All these efforts illustrate the spiritual connection with God in its purest form.

God's promises reside in his peace. Sabbath rest has taken on a new meaning. God is inviting his children of faith to celebrate his victory over death and the world. In Holy Communion God celebrates with us each Sunday his cosmic victory over all opposition to his Word, while at the same time God also renews our spiritual connection with him for the following week and, ultimately, for eternity.

The ultimate benefit on Earth in our spiritual connection with God, however, is the assurance that God will meet us at the rainbow bridge of divine grace. At the final step of our earthly journey, God is waiting to welcome home his faithful pilgrims. Let us, therefore, thank God for the spiritual connection. We also thank God for connecting us with Saint Stephen and Saint Paul, so that we can learn from their experiences. Most of all let us thank God for spiritually connecting himself to us to bring about our salvation from evil, sin, and death.

By the power of the Holy Spirit, all Christians are spiritually connected with God for eternity. As we now rest in the peace of God, God celebrates his life in us through our spiritual connection with him.

Conflicts in the world about faith issues will continue, but they have no control over spiritual wellbeing and happiness. We are not alone any more to confront our adversaries. The Holy Spirit is with us. And the Holy Spirit wields the Sword of the Spirit as the living Word of God on our behalf through the spiritual connection!

ACT II
THE CONFLICT OF THE NEW FAITH WITH THE OLD

Conflict over faith promise
Confrontation over Jesus Christ as the supreme revelation of God

Chapter 3

Conflict over faith promise

Spiritual conflicts are human aberrations of the way of God. God does not induce conflicts, nor does he encourage people to pursue a lifestyle of chaos where the ultimate goal is confrontation, especially in spiritual matters.

Human intelligence passed down through the ages by word of mouth warns us to stay clear of conflicts about religion. We are advised to proudly show our faith convictions in the cheerful smile of a soul whose sole source of confidence is God. Friends tell us to always encourage deeds of charity and compassion for an overall improvement of the human condition in the world. This is the work of love. And love has no time for conflicts.

Spiritual conflicts flourish when selfish motives gain the upper hand over faith and reason. Jesus Christ saw this behavior in people at the onset of his earthly ministry. The Jews of Jesus' day were jealously guarding their turf in the presumptuous belief that they alone were the true children of faith through Abraham, and with this promise they had definite privileges. They claimed in their presumptuous attitudes absolute ownership of God and his blessings.

The hostility to Christ centered not on faith inheritance alone but also on the finer nuances of human behavior toward God. Despite their boisterous claims, the Jews were powerless in their defense of the false notion about being the sole owners of God's promise to Abraham; neither could they defend the extreme presumption that God is supportive of Jews only.

The Jews clashed with Jesus on faith promise and several other fronts: faith definition and faith practice coupled with a self-centered tribal attitude toward God and personal behavior that was self-seeking and arrogant. They were intolerant toward other viewpoints, especially if the new realities interfered with the imagined privileged lifestyle based on their glory as children of Abraham. In their way of thinking Abraham was everything, and they scorned everyone else who dared to propose otherwise—especially anyone who claimed to be the Son of God with the implication that Jesus Christ is the Messiah.

The Jews of Jerusalem in Jesus' day were fighting an imaginary battle with Jesus, because the advent of the church and baptism by the Holy Spirit were years away. Nonetheless, they feared Jesus. Intuitively they felt that he was the Son of God and that he had authority over faith promise, but they did not want to admit it. Therefore, they scorned Jesus as they had previously scorned John the Baptist because he dared to expose the hypocrisy and falsehood on every front of arrogant faith assumptions. The Jews felt especially intimidated by Jesus' humility and faith integrity, even more so than they previously felt threatened by the Baptist's outspoken call to repentance and change. But the opposition to Jesus Christ at Jerusalem was not a unified front. Some ordinary people considered him a good man; others felt that he was leading the people astray. Christ loved the ordinary people, and he considered them as sheep without a shepherd. Christ's problems were not the ordinary people in the diverse walks of ordinary life; Christ's problem was the Jewish leadership—identified in John's Gospel as "the Jews." This religious elite were bursting at the seams with anger. They knew Christ was true to God's charge as the model of the godly life, and they saw in him a most obvious threat to their way of doing things.

The Gospel of John (8:12-59) recorded for posterity the climax of the confrontations. The raw anger of the Jews exploded when Jesus was true to the Word of God and presented himself as the light of the world sent into the world by God his Father. The Jewish leaders felt slighted because Jesus identified himself as the light of the world instead of the Jewish leadership. Ultimately, however, they did not want anything to do with the Son of God; they feared the onset of changes in their lifestyles.

A previous confrontation with John the Baptist opened the conflict. John called the Jewish leaders the way he saw them: "You brood of vipers!" (Matthew 3:7). To be sure, it was not a pretty description; it was true, but not gentle. They felt they deserved better in their leading role as authorities in the faith. But subsequently Jesus affirmed John's assessment verbatim when the Jews accused him of doing the mighty acts of God in the name of Satan (Matthew 12:34). Even harsher words resulted in the ultimate clash. Jesus formally denounced the Jewish leadership as "hypocrites" and "blind fools." They, in turn, responded with a fierce attack on the person of Jesus and his mission and work as the Savior of mankind. In reality, though, their attack was directed against God because God dared to think about changing the world of faith and religion, and in displeasure they objected to God's anointment of Jesus Christ as the Messiah.

Despite their objection to Jesus Christ as the light of the world, and in spite of their fears of imminent change, the Jews were powerless to stop God from bringing about the transformation of faith from meaningless Temple rituals to an active participation of God and people in the new covenant of

Christian love.

> Christianity was to be. God decreed it.
> God ordained the time for change.

Change is always a dreadful word for people who prefer the status quo and would like to continue the lifestyle of the past—especially those enjoying a privileged lifestyle. It was a terrible thought for the Jews that the glory days of David and Solomon were gone forever. Christ was disturbing a line of wishful thinking that had no future because the Christian covenant of love was to be the future. And the ultimate event happened. The Christian covenant of love fulfilled the Law of Moses. God's gift of faith is now acclaimed as the universal gift of faith to all people, including the Jews.

The Jews of Jesus' days guarded their presumptuous faith promise with unrestrained vigor. Nobody else was entitled to God's generosity but the Jewish people. So they questioned the rite of baptism by John the Baptist and called it an illegal act because John the Baptist did not have official approval from the Jewish leadership. The issue was not the water of baptism alone. Intuitively the Jews ultimately worried about the true Baptism by the Holy Spirit. They knew all about the role of water in the Jewish rite of purification. But future unknowns about the role of the Holy Spirit—and baptism by the Holy Spirit—frightened them. They were afraid of the day when the improved version of faith was coming between them, Abraham, and God.

And this is precisely what was going to happen by divine decree. The Holy Spirit transformed a ritual of purification into a living faith by baptism, a faith by the power of the Holy Spirit and, ultimately the spiritual connection with God. By the power of the Holy Spirit God has an active role in the Christian faith. He had entered the world in the person of Jesus Christ to be with his people. God himself is the Messiah, and the Messiah has come. God incarnate is now the Savior of all mankind. But there were other storm clouds on the horizon in Jesus' ministry on Earth.

Confrontation over Jesus Christ the supreme revelation of God

Whereas the God of the Old Testament is the God of prophecy, the God of the Gospel is the God of revelation by the power of the Holy Spirit. This statement is significant for our understanding of the self-revelation of God in Jesus Christ. For Christians all spiritual confrontations are over. The victory is won. Christ has won the victory for us on the cross. Christians are children of God, and the Christian story is a New Testament!

As we look at the Gospel, we see a righteous God and a loving father who wants an active role in the welfare of his children. By the power of the Holy Spirit, God empowers his faithful children with faith, hope, and love against fear, terror, and deceit. Past conflicts are history. The Christian life is the story of a new spiritual connection with the living God; our God has been active for billions of years.

Christ as the lord of his church speaks to us directly on all matters of faith. Our father in Heaven, the father of all who believe in Jesus Christ, has given Christ absolute authority over Heaven and Earth—and us.

We see God in Christ. This is the supreme revelation!

Christ is the foundation of our faith. This is central in our relationship with God. The Gospel proclaims this new revelation. The Gospel inspires faith. And it quickens life. God inspires us with the truth of his Word to constantly widen our horizons of faith. This has never been done in the past. God includes us in his spiritual work. Toward this end, God connects us spiritually with him to make sure that we are secure in his care as active participants in all his actions! The God of Abraham is active in the lives of Christians by the power of the Holy Spirit.

Moreover, the Father of Jesus Christ is also the Father of all mankind! The children of the world are his children in a true sense. The once distant God of ancient theology is available to all the children of the world just for the asking. He is always ready to help us. All we have to do is to call upon him in faith and truth: "The Lord is near to all who call upon him, to all who call upon him in truth" (Psalm 145:18) David prophesied about Christ.

Jesus Christ advances our already rewarding relationship into oneness with God, in which Christ is "the way, and the truth, and the life." (John 14:6) As we open our hearts to Christ, the Holy Spirit guards us with the Sword of the Spirit, which is the living Word of God. The Holy Spirit defends the Word and our faith convictions with all his might. The revelation we now experience is God living with us: "If a man loves me, he will keep my word, and my father will love him, and we will come to him and make our home with him." (John 14:24) In the presence of God truth is supreme. Truth leads to peace. And Christ includes us in his peace (John 14:27). From now on the Peace of God shelters us for eternal life.

God loves us, and he shares his life with us. What, then, is left to worry about? By the power of the Holy Spirit we now enjoy eternal life. This *fait accompli* is our salvation secured by God as the Christian covenant of love.

We are one with God, and Christ protects us from fierce worldly conflicts and deadly confrontations in a devouring world. Christ champions his disciples for eternal life in union with God. It is a new reality. It is a new faith! Great things await us now in the new reality in which Christ shepherds his disciples by the power of the Holy Spirit!

ACT III
THE NEW REALITY

The Holy Spirit
Christianity
The Era of Faith
The From/to method for spiritual fulfillment

Chapter 4

The Holy Spirit

Background

In an earth-shaking event Jesus Christ reveals the nature of God to a woman of Samaria. Christ speaks plainly about his father: "God is Spirit." Christ breaks tradition and ushers in the new age of absolute reality in which the spiritual connection with God is supreme reality.

The son of God follows up his awe-inspiring revelation to the Samaritan woman by telling the world at large the conditions for living with his father, the one eternal God: "Those who worship him must worship him in spirit and truth." (John 4:24) What is truth? Truth is nothing less than the model of the godly life of Jesus Christ. The God of all mankind is spirit, and truth is the condition for worship. In this truth the Holy Spirit is God Almighty present at all times throughout the world.

Pilgrim T. Homosapien, Servant of God, expands on this vital spiritual truth for the Era of Faith. Pilgrim explains: "Christ says, 'God is Spirit.' The Son of God is clearing up once and for all every theological argument about the identity, nature, and character of God. Christ commands: 'Worship God in spirit.' This alone satisfies the divine expectation of faithfulness and obedience in service to God. We submerge all worldly desires in the will of God, for our life on Earth is by the power of the Holy Spirit. We thankfully accept what Jesus Christ is telling us; newness of life has roots and connections that are spiritual, which no power on Earth can destroy. Christ commands: 'Worship God in truth.' Truth defines for all people the character of human attitudes and behavior. Applied truth is the model of the godly life of Jesus Christ. Henceforth we have no choice in the matter of truth but to abide with Christ, and live according to God's righteousness by the power of the Holy Spirit. God the Spirit is the Holy Spirit in the world."

Pilgrim closes his explanation on Christ's earth-shaking revelation to the Samaritan woman with the Word of God: "The new reality in the Era of Faith is now the spiritual connection. We derive our energy for life directly from God our Father 'by the power of the Holy Spirit.' The power of God is the power of the Holy Spirit in the world." We can be what God wants us to be. Our life in union with God is full of the melody of life that the Holy Spirit inspires within us.

The Holy Spirit is on center stage of life, directing our lives. This section is but a limited presentation of the activities of the Holy Spirit in everyday life. The discussion centers on a few of the highlights: (a) Background; (b) The Holy Spirit is God revealed in Jesus Christ; (c) The Holy Spirit saves us from evil; (d) The Holy Spirit is God's sole source for the spiritual connection; (e) The Holy Spirit is the presiding authority on faith and relationships; (f) The Holy Spirit is the presiding authority on history; (g) The Holy Spirit is God's teacher on truth and history; (h) The Holy Spirit leads us to God for every need; (i) The Holy Spirit and Sundays; (j) Baptism with The Holy Spirit; (k) The Holy Spirit in everyday life; (l) The Holy Spirit works the transformation of life; (m) The Holy Spirit helps us to become God's friends; (n) The Holy Spirit is our freedom; (o) The Holy Spirit is our future of promise.

The Holy Spirit is God revealed in Jesus Christ

*Life "by the power of the Holy Spirit" is life in
the majestic splendor of God.*

In the context of spiritual values, what does it mean when we say "by the power of the Holy Spirit?" Life by the power of the Holy Spirit is life in the majestic splendor of God's presence. And God works his will and purpose through us to make the world a better place. We witness to the world—and we confess before God—that we move and have our being in union with God through Jesus Christ by the power of the Holy Spirit. We submerge all human desires in the will of God for the purpose of our creation. Our needs are the needs of the Kingdom of God on Earth. In this relationship, the Holy Spirit is our guardian, teacher, and friend. We experience daily the presence of the Holy Spirit in our prayers. Saint Paul explains: "The Spirit helps us in our weakness; for we do not know how to pray as we ought, but the Spirit himself intercedes for us with sighs too deep for words. And he who searches the hearts of men knows what is the mind of the Spirit, because the Spirit intercedes for the saints according to the Will of God." (Romans 8:26-27)

The Holy Spirit is God revealed in Jesus Christ. This divine declaration clears up all speculation about the One God and fosters a common understanding of God in the Holy Trinity. The Holy Spirit is God active in the world in the hearts and souls of faithful believers. His life is our being. And in this relationship Jesus Christ is Lord.

The Holy Spirit saves us from evil

*The prime office of the Holy Spirit is to inspire us with the
Word of God, to protect us from the evil of tempting God, and*

to guide us in worshiping and serving God at all times.

Our God is a God who saves. This truth applies to all people in the world. The theme of salvation is the continuous thread in the weaver's hand weaving each individual mantle of salvation. We are children of God. Our loving father in Heaven sees to it always that we are properly dressed in his cloak of salvation. God has ordained human life on Earth to be lived by the power of the Holy Spirit to keep us safe from evil in our short pilgrimage on Earth. Our life in union with God is a mutual bond of love and admiration that evil cannot break, for the defender of our spiritual connection is God the Holy Spirit.

We welcome the Holy Spirit into our hearts and ceaselessly pray to sustain our souls as his home, for the spiritual life in the Peace of God is constantly threatened by the evil of a selfish world. As Christ's followers we are still living in the world; therefore, the world hates us as it has hated Christ. Out of concern for our physical welfare and spiritual wellbeing, Christ prayed to God on our behalf for the Holy Spirit to keep us safe from evil.

Evil in the modern world grows like the weeds in a bed of exquisite flowers. Therefore, each of us is responsible for weeding our flowerbeds of faith; as Christ the gardener is weeding the world's flowerbed of faith as the source of inspiration for his disciples. Christians are the flowers of faith. Since weeds rob the flowers of nourishment, weeds in the garden of life are aberrations of the way of God. The weeds in life rob us of nourishment for happiness. We cause the aberrations in the way of God through human shortcomings. Self-righteousness makes us falter in faith, and eventually we will fail in our commitment of faithfulness and obedience to God. Since the beginning of human spirituality, mankind has been extremely busy on its own behalf to escape the presence of God. Our poor attitude toward God is the common source of evil weeds among the flowers in God's wondrous garden of faith. Even though recorded history is only 4,000 years old at best, in this seemingly insignificant short period of time on the eternal time scale of billions of years people have been busily nourishing more weeds than flowers. The schemes to outsmart God and each other in unfair competition speak volumes.

Weeds are not the only disturbance to the beauty of an exquisite garden of faith. Multiplicities of other problems distract us from seeing God in the purity of his absolute reality. Among them is greed as the ultimate promoter of personal supremacy. Devilish greed has a strong partner in the lust for power. Lust for power is the sin that separates greedy people from God by encouraging them that it is all right to overpower and subdue friend and neighbor in the drive to individual greatness. The very people that once have lifted up a promising leader to prominence are now slaves to a tyrant. In radical situations tyrants kill their opposition just to remain in power. For example, Cain killed Abel to eliminate competition. In the more recent past, we have seen an evil tyrant killing masses of innocent people in the Holocaust. Tyrants use terror, death, and war to promote the rule of evil.

The world is full of evil. There appears to be no end to killing and suppression. People deny people the breath of life. People have killed the prophets of God. People have killed the Son of God. People ceaselessly threaten the servants of God in these modern times.

Why?

Why all the killings in modern times? Why all the threats to peace and family tranquility? Modern people are supposed to know better; we are better educated, and we are supposed to be more civilized than our ancestors were in ancient times. So we relentlessly keep asking the same question over and over again: Why? And we appear to be powerless to correct an evil situation.

Why do people kill brothers and sisters, the very young, the elderly, and especially those in the prime of their lives who are the promising source of leadership for building a better world? Why do we slaughter the future of promise in wars?

And then there is terror. Terror in the contemporary world is the zenith of irony. Terrorists kill or maim innocent people in the name of God. Other mundane examples of opposition to the way of God are arrogance, deceit, and immoral and unethical behavior in business and economics. Economic injustices are subtle ways of denying our neighbor freedom and happiness. Man-created fear and stress are evil ways that beat family, fellow workers, neighbors, societies, and even the world at large into submission and slavery. We have seen great evils in two world wars and the Vietnam War. The list of evils in a lackluster world is endless. Evil has no respect for God, people, and national boundaries. Evil sprouts like weeds when human nature rejects God, and the evil in human nature has deep roots.

Christ is shielding us by the power of the Holy Spirit against man-made calamities and all forms of evil in the modern world. By the power of the Holy Spirit, God empowers his faithful children with faith, hope, and love against fear, terror, and deceit. The prime office of the Holy Spirit is to inspire us with the Word of God, to protect us from the evil of tempting God, and to support us as we worship and serve God at all times.

The Holy Spirit is God's sole source for the spiritual connection

Spiritual fulfillment is complete when we joyfully live by the power of the Holy Spirit.

Jesus Christ opened his ministry in the spiritual glory of God: "The Spirit of the Lord is upon me, because he has anointed me to preach good news to the poor. He has sent me to proclaim release to the captives and recovering of sight to the blind, to set at liberty those who are oppressed, to proclaim the acceptable year of the Lord." (Luke 4:18)

God in Christ entered the world over 2,000 years ago to bring salvation to the children of Abraham, but the Jews did not see it that way. They rejected the Son of God on artificial grounds of pride as the heirs of Abraham. Their excuse for rejecting Jesus Christ was his claim to spiritual oneness with God. The message about his spiritual oneness with God offended the religious as well as the secular leaders of the Jews. Moreover, they were afraid that Jesus Christ was indeed God's Messiah who had come to uproot the status quo and force a cataclysmic change in behavior by implementing justice, equality, and peace among people according to the way of God! The Jews in Jesus' time were not interested in God's spiritual way of life.

Gentiles in the modern world keep falling into the same trap of spiritual opposition to God as did the Jews in Jesus' time. People in the modern world also want all the spiritual rewards that come from God without having to give up old habits. Nor are modern people excited about the opportunity to spiritually connect with God. We always postpone the required commitment of faith that spiritual connections with God demand.

But how can the servant act differently from the master he serves? God is the master. Jesus Christ as the Son of God is his Father's servant to help us return to God! As disciples of Christ, we are now his voice and his hands in the world to make the world a better place for everyone. Jesus Christ has given himself for securing our spiritual connection with God. Christ has opened the way for our life with God and, in return, he expects the same self-evident commitment from us if we are to attain the goal of a vibrant spiritual connection with God.

Pilgrim T. Homosapien, Servant of God to America in the Era of Faith, now exposes falsehood in contemporary schemes of self-righteousness: "Modern people wrongly assume that the same premise about human greatness that works success in the secular world also applies to the Kingdom of God. They argue: 'Why be a servant when you can be the master?' Modern people have no interest in spiritual connections with God as long as the secular world meets all temporary human desires. Modern people live for the day. They treat tomorrow as just another day of rewards by chance for personal achievements and self-glorification. They do not worry about sublime promises of living on in eternity. The modern attitude is facing trouble when trouble comes, while in the interim doing our own things. They dare to test God concerning life in eternity. Thus they are ill prepared to meet God at the rainbow bridge of grace when earthly life comes to a sudden end." Shortsighted human thinking has created a situation for which there is no solution when self-righteousness reaches its certain downfall. When the reality of downfall arrives, then the modern world cries out in despair: "Where is God when we need him?" This outcry is just another step in the self-glorification scheme. We are trying to shift the blame for spiritual neglect from man to God.

By the power of the Holy Spirit Pilgrim T. Homosapien declares the Word of God about self-righteousness. Thus says the Lord: "Be penitent. Change. Correct your attitudes and behavior, and align your commitments with my will and my purpose for you in my spiritual realm. Believe in me. Believe in Christ. Love me and Christ with all your heart, mind, and soul. Remember, your life is my breath in you. I am steadfast in my love for you. Accept the authority of the Holy Spirit as my presence in your life. I am glorified as the Holy Spirit works my will through you. I am your God. You are my children. I, the Lord have spoken."

Jesus Christ has singled out respect in relationships as the criterion for spiritual performance. He also established love for God and people as the sole qualification for the spiritual connection under the guidance of the Holy Spirit. These divine measures separate the worldly show-off from the truly dedicated workers in God's Kingdom on Earth: "Beware of false prophets, who come to you in sheep's clothing but inwardly are ravenous wolves. You will know them by their fruits. Are grapes gathered from thorns, or figs from thistles? So every sound tree bears good fruit, but the bad tree bears evil fruit. A sound tree cannot bear evil fruit, nor can a bad tree bear good fruit. Every tree that does not bear good fruit is cut down and thrown into the fire. Thus you will know them by their fruits." (Matthew 7:15-20)

Improvements in attitudes about life and living are already healing some damage in the contemporary world. We see greater respect for life. Young people in the modern world view life as the sacred right of every person. Children accept life as the true gift of love from God. Liberty and happiness are also advancing as God's indisputable gifts for every person in the world.

Yet, despite initial progress in human rights and respect for the individual, the time is here and now to push forward more aggressively in making justice, equality, and peace the new permanent world order. We must seriously examine our past, and we plainly must work harder on reform. We must let the Holy Spirit of God have the leadership role in reform. Christ promised the Holy Spirit 2,000 years ago. What can we really show in appreciation of a gift that is over 2,000 years old?

Unfortunately, our spiritual harvest in God's kingdom on Earth is meager. A firm human commitment to live by the power of the Holy Spirit is still missing. Baptism by the Holy Spirit is looked at with scorn. It is viewed by a majority of modern people as far-out religion. Thus spiritual fulfillment is left by the wayside.

God remains firm: "You must change. You cannot have your own way and hope to get away with it. I am your God. You are my people. I want your commitment of faithfulness and obedience to my word here and now. The choice is yours. But so are the consequences if you choose not to comply with my expectations of you. I, the Lord, have spoken!"

Human aspirations, traditions, doctrines, dogmas, philosophies, and worldly desires cannot save us. But God can. And God indeed intends to do so despite us! God confirms what he has been saying all along: "The Holy Spirit is my sole source for the spiritual connection."

This brief summary of divine grace at work to deliver us from the sin of self-righteousness is the true meaning of spiritual connections by the power of the Holy Spirit. The Era of Faith is here to stay by divine decree. We are part of it. Let us, therefore, joyfully submit to the Holy Spirit as God's authority, guide, comforter, and source of power in times of need. The Holy Spirit is our best friend! Spiritual fulfillment is complete when we joyfully live spiritually connected with God by the power of the Holy Spirit.

The Holy Spirit is the presiding authority on faith relationships

In every drama of life, the Holy Spirit is the spirit of truth.

God says: "I have made the relationship with my people a priority on Earth. I have fashioned you in my spiritual image for fellowship and communion. You are my voice in the world. You are my hands in the world to work miracles of healing. You are my peacemakers. And I love you. My love for you is always steadfast. I am always with you when you need me. I was present at your birth. I dwell among you now. I live in you as the Holy Spirit. Your life is my life. I am your liberty. Your happiness is my happiness." Indeed, God speaks the Word by the power of the Holy Spirit, and great things suddenly happen.

The dominant and recurring theme in our relationship with God is life in union with him through Christ by the power of the Holy Spirit. Since life in the modern world is a constantly unfolding drama of relationships, the Holy Spirit is always on center stage, directing our lives. The Holy Spirit is present in faithful believers to mold relationships in God's righteousness. In every drama of life, the Holy Spirit is the spirit of truth. The Holy Spirit is the presiding authority on faith. He reveals. He advocates. He counsels. He comforts. He saves. Even the worst among sinners who repent and stop their evil ways are saved!

While the Holy Spirit is the pilot of our souls and the working authority on faith relationships, Christ is the captain. As the Holy Spirit pilots our lives on the stormy waters of a troubled world, all we have to do is let go of ourselves. The Holy Spirit encourages us to trust God and his Word. We thankfully accept it. And we humbly obey. We rely on the Holy Spirit to keep our spiritual connection with God healthy and prosperous. In all worldly conflicts, the Holy Spirit manages our faith relationships, and he keeps our beliefs straight. God expects our willing submission to Christ and the Holy Spirit.

We submit to God because his Spirit is our breath of life. The breath of God is our spiritual character. Human life on Earth, therefore, is sacred, for the Holy Spirit imparts in us the sacred breath of God. Our life in the presence of God is spiritual union with God through Christ. Truly this is the greatest of all great relationships in creation. God is our Father in Heaven. We are his children on Earth. And all good things come our way by the power of the Holy Spirit for we breathe the breath of God.

By the power of the Holy Spirit, Christ is giving us glimpses into the true value of our spiritual connection with God. Christ speaks about a loving father. Christ leads us into the presence of a righteous God in a variety of parables. For example, Christ singles out the concerns of a loving father for his children on the run.

God is always patiently waiting for us, as a loving father is constantly looking for his children to be safely home and secure. God is relentlessly on the lookout for us, especially when we are running away from him. He does not want us to get hurt. He never abandons us. He loves us in spite of our stubbornness. God loves us even when we are insensitive to his love. The parable about the lost son illustrates God's generous love for his children.

In this parable, God is not only waiting, but he goes out of his way, and into our paths, to meet us. The Gospel writer Luke details the story of the lost son and the joyous welcome he was given by his father: "But while he was yet at a distance, his father saw him and had compassion, and ran and embraced him and kissed him." (Luke 15:20) In telling this great story, Christ inspires faith to boost our relationship with God.

Truly God is out in the world looking for the wayward who lack the ability to find him. The Holy Spirit is very busy doing the seeking and searching without ceasing until we are found. Why? The answer is simple. God says: "Your security gives me peace of mind. Your life in my presence is the focal point of our spiritual life together. With your life secure, I can focus on other things."

We are what we are because the Holy Spirit is a steadfast companion and a reliable friend. We are what we are because the Holy Spirit gives us comfort and encourages us to move forward, especially when we are afraid. Christ says that the Holy Spirit prays with us: "Whatever you ask in my name, I will do it, that the Father may be glorified in the Son." (John 14:13) The

Holy Spirit inspires us with confidence in God. The Holy Spirit inspires us to live according to God's righteousness. Christ is specific: "If you love me, you will keep my commandments." (John 14:15) The Holy Spirit supports our relationship with God and our relationships with people.

We are important to God and his Kingdom in the world. On our behalf, Christ assures us that he always petitions God to look after us: "And I will pray the Father, and he will give you another Counselor, to be with you forever, even the Spirit of truth, whom the world cannot receive, because it neither sees him nor knows him; you know him, for he dwells with you and will be in you." (John 14:16-17) We do not need to travel to the end of the Earth to find God. We only have to look within ourselves, and God is there! Indeed, the authority on faith relationships, the Holy Spirit, is living in each of us.

The Holy Spirit is the presiding authority on history

The Holy Spirit does for us what we cannot do ourselves: The Holy Spirit confirms the truth in history.

History is an integral part of the ongoing process of creation. Like creation, history never ends, unless human life on Earth comes to an end. History contains all the nuances of human attitudes and behavior. The human element in history makes history the Swiss cheese of civilization. Like Swiss cheese, history improves with age. Like Swiss cheese, human history is full of holes. Human ideas about life and living make it so. The immense forces of human egos then press the cheese of human history into shape. And history rolls on.

But absolute truth gives history a spiritual character, since God alone knows everything about truth and us. God alone knows the truth about our past.

The variables in history are countless, and they are beyond human comprehension. We may never know the whole truth.

"What is truth?" Pilate asked before condemning Jesus Christ to death. Our search for truth looks into the innermost parts of the soul for answers. So we ask soul-searching questions about truth. We ask: "When all is said and done, was our life truly worth living? Was our life what God had intended it to be?" We look to the Holy Spirit for guidance to these questions and all other questions on history. While absolute truth is eternal, human history is only 4,000 years old, and its truth is always in question.

So what do we do? Truth in some ancient stories is sparse or does not exist. Prehistory is speculation at its best. Ancient history has many theoretical assumptions and is based on fragmented knowledge. Myth and legend often punctuate the truth in ancient events. History, therefore, has many uncertainties.

Stories in ancient times were passed down by word of mouth. Storytellers were adding new trimmings and spicy flavorings to make the presentation of their stories more glorious and appealing to each new audience in time and place. Oftentimes history has been abused to control people. Some events were purposely altered or enhanced to realize the personal objective of powerful leaders. National ambitions oftentimes dictated truth.

Events in history, therefore, are subject to interpretation and judgment. What we consider documented history, too, is not flawless all the time. Spoken and written words are not always facts. The printed word is not always truth. Human ambitions—and human shortcomings—strain, taint, and stain the truth in gathering facts.

History will show, for example, how the American presidential election in the year 2000 was experiencing excruciating pain in accurately counting votes. History will show how the most technologically advanced nation on Earth failed in its responsibility to keep simple numbers straight. In the greatest democracy in the modern world, the wishes of the American electorate were subject to interpretation, debate, and judgment. Recent history in America is tainted by politics as five out of nine members of the United States Supreme Court established the presidential win. History will also show how some 300 votes of a total of millions of votes determined the outcome.

But history will also indict the remaining half of American citizens who neglected their civil duty to have a decisive part in the election process. After all, America is God's country. Our God-given freedom is based on rights as well as on obligations. Voting in a democracy is a privilege, a right, and a very important obligation. We must take seriously this obligation to keep our freedom.

We now ask the inevitable question that is on the mind of every responsible person in the world: If we can't keep current events straight—with the evidence right before our eyes—how certain are we about events thousands of years old? And we press on: The subject and object of history is truth. By what standards do we report history? Whose principles control the direction in recording history? Can we truthfully claim to know all the truth about past events with certainty and stake our lives on it?

We can't. History is people. Each person in history is an unknown variable. Every event in history has uncertainties of high degree. History is relationships. Can we accurately and objectively report on other people's relationships, if our own dealings with God and people are incomplete or in shambles?

We can't. Human beings have prejudices. It is part of the shortcoming in human nature.

But the Holy Spirit is the Spirit of truth. The Holy Spirit inspires seekers of truth in the confusing world full of uncertain history to keep searching and searching until the truth is found. In this never-ending process of securing truth, the Holy Spirit does for us what we cannot do ourselves in learning the truth of history—the Holy Spirit encourages us to keep on searching and searching using our faith until truth is found.

For example, by the power of the Holy Spirit, the Word of God tells us how Christ entered the world as the Son of God to transform chaos into harmony, falsehood into truth, and skepticism into faith. "And the Word became flesh and dwelt among us, full of grace and truth; we have beheld his glory, glory as of the only Son from the Father." (John 1:14) The living Word of God now guides history in the making. In this context, the Holy Spirit is the authority on truth. We accept as a matter of faith the work of the Holy Spirit throughout history as revealed truth.

Faith is a prime ingredient in truth. Faith does not require precise timing as to happenings in time or place. God accepts faith and trust in God as our willingness to see, listen, and learn. Faith prompts the conscience to accept revealed truth and then move on. God's truth supplies the answer. God has given us faith and a keen and rational mind to discern the truth about history as citizens of the world.

In all historic endeavors, therefore, the Holy Spirit prevails as the spirit of truth. The Holy Spirit guides us. The Holy Spirit lives in us to bridge the gaps of uncertainties. Knowledge by the power of the Holy Spirit is the most certain cure against confusion and doubt.

Thus we are not alone in our search for the truth in history. The Holy Spirit inspires our search. And the Holy Spirit walks before us into the unknowns of the future with the truth of the past. Truth revealed by the Holy Spirit is the most valuable legacy we can pass on to our children in their learning process about truth in history and the contribution of this truth to our spiritual freedom as children of God. The truth supported by the power of the Holy Spirit is sufficient for us to move on. Let us now learn how the Holy Spirit reveals truth in the teaching of history.

The Holy Spirit is God's teacher of truth and history

Truth is the essence of history.

Truth is the way God operates in the world. History is the way God teaches reality. Reality is facts presented in the light of truth. Reality is the substance used in building the bridges into the future.

The writer of the Gospel according to John links the way to truth and truth itself to the essence of life. We experience life the same way Christ's early followers did when he told his disciples: "I am the way, and the truth, and the life; no one comes to the Father, but by me." (John 14:6)

God values truth as it helps us to understand the present for building a better future. And God keeps blessing us with ever increasing amounts of faith for knowing truth. Truth is the strongest link to ultimate reality in the universe. Our constant search for truth, therefore, is important to spiritual wellbeing.

The Holy Spirit is the spirit of truth. He helps us to know God. He helps us to understand the world we live in. Jesus Christ confirms what we already experience: "But when the Counselor comes, whom I shall send to you from the Father, even the Spirit of truth, he will bear witness to me; and you also are witnesses, because you have been with me from the beginning." (John 15:26-27) Christ says on another occasion: "When the Spirit of truth comes, he will guide you into all the truth; for he will not speak on his own authority, but whatever he hears he will speak, and he will declare to you the things that are to come." (John 16:13)

God has made the teaching of truth and history among the noblest professions in the secular world. Truth is the essence of history. Truth bridges the gulf of falsehood and leads us into a brilliant future, for truth is God's dwelling place. The spiritual components of truth are revelations. The Holy Spirit is God's agent of revelation.

Revelations always start with the premise of who and whose we are. We are children of God. We are made in the spiritual image of God. We are dependent on God for truth through revelations. In the teaching of truth God cares for us as a loving father always cares for his dearly beloved children, who he wants to excel in knowledge and in truth.

As children of God we then do the work of our loving father. To become efficient in the secular world—and be smarter than the smartest of foxes—we must discern all we can about the history that the secular world is teaching. We then go beyond ordinary classroom learning and ask the Holy Spirit for help. The Holy Spirit shares with us God's experience of truth concerning human attitudes and behavior in historical events.

We soon will learn that the value of history is truth and not necessarily what the secular world declares as facts. Oftentimes there is a gap between worldly facts and divine truth. To close this gap we must reconcile what the world presents with what God sees. God's tools for doing this are faith and reason.

Facts are common everyday occurrences. Historical facts are recalled as a matter of routine from documented evidence to best available knowledge. But truth goes beyond facts. Truths are common everyday occurrences plus all the pertinent—and hidden—events leading up to them. Truth is the whole story. History is premeditated intent and subsequent action. Truth is what God sees in premeditated thought. Historical truth, therefore, is a matter of revelation by the Holy Spirit. Truth goes beyond the facts. Truth searches the hearts and minds of people. Truth leads to the clear understanding of facts. The Holy Spirit examines historical facts in the context of truth.

The Holy Spirit is the diligent guardian of truth, for the Word of God can discern human intent and aspirations. Truth alone affords the closure of conflicts. The greatest conflicts that require truth for closure are wars. Truth alone affords Sabbath rest for the people of God: "Let us therefore strive to enter that rest, that no one fall by the same sort of disobedience. For the Word of God is living and active, sharper than any two-edged sword, piercing to the division of soul and spirit, of joints and marrow, and discerning the thoughts and intentions of the heart. And before him no creature is hidden, but all are open and laid bare to the eyes of him with whom we have to do." (Hebrews 4:11-13)

Teaching truth and history are noble professions. More noble than teaching history and truth is being a teacher of the Word of God.

The Holy Spirit leads us to God for every need

There are many open questions in these modern times about spiritual life and how best to apply our spiritual aptitude for solving current problems and satisfying physical needs. The cynic will say that being spiritual does not put bread and butter on the table. "Just a minute, my friend, not so fast," God replies to the skeptic, "it is I who feeds you. Out of my abundant resources I provide for all your physical needs. I can go on forever telling you what I keep doing for you. Now, then, tell me, my friend, what are you driving at? What is your real concern?"

The Holy Spirit additionally speaks to the cynics of the world: "If your concern is bread and butter, let me tell you that your spiritual needs come first. I look after the health and wellbeing of your spirit. Meet your spiritual needs, and your physical needs are met as well."

The majority of worldly concerns need a spiritual solution. Unfortunately, this does not always happen. God says: "Instead of looking after your spirit, you promote mind over matter. I rank the human spirit above the physical nature of man." We are spiritual beings in the image of God. We must accept this reality and live accordingly.

But we are too stubborn to accept God's Way for us. The solution to spiritual needs is just a prayer away. Instead of looking for the solutions within us, we ask questions. And we have more questions than God is prepared to give the answers. Despite our stubbornness, the Holy Spirit leads us to God for the answers. And God answers our questions, and our needs. So we ask:

   – What is spiritual life?
   – What does living by the power of the Holy Spirit mean?
   – Does God really want me?
   – How do we change attitudes and behavior to be in compliance with the will and purpose of God?
   – Do we really want to live in peace and harmony with each other in the presence of God?
   – God wants us. Are we equally as excited in wanting to meet God?
   – In this jungle of worldly choices, God is waiting for our affirmation of faith. Are we ready to serve him? How do we transform lip service into action?
   – Are we ready to make a firm commitment to God in a world loaded with creature comforts and worldly pleasures?

At the crux of many of these ongoing conflicts is the Madison Avenue approach to life. Marketing "experts" tell us that we must want what we really don't need. And the news media living off advertisements is even more aggressive. There are pictures in newspapers and scenes on television of half-naked young women selling underwear and news at the same time. And then there is Wall Street. Although financial "experts" are known to be leading a gullible secular public astray, we listen. Are we ready to change all that? Are we prepared to give up sensual perceptions and our drive for pleasures and wealth?

Where do we go to avert total disaster? What must we do? We ask this question out of desperation.

Indeed, how do we go about changing our lifestyle for our own good, and the good of our family?

Peace and harmony are elusive to us today because we fail to pay attention to the Word of God. Despite our obstinate behavior toward God, God wants us back. How amazing!

This miracle is seldom talked about. By the power of the Holy Spirit, God is out in today's world to bless and support his children. God installed the Messianic age 2,000 years ago to help people live in his way of true happiness leading to eternal life. But progress in returning to God is slow. God has provided the roadmap, but we are slow to travel the road. We find ourselves on the road of true happiness when our life is a ceaseless prayer to welcome God into our hearts.

God hears us. And God welcomes our ceaseless prayers to make him part of the solutions to our problems! And he always acts to fill every need according to his plan for the best outcome of the problems facing us. By the power of the Holy Spirit, Christ is the way and the truth.

Since the incarnation of the Word of God 2,000 years ago, 100 generations of people have come and gone. And the world today acts as if nothing had happened. We can rest assured that on all matters of spiritual importance God is eager to help us with the solutions to our specific needs at hand. The Holy Spirit will lead us on God's way of truth that alone secures quality of life.

It is truly amazing how tolerant God is. He patiently waits for us to return to him. God does not force his will on anyone but patiently waits for us to come to him. By the power of the Holy Spirit, God says, "Time is my creation. Time is my gift to you. Time is on your side for your salvation." In the annals of time of billions of years, 2,000 years are but a single breath of God. His love for us is visible in each breath of life we take. Indeed, we live and have our being by the power of the Holy Spirit. And the Holy Spirit leads us to God for all our needs.

Jesus Christ explains the work of the Holy Spirit in leading us on God's Way of truth: "He will glorify me, for he will take what is mine and declare it to you. All that the Father has is mine; therefore I said that he will take what is mine and declare it to you." (John 16:14) Jesus Christ defined the role and the function of the Holy Spirit in the affairs of faithful believers as giving comfort and supporting life. The Holy Spirit is within us for support. The support Christ has promised is beyond human strength. It is spiritual support for deliverance from terminal circumstances. We are set free from any direct involvement in the ongoing cosmic struggle of light and darkness. The security we then experience is life in union with God through Christ. Christ advances spiritual truth: "It is the spirit that gives life, the flesh is of no avail; the words that I have spoken to you are spirit and life." (John 6:63)

The Word of God applies to every circumstance in modern life. Henceforth we defer personal ambition, status, glory, and honor in sum total to Almighty God. It further means that we submerge human aspirations and all drives for human superiority in favor of inspirations for advancing the Kingdom of God on Earth. Our priorities now focus on the public good and the wellbeing of people in our country and the world.

In our mission to fill the spiritual needs of people, we proclaim the risen Christ: Christ lives, believers also will live; the Holy Spirit prays with us for oneness with God. This is God's unique message by the power of the Holy Sprit about freedom and hope to every people and nation. In humility, and out of love for God and people, Christians are dedicated to serve God and people under the sublime sign of the cross. The cross of Christ is the powerful magnet of Christian discipleship and unity.

Christ foretold the unity of all people under the guidance of the Holy Spirit: "In that day you will know that I am in my Father, and you in me, and I in you." (John 14:20) Now the promise of Almighty God in Christ Jesus rings throughout the ages for all posterity to hear and live by: "If a man loves me, he will keep my word, and my Father will love him, and we will come to him and make our home with him." (John 14:23) In all this, the Holy Spirit will guide believers on the way of God for maintaining the delicate balance of faith and reason for the abundant life as destined by God. This is the Christian's blessing in a competitive world. We long for this support, for the modern world is a poisonous environment laced with opportunism, ruthlessness, and greed.

On the larger scale in the Christian community, the Holy Spirit is the divine authority presiding over all spiritual matters in Christ's church. It was by the power of the Holy Spirit that the church of Christ was made an extension of the Pentecost celebration for all posterity. The church of Christ has roots in human history. We know Christ's church in the world as the church militant.

But the church triumphant exceeds the limitations of the church militant. The church triumphant bridges gaps of doubt with God's eternal message of salvation and freedom from terminal circumstances. By the power of the Holy Spirit, the Word of God radiates throughout the church militant in every generation toward the goal of the church triumphant. The fellowship of believers is God's witness to the Gospel for humanity's salvation. The Holy Spirit reveals for faithful believers the truth about God. He sustains the faithful in truth and faith for the glorious life in the church triumphant.

The work of the Holy Spirit is specific to the needs at hand. He helps individuals with solutions to specific problems and needs as they arise. He works in the church militant to solve worldly problems. The Holy Spirit supports us to successfully reach the divine goal according to God's plan for the abundant life on Earth and, ultimately, full communion with all people in the church triumphant. The Holy Spirit is intimately involved in the affairs of everyday life—the blank check approach to solving human ills is not God's forte.

Therefore, by the power of the Holy Spirit, God retains control of the human pilgrimage on Earth to make sure we are secure in his care. Our mission in the world is to work for peace, justice, and equality. In these tasks, the Holy Spirit prepares the strategy and establishes priorities. At the same time, the Holy Sprit watches over our affairs, and keeps us safe from the Evil One. The Holy Spirit, at the bidding of Christ, protects, supports, and comforts his faithful believers. This is the will and the way of God for us.

The Holy Spirit bonds the Christian family in union with God through Christ. God speaks the Word. As children of God we accept his most outstanding gifts, the gifts of faith, hope, and love. Hence our pilgrimage in the Era of Faith is travel on the golden highway of God's righteousness. Only in this context can we find the true answer to our question as to how the Holy Spirit leads us to God for filling all of our needs, starting with spiritual needs, but also providing solutions to our physical needs as they arise.

The Holy Spirit and Sundays

Sundays are scheduled opportunities for meeting God in his house of prayer. We praise God in prayers of thanksgiving for his many gifts of everyday care and blessings. God has the leading role in Sunday worship. He receives each prayer of praise and thanksgiving as a sacred milestone in our pilgrimage on Earth.

But God also sanctifies Sunday as a special day of rest so we can properly reflect on his blessings. Furthermore, God wants us to prepare ourselves for doing his work in the days ahead and properly bring praise and honor to his holy name. Sundays are work sessions with God as he prepares our souls to see him more clearly in the work we do for him during the week until we publicly meet again in worship. Sundays are also days of pleasure for God and days of satisfaction for us. These public gatherings are mutually rewarding as God and each family enjoy happiness in each other's company in the remaining hours of the day.

God counts on us to meet with him each Sunday.

God looks at the practical side of our worship, and he wants us to grow in spiritual stature with each passing Sunday. God reasons that the average human pilgrimage on Earth is 70 years more or less and has about 3,640 milestones he now calls Sundays. But Sundays are more than the conventional milestones we know and work with in the secular world. In the spiritual domain, each milestone is a sacred opportunity for God to meet his children face to face in prayer. God looks forward to these opportunities of seeing his children as a united family.

God cares for us at these meetings. He does not want his

children to drift aimlessly in a world overburdened with confusion. Therefore, God teaches his Word every Sunday in public, and he wants to make sure that his Word is bearing fruit during the coming week. His criteria for evaluating spiritual performance at each Sunday gathering are similar to the criteria in the workplace for performance reviews. As the world is interested in the growth process of its workers, so is God. Especially God likes to see us grow as disciples of Christ. His goals for each Sunday milestone are readily discernable with ample help from the Holy Spirit. Among the milestones each Sunday are spiritual events with consequences that touch eternity:

- Prayer
- Holy Communion
- Reflections
- Joy, fun, and laughter

Therefore, God wants us to respect each Sunday as his special gift of time that is free of worldly interference. Work, shopping, and professional sports are not on God's agenda for Sundays. God does not want anything to come between him and us in our time together. When God implements his spiritual blessings each Sunday, he wants us in a joyful mood, sharing happiness and laughter with him. Laughter is important to God. Laughter is the most powerful tonic against fear, worry, and stress. God wants us to consume his blessings without stress. God desires us to be content and happy in his presence. God says: "Sunday is our time off from worldly business. I sanctified Sundays for my business. My business is blessing you. Let us enjoy each other, just us. The world will always be there." His goal is our spiritual renewal and quality of life. Here are the specifics:

Prayer

Prayer is bringing before God our worldly concerns. But the Holy Spirit also calls us to honor God as our Father in Heaven for the spiritual life we now share with him through Jesus Christ. Since we are free in the Spirit through baptism into the life of Jesus Christ, we are free to bring our petitions directly to God for resolution.

In our prayers, first of all, we honor God as our loving Father. We come before God empty-handed and in run-down spiritual conditions, but we leave transformed in his glory. God energizes us each Sunday as the light of the world. The Holy Spirit cares for us. The Holy Spirit provides for us. The Holy Spirit guides us to mountaintop experiences with God. Each Sunday experience with God is a new story. God keeps his Gospel stories alive in our hearts.

Unfortunately, things on Sundays are not always quite that simple and straightforward. As we listen to the preaching of the Word of God about faith, hope, and love, we also hear devastating words about hunger and homelessness, unemployment, family hardships, and suffering created by wars and the pain that God's innocent children experience in places of conflict and strife abroad and in our own land. Certainly the Word of God is pure, but human aberrations are plentiful to tarnish its glory in the physical world. Human ideas are always in conflict with the Word of God, even in Sunday worship. For instance, we have our own ideas about preaching and teaching. We have our own ideas as to how God ought to be worshipped each Sunday.

But there are also other practical problems to be dealt with in Sunday prayer. Foremost among them is the demand for a prominent position of the national flag at God's altar. Patriotism is a divisive issue in Sunday worship. It compels the faithful to compromise faith in favor of nationalism and political unity.

Human nature is prone to tell others how to live when nationalism rules the day. Thus we are our own worst enemies when it comes to conduct in God's house of worship. Inspiration and faith—the tools of the Holy Spirit for creating and maintaining harmony and peace on Earth—are downgraded when politics rules the day. People in the political world prefer their own ideas over and above the authority of the Word of God.

But salvation according to human politics does not work. Human ideas only dilute spiritual energies. We rob the creative authority of God when we promote self-interests for personal satisfaction. The greatest challenge facing the Holy Spirit each Sunday, therefore, is purifying the faith from politics and human concepts of religion. Religions are human ideas of trying to find God. In the Christian way of life, however, God has come down to Earth, and he is looking for us.

God does not want our worship on Sundays to be a ritual performance interspersed with patriotic jargon. God wants us to come to him for his blessings of love in the humility of heart, mind, and soul. God wants to make sure that our meeting with him in Sunday prayer improves the relationships with people around us in the family, the workplace, and the community. The Holy Spirit alone will carry us through the following week when we once again meet with God to thank, honor, and worship him.

Often we fail to meet with God to honor him in Sunday worship. We are headed for disaster when we neglect God, for at the same time we neglect our spiritual needs. This happens when we fail to acknowledge our total dependence on him. In our arrogance we dismiss any consequence due to spiritual neglect. However, the dire outcome is reserved for Judgment Day, when Christ will separate the faithful unto himself from the rest of the unbelieving world at the end of time.

Another great danger in the modern world is the commercialization of Sunday. God says: "Let stores, businesses, manufacturing, and professional sports do their things on their own time. I have ordained Sunday rest for God and families sharing laughter, having fun, and enjoying each other as families and friends. I am happy when my families in the world laugh with me in the great company of saints." God is not interested in competing with worldly activities on the Lord's Day. Therefore, let us celebrate each Sunday as the gift of time together with God. Let us honor God in prayers of thanksgiving on his day as the author and the authority of the Christian covenant of love.

Holy Communion

God ordained Holy Communion to prepare disciples of Christ on Earth for eternal life in union with God in Heaven. Therefore, God has made Holy Communion the highlight of the Christian experience as a reminder that Jesus Christ died for us once and for all for the forgiveness of sins and freedom from fear, terror, and deceit. God decreed Holy Communion as a spiritual event of the highest order.

The Holy Spirit now has the arduous task of communicating to each Christian that eternal life is contingent on life of union with Jesus Christ on Earth. Bread and wine are earthly symbols for the body and blood of Christ in this union. Christ has voluntarily given up his life on Earth. Christ sacrificed his body, and his shed blood confirms this sacrifice. We now take up Christ's broken body. The Holy Spirit therefore encourages us to continue Christ's life on Earth—by means of Holy Communion—until we are united with him and celebrate with Christ at the great banquet in Heaven (Matthew 26:29) his cosmic victory over Satan and his weapon of death. The Holy Spirit maintains in Holy Communion the continuity of believers and God through Christ's victory over death.

Holy Communion compares to a marriage. In a marriage,

husband and wife become one flesh (Genesis 1:24). The wedding banquet (Matthew 22:1-14) is a feast of celebration with joy and laughter. Similarly, Holy Communion is celebration throughout. There is no sadness. There are no tears. The air around God's altar is filled with heavenly joy. God rejoices with us as we become one in flesh with Jesus Christ by means of the living Bread that came down from Heaven. The Holy Spirit is master and servant at the Lord's Table during Holy Communion.

God is always generous in nourishing the soul with spiritual food. And he is patiently waiting for us to flock to his table of grace. His generosity seems endless as he serves us bread and wine, the everlasting symbols of life in union with Christ.

God calls the gathering of the faithful at his table of grace by its proper name, Holy Communion. By the power of the Holy Spirit, God sustains the feast as the holy communion of saints. It is holy, for God is in full charge at his altar. It is sacred, for God serves the Bread of Life, symbol of Christ's Body sacrificed for us so that in his death we have life. And God gives us wine, symbol of Christ's precious blood so that by drinking it we share with Christ his purity of faith in the covenant of Christian love.

God's goal in Holy Communion is covenant unity. God wishes a solid foundation with all Christians based on the life, death, and resurrection of Jesus Christ. Christ on the cross is now a personal experience at the Lord's Table. This connection makes Holy Communion a holy sacrament.

Holy Communion is truly a memorable event. In our selflessness before God at his table of grace, we receive more from God than we can ever think of giving. We never walk away empty from the Lord's Table. God is overly generous at his table of grace. He blesses us. He lets us live the holy life on Earth in the safe surroundings of his righteousness. God fills our cup of blessing at his table so we can be a blessing to others. Feasting with God at his table is the most important something for nothing in the world. It is real as the world is real. God works all this for our benefit. Holy Communion is a divine activity.

The body of Christ and his precious blood are an integral part of a reinforced spiritual connection with God. In this greatest of all happenings in creation, God sustains the faithful with pure grace—without human interpretation or contribution. As ordinary bread strengthens the body, the bread of life is food for the soul. As ordinary wine delights the spirit, the blood of Christ is spiritual drink. For this we praise God. Holy Communion is, indeed, a great feast of thanksgiving hosted entirely by God and serviced by the Holy Spirit!

Reflections

God reviews our actions of the past week each Sunday. The Holy Spirit is active on our behalf for a new week and a new beginning. The Holy Spirit thoroughly cleans the innermost chambers of our soul each Sunday, similar to our sweeping out all the dirt when cleaning house. The Holy Spirit is especially wiping away all the hidden dirt, similar to our cleaning the dirt we have swept under the rug. God is not interested in trash; neither does he want us to dwell on past failures.

Our sole reason for reflecting on the past is to make sure that our soul is clean for a bright future in a new week, a future full of hope and God's promise. These renewals of our spirit are answered prayers for immediate use. Faith and trust in God are strengthened. By the power of the Holy Spirit God inspires us with hope to enter the new week with determination and vigor, knowing in full confidence that he is with us. Our dreams and hopes are now God's Way of doing things. A bright future now beckons us to plant more seeds of faith for a richer spiritual harvest. All this is possible because God is planning our spiritual tomorrows with each Sunday.

Joy, Fun, and Laughter

Sundays are also "Fun Days" for the human spirit. Sundays are moments of spiritual bliss! We are spiritually free and secure from the stress and pressures of the secular world. Our time is God's time. Our life is God's life. Sundays are moments of joy for God. As we humbly praise God, we appreciate his mighty works. Our heavenly Father gleams with pleasure because he sees his children happy and free from anxiety. Like any father who is contended with his children in the world, God beams that big smile when we come to visit him in his house each Sunday. God is extremely pleased when we ask him to come home with us. This is what the spiritual connection is all about. God loves to be invited to the family meal each Sunday, and he loves to be part of our laughter for the rest of Sunday. Suddenly the week before us does not look bleak anymore, for we eagerly look forward to meeting God again in his house of prayer the coming Sunday.

Baptism with The Holy Spirit

Baptism with the Holy Spirit is our greatest spiritual gift. God specifically implemented this supreme spiritual reality for disciples of Christ. Christians accept this gift in faith. It was previously promised as our blessing through John the Baptist (Luke 3:16). God again is proven steadfast in his promise and the result, of course, is obvious (Acts 2:1-13). God once more is demonstrating his love for people as he previously manifested his love in a variety of ways from creation to redemption. God in Christ lives in us, and we share life with God. God in Christ sets us spiritually free, and we are children of God. God in Christ baptizes us with the Holy Spirit, and our spiritual connection is now *fait accompli*. We are friends of God, and as his friends we are empowered by the Holy Spirit to witness to the Era of Faith as the messianic age.

In our baptism with the Holy Spirit God sets us spiritually aside in the world to excel in the very same world as servants of God. The world has no more influence or control over us. The world may rant and rave about faith commitments and the spiritual connection, but God the Holy Spirit speaks to us directly: "Fear not. Be courageous. You are my friend. You and I are equal partners in teaching the Word; we are equal partners in healing; and we are equal partners in filling the spiritual needs of my people. Baptism with the Holy Spirit manifests your status as a spiritual being in the image of God."

Moreover, baptism with the Holy Spirit seals the timeless relationship of trust with the living God. In this divine act of salvation, we acknowledge our total dependence on God, while God acclaims us publicly as his children. The past is behind us. We are a new creation. God has sealed the Christian covenant of love in our baptism with the Holy Spirit.

Spiritual neglect is gone forever as the root cause of constant tension in the relationship of people and God. Gone also is our desire to be in charge of our destiny. Gone is our expecting the Holy Spirit to act according to our wishes. Gone is spiritual indecision as the origin of problems. These have created behavioral and attitudinal problems within us, and they have festered in the community as social ills. These social problems are now in God's hands, for we are baptized with the Holy Spirit.

We joyfully accept that we are children of God and that "justified by faith, we have peace with God through our Lord Jesus Christ. Through him we have obtained access to this grace in which we stand, and we rejoice in our hope of sharing the glory of God. More than that, we rejoice in our sufferings knowing that suffering produces endurance, and endurance produces character, and character produces hope, and hope does not disappoint us, because God's love has been poured into our hearts through the Holy Spirit, which has been given to us." (Romans 5:1-5)

Wishful thoughts about the Holy Spirit as the magical answer to prayer are banished. Spiritual apprehension is replaced with faith in the newness of life based totally on the righteousness of God. The Holy Spirit seals our relationship with God forever in the same way as Christ told his disciples: "You shall be baptized with the Holy Spirit." (Acts 1:5)

Baptism by the Holy Spirit opens for Christians the door to the Era of Faith in the messianic age. Christ's promises are now fulfilled, for God has done for us what we could never achieve. Baptism with the Holy Spirit is the prime event in the lives of Christians. God stepped into our lives. The Holy Spirit lives in us. The Holy Spirit prays with us! He is the helper, comforter, and guide God has promised.

We celebrate our spiritual freedom by the power of the Holy Spirit. We are free indeed through our baptism with the Holy Spirit!

The Holy Spirit in everyday life

Life by the power of the Holy Spirit provides the comfort and rest that Christ promised as the peace of God (John 14:27). Moreover, Christ promised success to all who live and labor under the guidance of the Holy Spirit according to the Christian covenant of love.

Christ is specific. He provides practical help to his weary workers in the demanding world: "He who believes in me will also do the works that I do; and greater works than these will he do, because I go to the Father. Whatever you ask in my name, I will do it, that the Father may be glorified in the Son; if you ask anything in my name, I will do it." (John 14:12-14)

While we do the work of God in the world, we are never alone. Christ does not leave us desolate: "The Counselor, the Holy Spirit, whom the Father will send in my name, he will teach you all things, and bring to your remembrance all that I have said to you. Peace I leave with you; my peace I give to you; not as the world gives do I give to you. Let not your hearts be troubled, neither let them be afraid." (John 14:26-27) The comfort and rest that Jesus speaks about is of a spiritual nature. It is true Sabbath rest. We share Christ's life in the presence of God by the power of the Holy Spirit.

What does all this mean?

With the promise of the Holy Spirit Jesus Christ does not project an easy life on Earth. Jesus does not imply that henceforth everything will be spoon-fed. If this is our expectation, then we have fooled ourselves. With any lofty attitudes about life we are creating wrong impressions about the presence of the Holy Spirit in our lives. Only false hopes will dare to rationalize that the Holy Spirit will help with all difficulties confronting us in a competitive world, with little or no effort from us. The reality of life in the Spirit is a far way off from such assumptions.

Christ had clearly stated that the Holy Spirit "will teach you all things, and bring to your remembrance all that I have said to you." (John 14:26) The emphasis is on learning the Word of God and remembering what the Holy Spirit has taught us. The Holy Spirit will help us to learn the truth about the Word of God for our spiritual wellbeing. The Holy Spirit will guide us in doing the work of God in the world. The Holy Spirit opens the avenues for Christian service, but we do the walking and the working. And the Holy Spirit champions us to work diligently in bringing our inspirations to their successful conclusions.

To be sure, Christ has demanding expectations. God has

prepared for us to do on Earth what he has ordained in Heaven. We must carefully listen to and learn what God has to say. Our job, then, is being the mouth, hands, and feet of God in the Era of Faith. False hopes will always encourage us to seek the comfort of the easy life. Human nature always wishes that things be done for us. But this is contrary to what Christ, by the power of the Holy Spirit, keeps telling us about everyday life on Earth.

Therefore, we must overcome all false impressions of self-glorification about our mission as servants of God. The world expects the easy life in return for discipleship in Christ.

Because a defiant world dares to proceed with false and pre-posterous assumptions about the spiritual essence of life, Christ categorically states that the world cannot receive the Spirit of truth: "And I will pray the Father, and he will give you another Counselor, to be with you for ever, even the Spirit of truth, whom the world cannot receive, because it neither sees him nor knows him; you know him, for he dwells with you, and will be in you." (John 14:16-17)

Disciples of Christ live the truth according to God's Way. We accept Christ's model of the godly life. Our hope is Christ's promise to share with us everlasting comfort in the presence of God. We know the Holy Spirit because the Holy Spirit lives in us. He is a definite part of our being in the world. The Holy Spirit is ultimate reality for believers. Our belief is not a supposition or far-out philosophy.

Christ never mentioned an easing of our responsibilities in the world. If anything, our responsibilities have heightened because the work we must do is the work of Christ by the power of the Holy Spirit. False notions about an easy and carefree life for Christians in a world of pleasure must be abandoned if a successful life in the Spirit is to begin. The comfort Christ has promised is spiritual wellbeing. We experience this comfort in a turbulent world as spiritual peace.

The Holy Spirit works the transformation of life

Life in the world is not always simple. It is contentious at best, even for Christians. As citizens of the world, we are always creating a set of situations within our minds and hearts opposite to God's spiritual intent for us. Our salvation is based on the grace of God, and the Holy Spirit is an integral part of divine Grace. But to the dismay of God, we distance ourselves from the Holy Spirit. We reject the guidance of the Holy Spirit to live in his comfort and peace. We must subdue all selfish desires to gain salvation and the favor of God. We must stop foolishly trying to force our definition about life on God. God expects us to submerge our goals in his will and purpose for us.

Why do we want a different framework from
what God intended for us?

How can a servant work independently of his master? How can rebellious servants claim to do their master's bidding when they do their own thing? Human beings are subject to God. The transformation of our lives in service to God is a tremendous burden on God. His faith in us to work the transformation of our lives is the true miracle of faith! Yet God trusts us to trust him. Our God truly is a patient and compassionate master.

What is our contribution to the transformation of our lives? Foremost, God is asking us to get rid of the notion that he will bless us without any effort on our part. Let us, therefore, free ourselves from the misconception that with his death on the cross Christ has earned for us a colorful life of wine and roses. Let us face the reality that we cannot do as we please and hope to get away with it. Time and again arrogant people encourage false hope. Hope in opposition to the will and purpose of God for all creation is false hope. Our contribution, therefore, is freeing the world of falsehoods.

Falsehoods are journeys of deceit into the unknown. But the future for Christians is known. God revealed himself 2,000 years ago in the person of Jesus Christ for humanity's salvation. So why behave differently from the truth of the Gospel? All the people in the world have an equal chance to true repentance. God is giving every human being the opportunity to share in Christian fellowship. Despite God's generous offer to have a voice in fellowship with him, the violation of God's way by people of all walks of life continues in the modern world— most of the time at an alarmingly advancing pace.

Lack of respect for the Word of God was the evil in ancient times. Lack of respect for the Word of God is the evil in modern times. Any witness to the Word of God that advocates the easy life on gold paved streets is a pipe dream. This unrealistic approach suits Satan perfectly. Pipe dreams produce unfulfilled expectations. They lead to frustrations and ultimate despair.

Satan likes to see us witness to the truth of the Word of God with sweet talk, for this is close to the forked-tongue charm of his character. Satan can't bear to see God's message of salvation and truth delivered to a sin-laden world with a clarity that is totally void of confusion and doubts. Satan wants us to soft-pedal the truth of the Word of God. Our lack of conviction and intensity of faith are his gain. Let there be no doubt, Satan stands to lose ground when the message of salvation by grace through faith is preached with boldness by the power of the Holy Spirit. Satan wants none of the boldness that the early disciples of Christ demonstrated during the Pentecost celebration.

Courage and enthusiasm in our witness to the truth of the Word of God is the way that the message of faith, hope, and love must be witnessed to in the Era of Faith. For this purpose God has blessed us with comfort and strength by the power of the Holy Spirit. And God transforms every doubt and fear into hope for the better life.

Boldness in declaring something we believe in is God's way for his servants to behave and act. If we claim to be bold, God is bolder than we are. Let us remember that it was God who took the first step in calling us. The call to serve God is extreme boldness on God's part. Toward the end of sustaining our boldness, the Holy Spirit counsels us with comfort, and he imparts in us the power of God. The transformation of our lives is complete when we experience the boldness of God.

The Holy Spirit helps us become God's friends

The Holy Spirit is the Helper to people everywhere—just for the asking. This was Christ's message 2,000 years ago, and this is Christ's message today. But the divine support is contingent on love: "If you love me, you will keep my commandments. And I will pray the Father, and he will give you another Counselor, to be with you forever, even the Spirit of truth, whom the world cannot receive, because it neither sees him nor knows him; you know him, for he dwells with you, and will be in you." (John 14:15-17)

Christ keeps telling his disciples over and over again that the Holy Spirit will teach us the entire truth about life with the resurrected Christ: "When the Spirit of truth comes, he will guide you into all the truth; for he will not speak on his own authority, but whatever he hears he will speak, and he will declare to you the things that are to come. He will glorify me, for he will take what is mine and declare it to you. All that the Father has is mine; therefore I said that he will take what is mine and declare it to you." (John 16:13-15) Christ is thus encouraging us to move forward boldly because we are friends of God.

Let us repeat the essence of the Word of God concerning our

friendship with God:

– The Holy Spirit will teach friends of God the true meaning of the spiritual connection with God.
– Friends of God share the cosmic victory over death and evil by the power of the Holy Spirit.
– Friends of God enjoy spiritual fulfillment as life in union with the resurrected Christ, who is promising us a permanent place in Heaven.
– Henceforth, spiritual unity is living with God through Christ in a friend-to-friend relationship.

By the power of the Holy Spirit, Christ tells us to rid ourselves of all misconceptions and false hopes. Christ instructs us to move away from the false prophets of worldly preaching who compromise the truth of the Word of God. Christ tells us over and over again to rely totally on the Holy Spirit as the true source for guidance and comfort in our new life as friends of God.

Unfortunately, situations in the modern world are different from Christ's vision for us. We want to be far removed from anything that has a spiritual connotation. We are afraid to give the Holy Spirit of God control over our lives, though the Spirit keeps telling us over and over again that we are friends of God, and it is God's will that his friends live in comfort and peace while still in the world.

Why are we so shy in accepting God's gift to be his friends? Why are we so timid to witness to God's presence in our lives? Our shyness is counterproductive to the working of God's grace. To celebrate our salvation, we really have no choice but to tell it to the world from our rooftops. This may sound extreme, but God's love for us is an extreme case. It doesn't matter what others may think about us when we tell them about our spiritual connection with God. What matters in life is how God sees us. Can a friendship survive when we are not truly active in the bond of friendship? This is even more troubling when we keep our friendship with God through Christ barely lukewarm. Any half-hearted commitment in the bond of friendship with God signals to the world our lack of sincerity to accept God's offer of friendship as the highest order in relationships.

True friendship is contingent on love, trust, and respect. We show our love for Christ by joyfully receiving what God is giving us: "He who does not love me does not keep my words; and the word which you hear is not mine but the Father's who sent me." (John 14:24) Christ made us God's friends. The Holy Spirit is our friend. The Holy Spirit asks for our love and respect. It is up to us to dispel the stigma that anything spiritual must be feared. We overcome this fear by inviting the Holy Spirit as an active partner in our lives—in the way of true friendship. We prove God's friendship when we welcome the Holy Spirit in faith, truth, and love.

Our ready response as friends of God, then, is declaring total dependence on the Holy Spirit for counsel, help, and comfort. The Holy Spirit, indeed, is the life-sustaining authority of the Word of God for all who believe. By the power of the Holy Spirit, we have freedom. Christian freedom is spiritual freedom. Saint Paul stresses that spiritual freedom must be honored as the crowning event in everyday life: "If we live by the Spirit, let us also walk by the Spirit." (Galatians 5:25)

Friends of God are ceaselessly nourished with the fruit of the Spirit: "The fruit of the Spirit is love, joy, peace, patience, kindness, goodness, faithfulness, gentleness, self-control." (Galatians 5:22-23) Above all, the fruit of the Spirit is our spiritual freedom, because we are friends of God.

The Holy Spirit is freedom

We confirm our freedom as freedom in the Spirit. The American Declaration of Independence reflects the glory of God in terms of truth, light, and life. Our lips speak the volumes of faith in our hearts: "The Lord is God. Our God and Savior is one God." We proclaim to the world that our life in the Spirit is the only means whereby salvation by grace through faith is assured.

By the power of the Holy Spirit, our confession of faith declares that God and Christ are one. We also confess that God entered the world in the person of Jesus Christ. "The Word became flesh and dwelt among us, full of grace and truth; we have beheld his glory, glory as of the only Son from the Father." (John 1:14)

We further confess Jesus Christ as the source of Christian faith: "He was in the world, and the world was made through him, yet the world knew him not. He came to his own home, and his own people received him not. But to all who received him, who believed in his name, he gave power to become children of God; who were born, not of blood nor of the will of the flesh, nor of the will of man, but of God." (John 1:10-13)

God responds to our confession of faith in the most constructive way. He inspires us to see and behold the unity of Father, Son, and Holy Spirit as ultimate reality and authority over our lives. God meets us face-to-face and indelibly impresses on our hearts and minds the reality of his presence among us. His truth is our blessing. God's blessing is our freedom by the power of the Holy Spirit.

The Holy Spirit is our future of promise

The Holy Spirit is Christ's legacy to secure for Christians our spiritual status as children of God. Christ lives in us. We are one with God. We live in Christ to the glory of God our Father in Heaven.

By the power of the Holy Spirit, Christ assured his disciples: "I will not leave you desolate; I will come to you. Yet a little while, and the world will see me no more, but you will see me; because I live, you will live also. In that day you will know that I am in my Father, and you in me, and I in you." (John 14:18-20)

In the meantime, the Holy Spirit is our best friend in our relationship with God. God says: "Your life is my life. I am your liberty. Your happiness is my happiness." By the power of the Holy Spirit, Christ has secured for us God's promise for eternal life: "If a man loves me, he will keep my word, and my Father will love him, and we will come to him and make our home with him." (John 14:23) Henceforth our future is God's future as God lives in us!

Christianity

Key words

CHIEF DOCTRINE OF CHRISTIANITY. The chief doctrine of Christianity is the divine declaration of the fellowship of love documented in Holy Writ: "He who has my commandments and keeps them, he it is who loves me; and he who loves me will be loved by my Father, and I will love him and manifest myself to him." (John 14:21) The believer's relationship with the resurrected Christ is contingent on love. Of the three theological virtues—faith, hope, and love—love is the greatest. Divine love is Jesus Christ alive in believers: Love unites people with God. Love keeps believers faithful; love has more power than any decree of law. Commitments based on love draw believers together in a permanent bond. Love embraces; love forgives; love never threatens, denies, or rejects. The love of God for people is the supreme example of Christianity's chief doctrine.

CHRISTIAN COVENANT OF LOVE. The Christian covenant of love is supreme reality for modern man. Its authority is God. Its sole source of power is the Word of God. Its purpose is to bond God and people in fellowship for eternity. The Christian covenant of love has ancient roots. Jeremiah first prophesied its future around 600 B.C. as an inward and personal relationship with God based on love. Jesus Christ formulated the new covenant about 2,000 years ago into the two Great Commandments in the relationship of people and God: love for God and love for neighbor. The Christian covenant of love supplants the ancient order of rituals and of laws.

Prelude

Christianity is a covenant relationship of God and people. It is an everlasting bond of love with the living God through Jesus Christ. The Christian bond is the oldest continuous spiritual connection in creation. Christians accept this eternal truth as a matter of faith. We believe in Jesus Christ as the Son of God. Christ and God are one from the beginning of time. He was the living Word of God in the creation of the universe. Even today, as God speaks his Word by the power of the Holy Spirit, Christ makes things happen in the world. In the Christian statement of faith, therefore, we rightfully claim that the Christian bond is the oldest bond of love. Our witness to this claim is Gospel truth. Inasmuch as eternal truth is contingent on faith alone for acceptance, no further human justification is called for.

God loves his children, and the Christian covenant of love is its manifestation. The Christian bond is powerful love at work at all times. God loves his Christian family as, indeed, a loving father loves his dearly beloved children. Christianity, therefore, is living proof that the bond of love with God is continuous since the beginning of time, and it will last—by Christ's promise—to the end of time.

On the strength of faith alone, therefore, we build bridges in the world to help all uncommitted people share the Christian goal of love through union with God. We help all seekers of truth cross the abyss of doubt and confusion. Christians follow the lead of Jesus Christ, who is the world's master builder of bridges in love and human understanding.

Christianity is a three-act drama. On center stage at all times are God and people. In the first act, God is calling people to worship and service. God calls us to make our lives living testaments to the Kingdom of God on Earth. The second act is our response to God's call. We tell the world that the will of God is supreme in human affairs, attitudes, and behavior. The third act is the process of faithful execution and witness to the will of God and his kingdom on Earth. By the power of the Holy Spirit, our witness is reliable information about our experience of God.

This three-act drama details the Christian mission and commission in the world. Christianity involves individual participation in the greatest drama in the universe: God wrote it. He directs it. And, above all, God is an active partner in the human drama of life on Earth!

Christianity is God's way to give human families purpose and meaning in life. God transforms us into giants of faith for teaching the world about his Kingdom. We walk in the will of God with fervor in teaching the Gospel of Christ. Christians are sheep on luscious pastures. We shall not want, for we follow where Christ, the Good Shepherd, leads us. We trust our shepherd.

Our shepherd is reliable. He constantly watches over us. He walks with us and knows all our needs. He guides us on the practical way of life prescribed by God. He answers all worldly problems facing us and, above all, he saves us from evil and

harm. Christ, our shepherd, is the shepherd of ancient prophecy. We are never alone.

The call

Christ calls individuals from diverse walks of life.

The privileged status of servant of God is God's way of
crowning his obedient children from all walks of life as champions of faith and truth. Election to this most honorable position
of servant of God in our life of union with Christ is the supreme
act of grace and the greatest achievement in life we can hope
for. Christ calls individuals from diverse walks of life—the humble from among the professions, the meek from among the
lowly, saints and sinners without discrimination—to follow him
in doing the work of God on Earth. Friends of God then live the
Gospel as a matter of faith.

The call sets the tone for serving God and neighbor in the
community. The call defines the conditions for service in terms
of time, climate, mission, and specific acts. Divine calls in modern times are quite similar to the instructions given to the
prophet Jonah in ancient times. God called him to preach
repentance to the people of Nineveh, but Jonah's response
was anything but joyous. Going to Nineveh and delivering
God's message of repentance and hope was the last thing in
the world he wanted to do. He wanted to be as far away as possible from Nineveh. He went in the opposite direction after
receiving his call from God. Jonah was prejudiced. He considered the people of Nineveh the enemy of his people and not at
all worthy of God's grace.

Often we too have our own ideas about our mission and the
work God wants to get done. Many of our prejudices are tied to
professional status or position in the community. But God

ignores all that. God chooses laborers in his Kingdom with a diversity of backgrounds, from doctors to floor sweepers. Unique backgrounds and a multiplicity of talents make us more effective messengers of the gospel of Jesus Christ. We are equipped to relate to people in dire circumstances when we have experienced life's hard lessons ourselves.

Jonah's call is a reminder to every faithful worker in God's Kingdom that the response to God's call must be as straightforward as the call itself. Our response must align with God's objectives for the future. God does all the rest. A faithful response will then bond God and people in the highest order of relationships. Immediately God makes us his friends.

God is inviting us to become part of Christ's Gospel team to touch human lives with the message of hope, salvation, and healing. To be sure, Christ had divine attributes and spiritual powers that excelled all worldly power. Yet Christ never presented himself on his own authority, as we often tend to do when we are experts in specific fields.

Christ always pointed to God as the ultimate authority. He never considered gathering the glory of God into his barn. Christ expects us to do the same when we serve the spiritual needs of people in God's name. Diversity of backgrounds and talents help us to meet his goals of humility. In our unified service to God and people, we see peers praising God as we do.

Christ used people from all different walks of life to cover the needs of all people at all times and in all real-life situations. He encourages us to be practical with our help, for we serve real people in their real needs. The Kingdom of God is not concerned with the theoretical or hypothetical. For example, a starving person has little interest in philosophy, nor is a homeless person who needs shelter in a deadly winter storm interested in the politics of government housing.

Hence God chooses teachers, doctors, lawyers, nurses, technicians, engineers, secretaries, electricians, plumbers, carpenters, and floor sweepers to cover the entire spectrum of human needs in the most practical way. God uses the talents of all his people. He needs workers with a variety of backgrounds and experiences to deliver the answer to the specific needs of the person crying for help.

We answer God's call to serve him because we see Christ in the other person. However, we are the ultimate beneficiaries of Christ's call. Let us know for certain: In each call God is giving us more than we ever can give away. God's contribution to the Christian covenant of love is far greater than any of the greatest sacrifices we can ever think of producing.

Servants of God are his agents to right the wrong.

By the power of the Holy Spirit, Christians focus on core problems of spiritual importance—as Christ did while on Earth—for God in Christ understands our needs most clearly. Hence we love God most dearly as a loving father because he always provides the best solution to our problem. Yet God listens to us. After all, we are his loving children. Then God sets us free in the Spirit so we can help others who are in need. God empowers Christians to serve in his name. We are called to holy living, for the God who called us is holy.

The transition from war to peace following the Second World War is a potent illustration of Christian effectiveness. People of faith from once-opposite sides of the conflict united to eradicate traces of evil. The humble and meek mended what was torn apart by the proud and the strong. Servants of God are his agents to right the wrong following any conflict. We do not seek the limelight and glamour; we do the work of God in humility. The Holy Spirit encourages us on the path of humility to pattern our service according to Christ's model of the godly life.

Jesus confirms eternal truth in his teaching by telling us that our service of love according to his model of the godly life identifies Christians with God's purpose: "When you give alms, do not let your left hand know what your right hand is doing, so that your alms may be in secret; and your Father who sees in secret will reward you." (Matthew 6:3-4) Thus the benefit of the call is freedom from pride. There is no need to explain or justify our work on behalf of God's Kingdom.

God will protect his faithful servants from all demands from a skeptical world. By the power of the Holy Spirit, God supports us when our attitudes and deeds as instruments of divine Grace are ridiculed as the work of do-gooders. The Holy Spirit shields us when we are branded overly zealous in living the Gospel as a matter of faith.

The presence of God protects us.

Evil will linger on to the end of time. Evil constantly prods the adversaries of the way of God not to stop pointing the accusing finger toward the friends of God as being not good enough. It is the nature of evil to discourage the faithful. Evil constantly shouts, "You are not good enough to be a servant of God."

Denouncing this mockery, Christ spoke, once and for all 2,000 years ago. He set the record straight on behalf of his disciples who are also his friends: "You did not choose me, but I chose you and appointed you that you should go and bear fruit and that your fruit should abide; so that whatever you ask the Father in my name, he may give it to you." (John 15:16)

God is our resource for helping others. Christians are no longer servants but friends of God. The bond of friendship always prevails even where the daily modus operandi is to divide and conquer. Christ has conquered the world. There is nothing left to divide! The presence of God protects us when we do his work. All other defense is unnecessary. Christians are free from vile attacks. Because we submit to the guidance of the Holy Spirit, a chaotic world has lost its control. Disciples of

Christ are accountable to God alone.

God, indeed, is our strength, and a mighty fortress in times of trouble. The secular world has no influence over us. Human wisdom is powerless. What God ordains, God also sustains. Friends of God have open access to his wisdom and power. The Holy Spirit is generous in helping Christians secure this status. Biblical literature assures us with certainty: "With God are wisdom and might; he has counsel and understanding." (Job 12:13) We rejoice in God's wisdom. We accept his power to act. We look to God for protection when worldly forces try to silence our proclamation of the Gospel.

Servants of God are instruments of change. Our work in the world is to transform the world. Our goal is to bring hope, justice, equality, harmony, and peace to all people in the world. God works eagerly with Christians to ensure the wellbeing and happiness of his people. In our work to right the wrong in the modern world, the Holy Spirit looks for souls who have fallen by the wayside when coercion forced them into hiding. We undo the evil of the theology of the sword. We help transform seemingly hopeless people into productive human beings. We are there when helpless children need us. The Holy Spirit does the rest.

God sees the human potential for goodness. He uses this potential when he creates saints. The historic example of the transformation of life is the fisherman Simon, who Christ called as a servant of God. After his encounter with Christ, Simon the fisherman became Saint Peter the Apostle. Christ called, and Simon answered. Christ invited Simon, and Peter followed. Though his pilgrimage on Earth was not always the easy travel on a smooth road, Saint Peter served faithfully. As Servants of God in these modern times, we have no choice but to always respond in God's name to the needs of people in our family, the community, and the world. According to the rule of grace, we do

God's work on Earth with a contrite heart and a humble spirit. We do not tarnish its quality with prejudice or pride.

God has two requirements for all who are called to serve him and people: faith, and faithfulness to the will of God and the needs of his kingdom on Earth. Following our positive response, God and Christ's disciples then work hand in hand by the power of the Holy Spirit toward the predestined goal for cosmic order, peace on Earth, and harmony among all the people of the world.

The mission

Our mission is to fill spiritual needs.

The call to become a servant of God is a gift from God. It comes fully equipped with the Word of God. It is ready for immediate use to bring glory to God. Hesitation in acceptance will tarnish its glory. Delay in execution will diminish its sheen. Christ has taught that God is the source of our being. God is the authority over us. God inspires us. God is our power and strength.

To better understand our involvement and God's expectations of faithfulness and obedience we are given the Bible as our sourcebook. The Holy Spirit reveals the Word of God for every need. The Bible is a reliable filter for the purification of faith.

Our primary mission, therefore, is to tell the world that God is out to bless and support his children. We proclaim God's Good News about our life in union with the life of the resurrected Christ: "For God so loved the world that he gave his only Son, that whoever believes in him should not perish but have eternal life." (John 3:16)

The participation in God's life sets the believer free according to Christ's promise: "If you continue in my word, you are truly my disciples, and you will know the truth, and the truth will make you free." (John 8:31) Truth is the core of salvation. Truth is the essence of life. We invite people to empty their earthen vessels of deep-seated problems. God invites us to submerge the past—sin, failures, and all—in the water of baptism. God tells us to start a new life with Jesus Christ. Water in the world is the active component in cleansing. In its spiritual sense, the water of baptism washes away all human shortcomings. Our new life is the abundant life—a life full of promise and hope.

Water purifies. In the water of our baptism God cleanses the mind in preparation for nurturing the soul. This is the foremost message of hope in our mission to the world. Life on Earth is an ongoing process of purification and sanctification in preparation of the abundant life. At the end of our pilgrimage on Earth, we will share with God his life, his liberty, and his happiness in Heaven. Our salvation is complete when we freely move in the Spirit of God on Earth and in Heaven! Christians now have the task of proclaiming the very same Gospel that transformed our lives to family, friend, neighbor, the community, and the world.

How do we do it? A positive and enthusiastic attitude to the Word of God is a good beginning. We then follow Christ's lead. We invite people to return to God. We talk about change. We focus on commitments. This is how Christ opened his ministry: "The time is fulfilled, and the Kingdom of God is at hand; repent, and believe in the gospel." (Mark 1:15) Sincere repentance, faithfulness, and obedience to the Will of God are essentials for restoring the spiritual relationship with God. In the renewed spiritual existence, health and happiness are as abundant as the waters in the river of life that spring forth from God's eternal fountain.

Unfortunately, not all people will take advantage of God's

generosity, especially in these modern times. Many people are not willing to give up certain creature comforts and old habits. Some are too frightened to let go of themselves and accept the way of God. To make sure that messengers of the Gospel do not take it personally when the Word of God is rejected, Christ tells us over and over again that we are not responsible for others who fail to accept his Word. The Book of Life is full of stories about incomplete lives. God says: "Many are called, but only a few are chosen to serve God and people faithfully."

Spiritual indifference is rampant in the modern world—but there is hope. God has willed to save humanity on the strength of a few believers. Therefore, dedicated servants of God persevere in their witness. We continue to bring the Word of God to people in need of inspiration. The concept of a remnant of faithful people saving many has ancient roots. The story in the Old Testament tells about Abraham—the world's ancestor of faith—and how he bargained with God to save Sodom and Gomorrah from annihilation. Amazing grace worked salvation miracles in legendary times some 3,900 years ago. Amazing grace works salvation miracles today!

*God sends his servants into the world to
make the world a better place.*

Salvation stories in modern times are accounts of bravery and personal sacrifice. Parents do not give up on their children. Brothers save brothers. Sisters look with selfless love after siblings and ailing parents. Young soldiers die in defense of freedom for family, friend, and neighbor. God lets the bad coexist with the good as a matter of divine tolerance. God prefers to see the good in us instead of condemning our bad behavior. God has high hopes that each of his children will eventually see the light of truth and change poor attitudes and correct bad behavior to make the world a better place.

God is patient. His love for us is steadfast. His love for even the greatest sinners among us is recorded in the Bible. We read how God showered his love on the prodigal son upon his return. God felt pain when the older brother was complaining about his generosity. God is a loving father! His way of dealing with us is healing and saving. This is the prime reason for God sending his Son into the world to make the world a better place for all his people. Christians, therefore, carry the Gospel as the central theme in the Christian covenant of love to fill the spiritual needs of people.

Christ's instructions to his first 70 missionaries were to leave all excess baggage behind—including personal opinions and prejudices—as he sent them into a hostile world to deliver hope: "I send you out as lambs in the midst of wolves. Carry no purse, no bag, and no sandals; and salute no one on the road. Whatever house you enter, first say, 'Peace be to this house!' …Heal the sick in it and say to them, 'The Kingdom of God has come near to you.' " (Luke 10:3-5,9) Christ also warned his first missionaries about any negative outcome: "But whenever you enter a town and they do not receive you, go into its streets and say, 'Even the dust of your town that clings to our feet, we wipe off against you; nevertheless know this, that the Kingdom of God has come near.' I tell you, it shall be more tolerable on that day for Sodom than for that town." (Luke 10:10-12)

Despite turmoil and rejection, God wants our service in his name to be a rewarding experience. When the 70 returned from their mission with great satisfaction, Christ accepted their enthusiasm. Yet he added to their joy the heavenly flavor: "Do not rejoice in this, that the spirits are subject to you; but rejoice that your names are written in Heaven." (Luke 10:20) This is

Christian satisfaction: God retains control of our mission to make the world a better place. God desires quality of life for all his people. And he helps us bear our disappointments when our efforts on behalf of his Gospel fall on fruitless soil. God rewards all efforts on behalf of his Kingdom by entering our names in the Book of Life.

The world we are trying so hard to make a better place is the immense four-dimensional space-time continuum of God's creation. God had sent his servants to reform the world on many previous occasions. His intentions were always to make the old world of sin and rebellion new and a better place for his people to live in. History bears witness to past efforts.

Prophets of old, from Abraham to Jesus Christ, have labored extensively on behalf of the Kingdom of God. The life, death, and resurrection of the Son of God have become the model of the godly life.

Sages in every generation have provided guidance on faithfulness and obedience to the will and purpose of God. They shared time-honored faith with young people. Their teaching helped young men and women spiritually in charting their future.

Philosophers challenged the world as seekers of truth on faith, spirituality, moral values, and science. Philosophy and religion have worked at opposite ends of the spectrum at times but always toward the same goal for improving the lot for humanity.

Scientists from Copernicus to Goddard have labored relentlessly for progress in science. These champions of truth worked uncompromisingly in the stressful environment of a highly skeptical world—a world full of scorn—but their achievements are extraordinary triumphs.

People of faith from ordinary walks of life have risked life and fortune to support prophets, sages, philosophers, and scientists. All achievements would be incomplete without crediting their contribution.

The world will experience constant evolution because of Christian witness. God, however, is the steadfast Word. Let us remember that the Christian covenant of love is a living testament in the hearts of believers. Thus the Word of God lives on!

The missions of God's servants have cosmic effects.

We are asked to work for equality, justice, and peace for all people everywhere. God protects and guides our activities in the search for truth by the power of the Holy Spirit. The Holy Spirit teaches, admonishes, and corrects. Instructions are designed to bring us into compliance with God on all matters of truth. Christ has clearly said: "If you continue in my word, you are truly my disciples, and you will know the truth, and the truth will make you free." (John 8:31-32)

The Word of God is truth. Truth opens wide the horizons to everything that is important in the relationship of people and God. God does not want us to sail into the wild blue yonder ill prepared or poorly equipped. In the immense space-time continuum, the Holy Spirit is our guide.

What is a deed of charity done in secret? The deed done in secret is a kind word of encouragement without expecting anything in return. It is the giving of material support without strings attached. It is the cheerful smile. It is the wink of the eye that signals encouragement for young people. All contributions to the wellbeing of others without fanfare are deeds done in secret. Servants of God are blessed with talents of gentleness for promoting the Kingdom of God on Earth gently and gracefully. We give away what has been freely given to us.

We use the miraculous power of God to brighten an otherwise seemingly dismal day for the disheartened, the hopeless, and the panic-stricken. God approves our giving and adds his blessing to the happiness of others. God works his love through us by the power of the Holy Spirit to make the world a better place for all his children.

Kindness, love, and encouragement are acts of the Holy Spirit in teaching children the true meaning of grace. Children are inspired with hope to appreciate spiritual wonders. We give hope to children in supporting their journeys of faith to mountaintop experiences with God. We are instrumental in helping children meet God face to face. The missions of God's servants, indeed, have cosmic effects because we help Christ forge the chain of Christian continuity from the here and now into eternity.

God charges us to protect nature and the environment.

There are additional concerns in our mission. These involve us in preserving a pristine environment for future generations. We acknowledge the importance of nature to the overall harmony in creation, and we are now asked to promote it. Our reverence for nature proclaims God as lord of the universe. We help preserve the pristine state of lakes, streams, and forests. We protect open spaces. We shield the wilderness from human intervention. We help in creating laws against pollution. Clean air is essential to life. Clean air is important to all creatures of land, air, and sea—and that includes human beings. We are as healthy as the air we breathe and the water we drink. By the example of our lives we teach children to align their attitudes and behavior with the divine objectives for the purity of natural resources in God's plan for Earth and universe. Respect for nature glorifies God.

*Spiritual life is a journey on the high road of
God's righteousness.*

The modern world is full of diversions. The easy roads that appeal to the pleasures of the eye are many. Young souls are constantly on the verge of becoming lost in the quagmire of modern life. Their ambitions promote unrealistic goals. Young people will need all the support we can provide to help them overcome the temptations to choose the easy way of life that leads to their destruction and death.

Our mission is to convince the seeker of truth that man is born spiritually free to serve God with haste and determination. We help children of God walk the high road of God's righteousness. We teach the truth of the Word of God. And we provide the assurance that at the end of each pilgrimage on Earth God is waiting at the rainbow bridge of grace to welcome home his faithful pilgrims.

Salvation is God's promise to take care of his friends.

The modern world is a mission field full of people with social, physical, and spiritual needs. In this environment, our faith, trust, and hope in God are pillars of strength to help the hopeless overcome their growing pains.

Education is the answer to many social ills. "Why," people ask very pointedly, "does a fast-food chain entice children away from learning to work for them at cheap wages without benefits when they should be doing their homework assignments and preparing themselves for a promising future in the highly competitive world of greater rewards? Why do national food chains entice young people with jobs and money, tiring them out, when they should be studying and enjoying life in their youthful years?"

Legions of the elderly need to have their faith assured in the hope of God's promise that life, indeed, is eternal. Many of them have vainly labored all their lives long—but with only good intentions. They have never realized spiritual fulfillment.

Servants of God, therefore, bring hope to all people in need of hope—even to the worst. Salvation is not influenced by human prejudice. Salvation is God's promise to take care of his friends. We help people become friends of God. Servants of God, therefore, labor in faith in their mission to prepare all of God's children—young and old—for a safe voyage to eternity on a calm sea in vessels of hope. Christians are not alone in doing God's work in the Era of Faith. Christ says: "I am with you always, to the close of the age." (Matthew 28:20)

The action

The road called Change

In the eyes of God, *change* is doing what we *should have* done in the first place!

God is not interested in good intentions or promises. God wants action! Jesus Christ demonstrated God in action when John the Baptist sent messengers to ask Jesus if he was indeed the Messiah. Jesus answered John's question head-on: "Go and tell John what you hear and see: the blind receive their sight and the lame walk, lepers are cleansed and the deaf hear, and the dead are raised up, and the poor have the good news preached to them." (Matthew 11:4-5) By his actions Jesus changed the fortunes of the less fortunate and the suffering. As we see Jesus in action, we see changes taking place. Change gives birth to actions; action is the fruit of change. Jesus changes people's lives by filling their spiritual needs. Once spiritual needs are met, the physical needs will also be met. And the result is chain reactions. Success breeds success.

In teaching practical piety in the Sermon on the Mount, Jesus Christ uses action words in the much-celebrated Golden Rule. Christ says: "Whatever you wish that men would *do* to you, *do* so to them." (Matthew 7:12) Christ does not want us to stand idly by and contemplate empty words when things are wrong. Jesus Christ wants action. The action word is "do!" The road called Change is the correction of remorseful deeds. The road leads us to action for a future that is aligned with the will of God and his purpose for creation.

God's prophet Jeremiah called on the ancient people of Judah and Jerusalem about 2,600 years ago for a complete moral change. His warning dealt with justice and equality. In a temple sermon the prophet called on the people to amend their ways: "If you truly amend your ways and your doing, if you truly execute justice one with another, if you do not oppress the alien, the fatherless, or the widow, or shed innocent blood in this place, and if you do not go after other gods to your own hurt, then I will let you dwell in this place." (Jeremiah 7:5-7)

Jesus Christ addressed justice and equality by going beyond the simple precepts of the law. He spoke about achieving true greatness in answer to the question as to who is the greatest in the kingdom of Heaven. Christ tells us that true greatness is having faith and trust in God like a child's love for the father whom he adores. Christ says: "Truly I say to you, unless you turn and become like children, you will never enter the kingdom of Heaven. Whoever humbles himself like this child, he is the greatest in the kingdom of Heaven." (Matthew 18:3-4)

Our love for God—i.e., a childlike trust in God—moves us to constantly update, adjust, and correct our attitudes and behavior. This, of course, is the greatest reason of all for change. We want to please our heavenly Father. The Holy Spirit directs the changing of attitudes and behavior in our relationships with God as well as people.

Our life in union with Jesus Christ is serving God as his messengers of hope for people of hopelessness. We instill hope in people by bringing to them the Gospel that God's Kingdom on Earth is here. It is real. We talk about what God has done—and continues to do every day—for all who believe in Jesus Christ as God's savior and redeemer. By the power of the Holy Spirit, God heals. He spiritually frees us from stress and distress. He blesses all his people with life, liberty, and happiness. God is giving us a new beginning in a new era. The Era of Faith is a future full of grace and blessings of hope.

We are now friends of God. We let the Holy Spirit speak the Word of God through us to emphasize the importance of God's rule in the world. We invite our brothers and sisters to this process of change to show them that we are all one in God and subject to his rule. Change implies that we are like clay in the Potter's hands. God shapes our posture, character, and relationships as we yield to his rule in absolute faithfulness and total obedience. Because we are willing to change, God blesses us with grace to make us potent and powerful. We are now vibrant for bringing the Gospel of Jesus Christ to fill the spiritual needs of people. To be sure, we are still citizens of the world. But we are special. We are Christians!

The first act in this drama of transformation is God calling people. God builds bridges across impassable gaps to help us live in harmony and peace with other people. And the road of Change is our last opportunity to correct attitudes and behavior. Once we are on the high road of God's righteousness there is no tolerance for human idiosyncrasies—and there is no turning back. Faithful pilgrims on the high road of God's righteousness travel at full speed to bring the Gospel to people in need of hope and help from God.

The second act in this drama of new life is the Christian's response to God's call. Christ asks us to submerge all human desires in the waters of our baptism. He directs us to apply all our energy to the needs of the Kingdom of God on Earth. The scripts for the second act are the stories of individual changes as they unfold.

Christianity on the road of Change is full of stories.

The third act in the drama of Christian life is our submission to the Holy Spirit. The Holy Spirit is God as supreme reality— and ruler—living within us and in the world. The Holy Spirit guides us in all matters of faithfulness and obedience. We are children of God who bring glory to his holy name. The rest of the world who see and observe our attitudes and behavior in this relationship of supreme realities have no choice but to emulate the harmony, justice, and peace we make known as the Gospel of Christ. In the presence of God all other needs and concerns are trivial.

God always responds to each of our concerns in due time, and in a way that satisfies himself and us. The Holy Spirit provides guidance, and he comforts us in our specific times of need. The Holy Spirit constantly watches over us to meet our spiritual needs, and he provides for our physical welfare.

The forum

God designed the forum on the Era of Faith to address the concerns on matters of faith and spirituality for the Christian community. The focus is on spiritual wellness insofar as spirituality touches every facet of daily life. Throughout time, religion has played an influential role in shaping attitudes and behavior. In their religions, people are trying to reach up to Heaven in hopes of finding God.

By the power of the Holy Spirit, God made religion the forum for change. He transformed worldly religions into Christianity. In the Christian covenant of love God entered the world, and he is searching for us to return to him. The Christian community throughout the ages has witnessed reforms that purify the faith. This forum, however, will examine contemporary changes in the context of the From/to method for spiritual fulfillment. It will further highlight the contribution of positive changes to the growth of Christianity—and civilization (see From/to in the following section).

The positive results of these changes are improvements in social attitudes and personal behavior. Christianity in the past has experienced many successful transformations in human behavior from senseless witchcraft to ever-increasing appreciation of faith in our relationship with God and neighbor. Christianity has proven to be a reliable component in the transformations of human lives from utter chaos to serene order in the presence of God. The benefits to societies are social and political improvements with ever-increasing independence for the human spirit. Christianity has played a major role in advancing civilization.

Reforms of religious traditions are essential to align Christianity with the needs of the Kingdom of God in time and place and also to satisfy the needs of people. Christian history is a series of stories, each story significant to its time and place. When the human mind is left in charge to make changes, changes encroach on freedom and faith, for human nature likes to control people and circumstances and even tries to manipulate God. If this were allowed to happen, then faith as the strong link in our relationship of trust in God could suffer.

Christianity is the major system of belief in the Western

world. The basis of Christianity is revealed truth. God is in charge; therefore, Christian faith is not subject to human change. The revealed truth for Christians is clear. Jesus Christ came into the world. He lived among us. He taught the Word of God as a reliable teacher of truth. Christianity prospers because God is the author of divine truth.

There is more to Christianity.

The discussions up to this point have focused on the human angle. But there is a spiritual angle to the Christian story. It shows how to overcome human ideas and idiosyncrasies about life and successfully live life as God intended it to be lived. The spiritual quality of life addresses the physical problem of human stress. The main point of God's involvement in human stress and worldly struggles is that Jesus Christ experienced stress and struggles. Hence, Jesus Christ knows what it takes to save us from bad or intimidating situations and, ultimately, to free us from terminating circumstances in a healing process that is entirely God's doing. Christ experienced stress. Therefore, he is truly qualified to help us overcome stress since he knows what stress is all about. Christ became a hobo for our sake in order to be practical with help for all the hobos of the modern world. Above all, Christ died for us! His promise to one of the criminals that he would be with Christ in paradise was practical help in the first degree. Christ's words were genuine comfort. He knew what it felt like to be an outcast. But this is not the end of the Christian success story. God raised Christ from death to eternal life, and the Holy Spirit now helps us at the bidding of the resurrected Christ.

Christians can now bask in God's glorious Easter message: "Christ is risen." This act of God signals the greatest change in the relationship of people and God since the beginning of creation. Our response, "He is risen indeed," assures our deliverance from terminating circumstances and leads us to eternal life in the presence of God. Jesus Christ died, and God raised him back to life in an indisputable witness to God's power and eternal truth. History thus confirmed the essence of Christian faith. Christians are blessed with the only powerful faith on Earth: Its essence is one eternal truth and one universal salvation for all people. It is important to notice that the emphasis is on the unity of God and people.

The intent of this forum on the Era of Faith is to apply Christian faith perspectives to the daily spiritual needs of individuals. This forum on faith contains all the essential seeds for successful survival in the temporary world at home, in the community, in the workplace, and throughout world.

Theology in the workplace is a beneficial overflow from God's reservoir of faith into places of employment. God wants us to carry his Word into places where Christians spend a great deal of their time. As economies evolve, new needs arise. Theology in the workplace examines secular needs from a spiritual viewpoint. These require new themes for hitherto unknown situations. God provides the solutions for every new event facing Christians in an uncertain economy. By the power of the Holy Spirit, God supplies a multitude of seeds of faith to meet every need in time and place. It is now up to Christians to nurture God's gift of faith and come up with viable and affordable solutions to the multitude of human problems as they arise in the workplace.

But the problems in the community are also overwhelming. Foremost among our concerns in the contemporary world are families, children, and drug abuse. God shares our needs for strong families. God appreciates the value of harmony within the family unit and its contribution to each family member. The Christian family is of immeasurable value to the community.

Families have a vital role in the advancement of civilization.

Children are the focal point.

The current agenda for the forum on faith and spirituality has 20 subjects dealing with contemporary issues of interest. The background for all topics is the Era of Faith—the shifting of the ages, the Messianic age, and a new beginning for all who believe in God. Children are the focal point in the forum on faith and spirituality. A close second is caring for nature and the environment.

Children ultimately must make sense out of what they are inheriting from their elders. The burden is on the children of the modern world to improve on the faith of their forebears and then excel in it. The children of the modern world are the true heirs of the blessings from God, but they are also forced to deal with the curses of past events. Previous generations have grievously exploited the inheritance of children.

For example, nature—the most visible of God's gifts—has been disenfranchised, raped, and then abandoned throughout the ages. Second, the economy has been abused by a privileged few. Unscrupulous manipulators have made fortunes at the expense of fellow men and innocent children. Economic injustice remains prevalent in modern times. The future wealth of children is consumed in government deficit spending as greed puts its ugly face in the forefront. Even God's greatest commandments—to love God and neighbor—have been relegated to second-class status of the "also ran" as modern people promote self-interests.

In all human aberrations, amazing grace throughout the ages has proven to be reliable in supporting a faltering humanity. God is steadfast in his love towards faltering humanity despite humanity's dealings against him through denial and outright rejection. God in his Grace offers wayward humanity a new beginning. Against all human ambition stands the Word of God. All it asks of humanity is faithfulness and obedience to the Will of God and a positive response to the needs of his kingdom on Earth. "Come, listen, and learn, my children," is the Master's call. And God patiently waits for his children to answer.

Christianity is not an invention of the human mind. Modern Christianity is not a refined and polished philosophy of ancient thinkers. Christianity is God in action. Christians are called by God to do his work on Earth. Our mission is to fill spiritual needs.

Forum topics:
– Do we exist in an identity crisis?
– Christianity, nice people, and the real world
– Life in the world despite the other person
– Surviving trials and temptations
– Knowledge, truth, theories, and opinions
– A matter of economics
– The Bible
– God's prophet Elijah and his challenge
– Family
– Family and work
– The church
– God's truth
– Work
– Government
– Justice
– Tension resulting from human interaction
– The true value of the earthly life
– War and peace
– The peace of God
– The Era of Faith

The finale

The Gospel of Jesus Christ is the Book for modern times.

The forum on faith and spirituality is God's forum. Our future is in God's hands. God gives us infinite opportunities of faith to strengthen our relationship with him.

The Gospel of Jesus Christ is the Book for God's eternal message of hope to his people in modern times. We accept Christ's Gospel as truth in faith. We live the moment in God's truth!

Christianity is God in action, and the Gospel leads the way. As we learn all we can from the Book about the love of God and his gift of faith, our commitment of trust in God will make us free by the power of the Holy Spirit!

The Era of Faith

God speaks and blesses us with faith to live in his presence. His inspirational message is hope for a new beginning. We believe the Lord and answer his call by being faithful and obedient to the Word of God.

Key words

ERA OF FAITH. The Era of Faith is an act of God. (1) The Era of Faith is the timeless state of reality in its purest spiritual form. By divine decree the beginning of time is not defined. And the end of time remains the secret in the hands of God, the Almighty Creator of all that is and all that ever will be. Securely nestled between the beginning and end of creation, the Era of Faith is the time for performance in real-life situations. Real-life drama unfolds as relationships. The Era of Faith is the proving ground for humanity as spiritual beings in the image of God. Spirituality and relationships define the era. Justice and peace are its manifestations. (2) The Era of Faith in time and place is an inspirational forum for relationships, faith, hope, love, equality, justice, peace, trust, and truth.

CHRISTIAN COVENANT OF LOVE. The Christian covenant of love is supreme reality for modern man. Its authority is God. Its sole source of power is the Word of God. Its purpose is to bond God and people in fellowship for eternity. The Christian covenant of love has ancient roots. Jeremiah first prophesied its future around 600 B.C. as an inward and personal relationship with God based on love. Jesus Christ formulated the new covenant about 2,000 years ago into the two Great Commandments in the relationship of people and God: love for God, and love for neighbor. The Christian covenant of love supplants the ancient order of rituals and of laws.

Background

The circumstances leading up to God's action in creating the Era of Faith were to give his people one more chance to honor God and respect neighbor. God is taking our future into his hands, and he is correcting the life-threatening circumstances in the shortcomings of human nature.

The historic "from" in the Era of Faith

God's prophet Job laments: "If people would only listen."

"Oh, for a thousand years," God's servant Job moans in

Heaven, "if people would only listen: Stop living in arrogance, self-indulgence, and self-righteousness."

This is Job's testimony: "I practiced arrogance, and I was victimized by the arrogance of others. Arrogance pierced my soul, numbed my senses, and paralyzed my spirit—arrogance is the most vicious of the poisonous arrows of evil.

"I practiced self-indulgence. I totally relied on my own ideas as to who God ought to be and what God could expect from me. Much of my good behavior and many of my charitable deeds were even praised by God—up to a point. God eventually made my good behavior and humanism the evidence in my trial to indict my sin of self-righteousness.

"Ultimately, God proved me in the wrong. I repented. God rescued me from evil. And God blessed me with eternal life in his presence."

God declares: "My human beings, indeed, are poor listeners."

Thus says the Lord: "My people are so very slow in learning my will. And they are even slower to accept life in my Kingdom. My will is the foundation of relationships with me. And freedom in peace is my blessing. Knowledge of my will is a prerequisite for working with me.

"I have provided the Bible as my textbook on relationships. Unfortunately, only few people read the Bible consistently. Even fewer people study the Bible earnestly for the value of inspirational and revealed truth. Foolish people! Is your cleverness in the world greater than the wisdom of God?"

And God laments: "Why is it so hard for my children to accept my love? Why is it so difficult for my people to practice love in return for my love? Why won't my people live with each other by the Golden Rule? Why are my people so arrogant and why do they reject life in the peace of God?"

And God declares: "It is my will that all people live in harmony on Earth. It is my will that my people are my light for the world. It is my will that my people live the abundant life in evidence that brings glory to my holy name."

God now puts us to the test: "Why are my people so rebellious toward me?"

God identifies the evil in human nature as the cause of rebellion: "My people go after short-term goals. They seek the pleasures of the secular world, and they neglect faithfulness and obedience to the Word of God. My people substitute time-limited worldly satisfactions for my eternal gift of infinite happiness and the joys that are pleasing to me."

And God authenticates his address to all his children in the world with the divine signature: "I AM the LORD. I AM the Almighty God of creation of the universe and you. I AM the Almighty God of everything you are. I AM the Almighty God of past, present, and the future. I AM!"

God keeps looking and looking. And what he sees over and over again are our ill manners toward him and faithlessness among his people. Relationships in the modern world are in shambles. Disrespect, dishonor, and distrust punctuate everyday life. We fight wars. We kill people. We live in the modern world as if there is no God.

The prelude to the Era of Faith —the initial gift of faith

God initiated the gift of faith to Abraham some 3,900 years ago. In the following years God was always near to help the children of Abraham. The sad news is that the human ancestors of faith and promise throughout the ages have scorned faith and ignored the promise. They lived in utter contempt of

God and his newly extended gifts of faith, hope, and love. Modern people continue this foul trend of disrespect toward God and people through sweet talk, meaningless lip service, and feeble prayers for help in despairing times of need. God is now changing all that. His renewed focus is on the purity of faith.

The From/to method for spiritual fulfillment is an integral part of the new era. God is generous. From/to provides the methodology for change. God gives us direction how to apply it to make faith, hope, and love the power for action in modern life.

God has reserved judgment until the end of time about our use of his spiritual gifts. He has blessed us abundantly with them for the Era of Faith. As a loving Father, however, he wants all of his children safely around him. This is his natural parental desire. Let us remember that God was once human in form. He experienced for himself human life and human desires. God entered the world in the person of Jesus Christ. God became one of us in the world. He did it to solely make us one with him in Heaven.

God wants us, and we need God

The Era of Faith is an act of God. God has selected family, education, and relationships as his priorities for people in the Era of Faith. He expects us to live in harmony and peace. God stresses education for improving relationships and family harmony. The Word of God is the absolute authority in the Era of Faith.

Before us is faith. God asks us to improve our bonds in the spiritual domain.

Before us is justice. God asks us to reform and improve our conduct in the secular world.

Before us is equality. God asks us to let our light shine bright in promoting respect for all children of God.

God says: "Faith, justice, and equality illustrate my love for all people." Thus we have an active role in his love. God works zealously with us to achieve this goal.

The unity of God and people

The unity of God and people makes the Era of Faith a relationship of trust not experienced previously.

This unity is captured in the Gospel of Jesus Christ as the Christian covenant of love. Two things are absolutely certain in this new covenant: God wants us, and we need God. The unity of God and people makes the Era of Faith a relationship of trust not experienced previously. Our firm commitment to live in God's righteousness manifests it to the world. We are partners of God in the Christian covenant of love.

Opposition to the Era of Faith

We will not have to face the consequences of any ill-conceived behavior until Christ confronts us in the Day of Judgment. When that day comes, only then will we distinguish good behavior from bad. In the meantime, opposition to God's rule in the Era of Faith may flourish. The most common opposition to the will of God is human ideas on faith and religion, and

a close second is forcing our ideas on meek and innocent people by telling them how to live.

Life away from God has been the dilemma of people in ages
past. But God is changing things now. The Christian covenant
of love is the outcome of change.

Our love for God and people makes love the common ground

God promises newness of life to all members in the Era of
Faith. The Christian Covenant of Love is the sole manifestation.
God loves us. And our love for God and people makes love the
common ground in the Era of Faith. All other things in life are
subordinate to the principle of love.

Our response to God's invitation is a resounding declaration
of faith and trust in God: "We need you, LORD, and we welcome you!"

Jesus Christ reveals spiritual truth for the Era of Faith

"The wind blows where it wills and you hear the sound of it,
but you do not know where it comes from or whither it goes; so
it is with every one who is born of the Spirit." (John 3:8)

By the power of the Holy Spirit, God transforms life, and he
creates a holy people for fellowship and service. The Holy Spirit
and the spiritual are God's gift of newness of life. Christ says,
"You must be perfect, as your heavenly Father is perfect."
(Matthew 5:48) We are free in the Spirit from human stress; the
Spirit sets us free from all man-created problems. Life, liberty,
and happiness are the new spiritual creation.

Jesus Christ tells us about his Father

"God is spirit, and those who worship him must worship in spirit and truth." (John 4:24)

Jesus Christ encourages the world to seek spiritual values. The righteousness of God is our greatest treasure on Earth. The Holy Spirit lives in each of us to help us reach this goal. God is calling all faithful believers in Christ to live in his Father's fortress of truth, where love, peace, and harmony is the greatest treasure on Earth. The Word of God is the free pass for entering the Kingdom of God on Earth. To be sure, we have our work in the world. But we return for rest to our Father's fortress of truth after each day's tough labor in the self-centered world. We joyfully greet the sunrise. We enjoy the sun at high noon. We thank God for the majestic sunset. And we look forward to greeting another sunrise for a new day! On occasion God blesses us with rainbows.

The From/to method for spiritual fulfillment

The method

The From/to method for spiritual fulfillment is a dynamic approach for turning visions into reality. This process applies to every discipline in life. Faith is the prerequisite that makes it work. Reason is the partner by which all things then happen. Faith and reason are powerful tools in the modern world for bringing about positive changes for improving the human condition.

Human knowledge does not always have the answers to the many intricate problems in our lives. And reason is frequently burdened with unnecessary baggage of traditions. Some humanly imposed traditions make it impossible for the human mind to reach beyond them for answers. Severe problems in life require faith solutions. It is a true saying, "Where reason fails faith prevails!" In all situations where human intelligence is powerless to solve social ills and personal problems, the power of faith works miracles. Faith works the way of God. Faith is above and beyond human knowledge.

The process

Faith unlocks the gates to Heaven. Faith opens wide the doors to the mystery of life. Faith together with reason becomes a vigorous partnership for spiritual growth in the modern world.

The From/to method is God's way for spiritual satisfaction. The driving force that determines success is faith. God makes things happen in life because we believe. The working tool in the From/to method for spiritual fulfillment is the combination of grace and faith.

In the beginning God established a spiritual connection with his human creation as the personal bond between God and people within the controlled environment of paradise. In this setting all things were possible because mankind lived in the presence of God.

The universe, however, witnessed this for only a short time. Man rebelled. Our ancestors created the current problems long ago in paradise by denying the authority of God. Hence God forced us to be part of the solution to man-created problems in the world ever since. The human input, therefore, is an essential ingredient for success in turning things around.

We must work hard in the world to make these visions come true.

We must work hard in the world to make relationships succeed.

The secret, and stepping stone to spiritual success, is choosing right over wrong. Freedom of choice is a very ancient concept in human motivation. Motivation is driven by faith. Faith creates additional motivation toward success.   Success strengthens faith, and old faith makes room for new faith.

By the power of the Holy Spirit, faith and intellect—i.e., human knowledge and reason—are the greatest motivational forces in the world. They determine destiny as they steer the frail earthly vessel of the soul in the right direction for a healthy spiritual life in the world and, ultimately, life in union with God.

The From/to method has a major role in restoring the spiritual connection with God. Relationships with people also benefit because we commonly share the peace of God. In the From/to method for spiritual fulfillment, God helps people with the answers to the multitude of humanly created problems.

The descriptive trademark of From/to is ***From* chaos *to* order.**

In the beginning of time God decreed cosmic order. Harmony emerged out of chaos. God has endowed the human spirit with all the necessary energies to maintain a similar order in the world. Faith is the key to unlock these energies to make things happen. As children of God, we have the power of God within us. We are his instruments of change. By the power of the Holy Spirit, we are charged to create harmony, and we work for peace through justice.

By the power of the Holy Spirit, we help maintain relationships.

By the power of the Holy Spirit, we witness to the Gospel about life in the peace of God.

God has given us power to promote right over wrong, light over darkness. God is giving us spiritual freedom for a healthy body, mind, and spirit to enjoy life to the fullest capacity of our being.

The From/to Process is simple:

A + B = C,

Where **A** is Vision,
           B is Reflection,
           C is Reality, Quality of Life

This is how From/to works when put into language we all understand:

Vision

Inspiration
Revelation
Aspiration

PLUS

Reflection

Assessment of issues and facts
Decision
Commitment
Change

EQUALS

Reality

Unity with God
Spiritual fulfillment
Realized secular goals
Quality of life

From/to unfolds as a *vision*. Inspiration, revelation, and human aspirations join in as equal partners in support of the human spirit.

Reflections provide visions with specific feedback. We focus on life within the context of our environments. We learn from historical events. We then decide on the action. We follow up with commitments. The result is change for improving the human condition. Relationships are manifestations of vision and reflection. Reflections, in many instances, take us to the Serene Expanse. In these fortresses of nature, we can sort out issues and facts without interference or worry. At the Serene Expanse, nature caters to human needs.

Reality is spiritual fulfillment on Earth. In this harmonious state of physical existence and spiritual wellbeing in the world, God walks with us in everyday affairs. We properly call it fulfillment—*Quality of life* in its purest form—because we move and have our being in the presence of God.

Fromto is the blessing that helps us to get from the here and now in the world to eternity in Heaven. We have achieved spiritual fulfillment when our whole being is in harmony with God and one another in the world. Abundant life, liberty, and happiness are the attributes of spiritual fulfillment. In our relationship with God—our Father in Heaven—we dedicate our whole being to bring glory to him so others may also believe and know God. Our happiness on Earth reverberates as joy in Heaven.

The action

God has blessed humanity with freedom of choice to help us set goals in life. Our primary goal in the short pilgrimage of 70 years, more or less, is love for God and neighbor.

By means of grace, God inspires faithful believers toward this noble objective. He prepares the road. His road map is the Word of God. He supplies the time and all necessary resources. We are his tools. We are in full compliance when our aspirations align with God's inspirations for his will and purpose for all creation.

Reflections have an active part in the motivation process. We use the human mind as the reservoir of ideas for our action. God encourages us to use our minds to the fullest extent of our abilities and talents. God admonishes us to be productive in living up to his righteousness: "Do this for the good of yourself. Do it for the good of your family. Do it for the good of your country. I have given you all the potentials to excel in everything that you do for the ultimate good of my kingdom on Earth."

When our minds are made up, and all essential commitments are in place, we then step into action. We courageously challenge the world we live in to know God.

Illustration I: Social reform

Making the world a better place

We challenge the world to remove barriers of arrogance, greed, envy, conceit, deceit, insolence, prejudice, injustice, inequality, and wars. We challenge the world by the examples of our lives.

Curing the "Monday through Saturday" syndrome

We help free people from the evils of Mondays. In these situations, the pious sheep of Sundays are devouring wolves on Mondays. We challenge fellow workers by the examples of our lives.

Love for God and neighbor

We help people realize their true identity as the image of God. The purpose of human creation is to work the goals ordained by God. Only in this context are people in the image of God.

Sharing the victory

We claim victory when our whole being lives in spiritual harmony with the rest of God's creation. Victory is our fortress of light and truth. The Holy Spirit guards the unity of God and people with the Sword of the Spirit. The living Word of God sustains us in all that we do. We live securely in the world according to divine promise. Faith confirms this reality as eternal truth. We then happily share our accomplishments.

Illustration II: Literature reform.

From vision *to* value and reality.

Pilgrim T. Homosapien says: "The literature of any nation defines the future character of her people." Pilgrim summarizes the sad condition of intellectual life in the modern world:

"Literature is neglected, misused, and abused. Illiteracy further compounds the problem of spiritual ruin. God is saddened by the illiteracy of young people."

"Why focus on literature," the world's reformers ask, "when there are so many homeless and hungry people?"

Pilgrim's answer is straightforward: "God wants people to cure the cause of their problems. He is not looking for Band-Aid solutions of the symptoms. Literature is the cause of many social ills. Literature is important because literature prepares young minds for the future. We teach children with our literature. The written word is passed on from families to communities to nations. Literature is a key element in improving the human condition in the world. Literature is the instrument of choice in teaching."

Literature helps build character. We educate our children with the written word. They learn in early childhood from stories we tell and read. As minds then develop and grow into adolescence, young men and women read all they can. Inquisitive minds appreciate the written word as the tool for widening the spiritual horizons.

Literature is more than just entertainment. In adulthood we consume the whole spectrum of information, from books to newspapers. Literature is information. Literature also provides models and explanations. Historic literature tells us about the past for improving the future. Educated minds gather all this information for building bridges of trust in relationships.

Social change and reform in literature

Pilgrim T. Homosapien now sets the stage for reform in world literature: "What we teach our children today is what societies are going to experience tomorrow." Pilgrim's proposal for human greatness is to stimulate the mind and nurture the intellect to realize its fullest potential in relationships that are pleasing to God.

He denounces sensationalism in literary promotions: "There is madness in arousing the emotions. Sensationalism is short-lived. Faith and reason are forever. Faith and reason alone will lead children to mountaintop experiences."

Therefore, Pilgrim T. Homosapien, Friend of God, courageously breaks rank with the literary and news establishments of the modern world in protest of sensationalism: "Publishers in the modern world should not print books and sell newsprint for the sake of selling, making money, in a devilish scheme to control public opinion."

God says: "Take control of literature and the news and you control the world."

And Pilgrim concludes: "Fear, intimidation, and propaganda are evil aberrations of truth in the printed word. News 'stories' on television and radio to sway public opinion are the evil of the spoken word. Editorial propaganda is a great evil. One of the greatest evils is the control of public opinion through literature and propaganda. Furthermore, the repetition of the same news items over and over again is despicable to common sense and an offense to human intelligence."

Freedom of the Press

Pilgrim T. Homosapien indicts the lofty attitudes of the press: "What you consider intelligence of the world is foolishness in the eyes of God. Your ambitions are not truth but the enslavement of people through the control of public opinion.

Why do you print sensationalism for money? Why are news stories decorated with tempting ads depicting young women selling underwear? What is the moral behind this story?

"Your end product is the manipulation of public opinion. In your drive to control people, you exploit the emotions. Why do you go for temporary financial gains at the expense of truth? Why do you want to spoil the bright future for our children by hammering to them the same story over and over again?"

Pilgrim's lament about the freedom of the press is an ongoing concern: "Don't drug young minds in their formative stages with disguised truths or half-truths to make your stories more appealing. Don't exploit the emotions of our children. Nourish their minds with truth. Encourage the human spirit with truth, quality, and substance in journalism. But also enrich the young minds with eloquent style. Take care of the minds of our young people; they are the future of America. In your writings, therefore, encourage the young spirit to do well. But you must do well first. Everything else will fall into place by divine decree."

Pilgrim T. Homosapien now defines a new tenet for freedom of the press throughout the world in the Era of Faith: "In God we trust for truth, ethics, and value in the spoken and written word."

Reaping the fruit of literature reform in the modern world

Pilgrim is confident that new prospects of hope among young people in the modern world will enhance the human condition in the future. At the core of hope are willingness, readiness, and a strong desire for reform. Pilgrim T. Homosapien predicts progress: "Reform will be the new order of the day. A tender breeze of inspiration and vision is moving across the American literary scene. In its wings are the seeds of change."

The result

Pilgrim T. Homosapien quotes ancient wisdom: "Understanding the root cause of social ills and behavioral problems in societies is the better part of the solution for improving the human condition in the modern world." But knowledge alone is not the only solution.

People must be willing to change. People must be ready to correct social shortcomings. Hence a conciliatory environment is fertile soil for progress.

Who benefits from the From/to method for spiritual fulfillment?

Pilgrim is generous. He spreads the wealth. He prophetically states: "Everybody shares in the spiritual wellbeing of people and nations. Reform is an essential part of spiritual wellbeing. In reform, the emphasis is on people; specifically the focus is on people helping people. Progressive nations are nations on the center stage of reform. Literature and news reporting have an important role in improving the human condition."

ACT III
DIVERSITY

Key ingredient in the melting pot for faith, hope, and love
One God, one Word, one Voice
Diversity perspectives
Storm clouds on the horizon
Unity through diversity
Diversity of world religions
Current diversity assessment

Chapter 5

Diversity is as old as creation. God purposely created diversity for the perfect functioning of the universe. Unity through diversity is a creative wonder of human life on Earth.

The universe is diverse as the stars in the sky; yet the universe is one universe. People are diverse as the grains of sand by the sea; yet humanity is a single entity in that we are all children of God. The examples of diversity in creation go on *ad infinitum*. It appears that creation itself is a cosmos of diversity. This implies that created things perform best in an environment of other created things.

Earth itself is God's model of diversity. Its resources are bundled together to meet the cosmic requirements of the diverse galaxy of the Milky Way. Six diverse continents melt into one unique sphere to fill the needs of the next order of diversity. Small planet Earth has a definite role within the family of diverse, yet unified, celestial systems.

Key ingredient in the melting pot for faith, hope, and love

Diverse groups of people from six continents melt into the one and only human race to make it uniform, but different attitudes and beliefs among these separate groups of people make the human race, so we properly call the world a uniform enterprise with diverse features.

Humanity is uniform as God's family, but varying attitudes and multiple religions make humanity diverse. We see God's hand in this contrast of diversity and uniformity.

God frees us from worldly hang-ups about race, cultures, and methods of believing in him. God sees all of us as his children. This is precisely the strength of the human family in the world: We are *all* children of God. In the eyes of God our Father we are uniform, but in the eyes of the world, we are diverse.

We experience the contrast of diversity and uniformity in numerous other ways. The diverse world unites for reasons of strength according to political preferences, which are then incorporated into law. Yet God calls us all his children, and he affords us his protection under diverse circumstances.

While the Word of God prompts us to strive for unity through diversity in the world with tolerance for other points of view, faith and trust in God require that we live out the purity of the Word of God. The tension between diversity and uniformity is ultimately resolved when our pilgrimage on Earth comes to its end; only then will all the diverse souls spiritually unite with God in Heaven and proclaim with one voice the only truth of value: "The Lord is God. Our Lord and Savior is one God." In the world we experience unity through diversity; in Heaven unity is unity without qualifier, for eternal life is life in union with God.

God provides religious diversity in the world as the fertile soil for growth in faith. Though there are different methods of believing, humanity has but one common goal: To support each other as spiritual beings in the image of God.

Jesus Christ is God's advocate for diversity in human attitudes. Christ promoted unity through diversity when he issued the Great Commission to go into the world and make disciples of all nations. He sees diversity as a huge field of people, all starving for God's love and his blessing.

In the Christian covenant of love, diversity germinates love. Diversity makes love grow as believers support each other in faith. In his love for all people Christ lives and works within us to help Israelis, Greeks, Arabs, Africans, Chinese, Indians, and white Europeans and members of all other cultures achieve harmony and peace. In the Christian covenant of love, national interests or ethnicity do not stop God from sustaining the unity through diversity of his people.

Religious diversity in America is the most viable illustration of God's melting pot for faith, hope, and love. Spiritual life in America is diverse as the grains of sand by the sea. The pilgrims of America make it so. Foremost among these are the immigrant-pilgrims of modern America. They shaped a way of life hitherto unknown in the world. And native-born Americans continue this trend of unity through diversity as the heirs of pioneers from nations near and far.

American Indians are worthy of special recognition in this unity through diversity presentation. Modern American Indians are the sons and daughters of explorers. Their ancestors crossed the Bering Strait thousands of years before the Sumerians invented cuneiform writing in the ancient land of Mesopotamia. American Indian explorers heeded the inner call to pick up and move—undoubtedly leaving known comforts behind them—long before God called Abraham to leave the city of Ur in ancient Mesopotamia some 3,900 years ago.

In concluding this presentation on diversity and uniformity, let us listen to the Word of God recorded by Saint Paul: "For as in one body we have many members, and all the members do not have the same function, so we, though many, are one body in Christ, and individually members one of another. Having gifts that differ according to the grace given to us, let us use them: if prophecy, in proportion to our faith; if service, in our serving; he who teaches, in his teaching; he who exhorts, in his exhortation; he who contributes, in liberality; he who gives aid, with zeal; he who does acts of mercy, with cheerfulness." (Romans 12:4-8)

Promoting peace and harmony in the diversity of God's great people in this huge melting pot called America is the only tribute that God is asking for.

One God, one Word, one Voice

Success in religious diversity requires a firm commitment to one God, one Word, and one Voice. The one voice, of course, is the Holy Spirit revealing eternal truth and speaking the Word of God to current needs.

"The LORD our God is One God" is an ancient proclamation; and it remains God's message of hope for people in these modern times. The Holy Spirit may speak in different languages, but his Gospel carries the same message for all people in the world. It is a simple message of love and hope.

God entered the world in the person of Jesus Christ and made Christianity his way of believing. By the power of the Holy Spirit, Jesus Christ is speaking in one voice the Word of God. Christ is the one voice that God wants us to hear!

Christianity is not just a religion but is also a way of life. In the

Christian faith, God is reaching down to Earth to be among his people. We hear the Shepherd's voice and, like sheep, we follow willingly, faithfully, and obediently.

In all other religions, people are constantly reaching up to Heaven in hopes of finding God—not knowing the one voice God speaks by the power of the Holy Spirit.

To transform diverse world religions for hearing the Word of God in one voice, God has installed the Era of Faith. In the Era of Faith, people are helping people to make the world a better place. They will succeed because believers in God listen to the one voice of God's anointed Savior for the world.

Christians hear the Word of God as one voice. We hear the Master's voice calling us and respond accordingly. Christ's work of preaching and teaching the Gospel is now our work. And we speak in one voice by the power of the Holy Spirit according to Christ's charge to "make disciples of all nations, baptizing them in the name of the Father, and of the Son and of the Holy Sprit, teaching them to observe all that I have commanded you; and lo, I am with you always, to the close of the age." (Matthew 28:19-20)

Witnessing to the Gospel in one voice by the power of the Holy Spirit is the most rewarding experience in life. We are rewarded for doing so. Christ sees to it that our names are recorded in the Book of Life because we are witnessing to the Gospel with one voice by the power of the Holy Spirit.

Does speaking in one voice by the power of the Holy Spirit about God and his Gospel cancel the concept of diversity? Do we lose our identity by subscribing to the one voice precept? The answer to both questions is a definite no. God is the source of uniformity and diversity. While uniformity in the Spirit is God's way for Christian witness, diversity in the Spirit is God's prefer-ence for living the spiritual life.

The relationship of God and people is freedom for all of God's people. Toward this goal, we are one with God. God does not want our spiritual freedom to fall hostage to traditions, doctrines, or a single definition of faith that is only to the liking of any one group of people in control at any given moment. Therefore, diversity will always be.

In the Kingdom of God, God recognizes his children according to faith and trust in him. He acknowledges being the father of Africans, Asians, Australians, Europeans, North Americans, and South Americans. National boundaries don't matter. Faith and trust in God surpass all artificial human separations.

Diversity Perspectives

Out of more than 6 billion people in the modern world, major religions prove the rule of diversity.

Major Religions Ranked by Number of Adherents

	Number of Adherents	% Of World Total
Christianity	2 billion	33
Islam	1.3 billion	22
Hinduism	900 million	15
Secular/Nonreligious/Agnostic/Atheist	850 million	14
Buddhism	360 million	6
Chinese traditional religion	225 million	4
Primal-Indigenous	150 million	2
African Traditional & Diasporic	95 million	1
Sikhism	23 million	0.3
Judaism	14 million	0.2

Source: www.adherents.com—Approximate estimates—Last modified 6 September 2002

Storm clouds on the horizon

When the children of God fight each other about human concepts of religion they are fighting God. For instance, Jews and Muslims are part of the family of God, yet they are carrying on vicious engagements in Palestine. And in the former nation of Yugoslavia Orthodox Christians and Muslims have been killing each other to promote human ideas about ethnic purity. And in Northern Ireland Christians have been killing Christians as Protestants and Roman Catholics desire control of a small piece of land and its people out of "love for God." These family fights are worrisome to God and terrifying to people. God demands a stop to this human insanity, but people do not listen. Jews, Christians, and Muslims must remove the evil of hate from the face of the Earth. Peace through justice and equality is God's way to live in harmony as diverse families of God.

The tragedies in America on September 11, 2001 were religious insanities beyond description. Muslim extremists murdered innocent children of God. Such satanic acts create festering scars in the lives of suffering families. If the god of terrorists and suicide bombers—and all others who sacrifice their young and promising lives to be damned forever in the name of religion—is indeed some kind of a god, that god must be the god of the damned. The notion that suicide in the name of God is not suicide but sacrifice for a cause is as insane as the act of murder. To prevent the murder of innocent people from happening again, therefore, is the responsibility of the entire Muslim community. They must clean house and remove the evil of terrorism if Islam is to remain a viable member of God's household of faith. Religious extremism, suicide, and murder have no place in God's plan for his human creation. But Jews and Christians share an equal responsibility to live with our Muslim brothers and sisters in respect, economic fairness, equality, and justice.

Unfortunately, there are other troubling clouds on the horizon. Tribal warfare throughout Africa is killing millions of innocent men, women, and children through murder, starvation, and disease. Peace-loving people are denied the essentials of life; food and medicine are not there when needed.

The list of killings in the name of God throughout the ages is a shamefully huge list. This list is written by Satan in blood and will continue to be written until the faithful people of God rise up, clean house, and stop all killings in the name of God.

Unity through diversity

God's system of diversity is a blessing for everybody. God is asking the various people of the world to treat each other with equality, justice, respect, and honor and to reach out to each other in the peace of God. Let there be no doubt; we indeed are our brother's and sister's keepers with regard to God's precious gifts of faith, hope, and love. God is the Father of us all.

Every person in the world has the right to see God as Father. Everybody in the modern world has the right to speak with him in prayer. Prayer is the leading manifestation of unity through diversity.

Prayer is Gospel truth: God loves each person who prays to him. Prayer releases the love of God. Pure love is prayer at work in the world to unite people and God. Prayer alone can fill the crevices of hate and bridge all kinds of man-created pits standing in the way of relationships with God, family, and neighbor. God's answer to our prayers is the miracle we all have a right to hope for.

By the power of the Holy Spirit we do our best to help our suffering brothers and sisters throughout the world. Doing what Christ wants us to do is noble and honorable work. It is God's Way to prove that religious diversity is a good thing.

Unity through diversity is God's predominant theme in the Era of Faith.

Diversity of world religions

God continuously welcomes into his household of faith the masses of people from the diverse religions of the world. As God made Abraham his child of faith some 3,900 years ago by calling him directly, so God today invites the whole of humanity to become his children of faith. His precious gifts of faith, hope, and love are available to all!

Current diversity assessment

How viable is unity through diversity in modern America and the world?

God as the author of diversity is dismayed that unity through diversity is marginal at best in contemporary America and a disaster throughout the world.

A lot of work remains for the children of America, Palestine, Northern Ireland, Afghanistan, Iraq, and the numerous countries in Africa. The children of the world keep inheriting a corrupt system of intolerance and hate. It will be their challenge to implement the Word of God for harmony and peace in places where their elders have given only lip service or, in severe situations, have instituted their authority above the authority of God over the lives of people.

ACT III
FOCUS ON THE NEW REALITY

Family
Family and work
Economics
Education
Relationships

Chapter 6

Family
(Selection from *I.D. Crisis*)

God's contributions to families are faith, hope, and love.

Love is essential in family unity and harmony.

As disciples of Christ we are all members of the family of faith. We claim restored fellowship with God through salvation by grace through Jesus Christ.

But within this large family, each unit is a sacred entity in itself. God has ordained the separate existence of human families so that individuals can strengthen each other for worship and service.

The sanctity of the family is an acknowledged fact among faithful believers. God has blessed its existence with the promise of posterity. In proof of this statement let us recall the teaching from the book of Genesis: "Therefore a man leaves his father and his mother and cleaves to his wife, and they become one flesh." (Genesis 2:24)

In further explanation of God's purpose concerning the family unit, Jesus speaks about divorce and adultery. These have been subjects of concern since the Law was given to Moses. They have a direct influence on the performance of family life. In these discussions, Christ cites the Scriptures to demonstrate their validity and truth.

Christ says: "Have you not read that he who made them from the beginning made them male and female, and said, 'For this reason a man shall leave his father and mother and be joined to his wife, and the two shall become one'? So they are no longer two but one. What therefore God has joined together, let no man put asunder." (Matthew 19:4-6)

Saint Paul expands on Christ's teaching on the family as a unit set apart for God's purpose and service. His teaching implies that the family has a similar significance to the world as the church does to Christ.

Paul cites love as the coherent agent that holds the family together. Love is essential in family unity and harmony. Saint Paul speaks further in terms of mutual respect and reciprocating concern: "Be subject to one another out of reverence for Christ." (Ephesians 5:21) These components are inherent in the rule of grace. God through Christ has chosen us for holiness, but our response in faith is necessary to put God's plan into action.

We must, therefore, value and honor the
family as an instrument of God.

As God and people then work together for the advancement of the Kingdom of God on Earth by means of the church, so does solid family life advance civilization on Earth. Saint Paul uses the example of husband and wife in this demonstration (Ephesians 5:21-33). His theme is analogous to the teaching in the Gospel, where the church is identified as the bride of Christ. The bond of marriage is evidence of a strong church as well as a sign of vitality within a happy family.

We must, therefore, value and honor the family as an instrument of God. It has specific significance in mankind's journey on Earth. God intended the family to be a haven of rest from the daily weariness of soul and body.

Within the family we give and receive physical support and emotional encouragement. Society also benefits because the stability of family life provides a sound basis for progress.

A stable home environment is also rewarding for personal advancement in faith. Spiritual growth is a building process that requires a sound foundation. Besides these benefits to individual life, the family also enhances a more meaningful continuation of civilization. Let there be no doubt, the family is an essential part in God's plan for creation. This has been made obvious through an overabundance of God's blessing when Jesus Christ is the center of family life.

To be sure, Christ has singled out individuals who believe and do the will of God and called them his family (Matthew 12:50). But Christ also chose children—the very element that assures human posterity and who are the fruit of love between husband and wife—as examples in the teachings about the Kingdom of God. We see God's message about humility (Matthew 18:4), temptations to sin (Matthew 18:6), and the availability of God's kingdom (Mathew 19:14) brought to people by way of a child's experience.

These statements encourage us to be more assertive in our views about the family's contribution to the church. They beckon us to categorically affirm that the family of God flourishes because of people who practice at home what they publicly confess in church. The fruitful environment of a happy family life lends support to God's message of salvation. The home is the right place for the Gospel of Christ to mold the lives of young people. History is full of successful family participation in the growth of Christ's church ever since its formation at Jerusalem.

The worshiping family translates divine force into work. The power within families is so immense that mountainous obstacles vanish before it. Its power is only diminished when worldly ambitions sever the tie of restored fellowship with God. Then the family unit disintegrates because of the resultant disharmony and hate.

The family that is made in Heaven, to borrow the cliché of the world, is ordained by God. It knows its responsibility to God as its first and most important requirement for existence. Such a family then works harmoniously to fulfill its responsibility.

This is the only way that the purpose of God can be fulfilled for perpetuating faith and civilization. Within such a framework, selfish ambitions are submerged.

Our foremost concern is the happiness and well-being of the other person simply because we want to share our abundance of God's blessing. We do it joyfully, for we ourselves feel secured in Christ. We know that we are well taken care of.

It is quite plausible to say that this is nothing but talk. It sounds good, but such a state is only utopia. It cannot be achieved in real-life situations. Human nature is contrary to all that is good and nice.

The problem really is the evil of human nature. Therefore, let us control human nature so that it has no influence over the family of God. The Word of God and the teaching of Christ are sufficient to sustain believers in Christ's model of the godly life.

The world that is totally absorbed by human nature does not know Christ, or his teaching, or the model of the godly life. The world is not interested to hear that God expects of it faithfulness and obedience. The world has its own agenda of doctrines and teachings.

Because the unbelieving world rejects the Word of God, it will never have an active part in it. Nor will it know the peace that the Word of God provides for all believers. Thus, the family in the world outside the will of God is in real trouble.

"My mother and my brothers are those who hear the Word of God and do it." (Jesus Christ in Luke 8:21)

The family of believers is the Church of Christ. Christ when identifying eternal relationships, singled out this truth: "My mother and my brothers are those who hear the Word of God and do it." (Luke 8:21) Consequently, it must act as light for the world and reflect the glory of God through Christ, who is the family's own beacon unto life eternal. The life of the Christian family is like a relay lens. It receives and then magnifies the glory of God. This kind of response substantiates the word of Christ: "Let your light so shine before men, that they may see your good works and give glory to your Father, who is in Heaven." (Matthew 5:16)

The world that refuses to receive Christ is totally ignorant of grace and salvation. Because of this very ignorance, people in the world call the life in the Spirit utopia.

Because the world does not know Christ, neither will it understand matters concerning the Spirit. The world's only interest is in shortsighted goals and objectives. Therefore, it has set up institutions that are supposedly highly efficient in dealing with family matters. But, in reality, these organizations are many times ineffective, even by the world's own evaluation and standards.

Any shortcomings are explained away. In worst-case situations, they are covered up and lied about. Yet we find people in these worldly institutions exerting pressure on the family life of others.

Administrators of government programs dealing with family structure and coherence work according to legislated objectives. There is no freedom of choice in the working of the law, even though some family discords before social agencies warrant a less rigid treatment.

This is especially true where family problems fall within gray areas, where either circumstances or law are not clearly defined. What a strong family could remedy with a simple reprimand when one of its members strays becomes a case for the social worker.

For instance, young people, who are still in the formative stages of their lives, are drawn into the system of government machinery, where there are no provisions for emotional support to sustain a second chance. Past behavior and future guidance become fixed as a matter of record, even though the opportunity of a new beginning—so essential to the correction of social attitudes and behavioral patterns—should be flexible enough to accommodate specific needs. This is found within healthy families who work the principle of love.

The formality of government proceedings alone brands a person for life, and a marginal situation can become hopeless. Let us consider the story of Karl, a spirited 16-year-old whose young life had always bordered on chaos because the family environment was predictably unstable. He was unwanted by his stepfather and unwittingly rejected by his mother because she felt her new family threatened because of him. There was no place for Karl in the new home. In a moment of foolishness, Karl was reckless and had destroyed property.

His family formally rejected him as a stubborn and destructive child, and he was temporarily put in a correctional institution. At the time of his commitment, no provisions were made for Karl's future or guardianship; his mother retained control.

After serving his debt to society, Karl was released with a commendation for his model behavior. He returned to his town, but he really had no place to go. He dared not enter the family home. He opted for shelter in the barn of a nearby estate, lit a cigarette, and fell asleep. Exploding flames burned the place to the ground and with it also went all hope for a better future. His life was saved. But society now looked at him as a criminal.

Karl was held responsible for illegal entry and setting a fire, while those involved in his predicament leading up to this ordeal were absolved from all blame. People reasoned that it is impossible to predict what kids will do. "This fellow should have known better; he deserved what was coming to him." Many children, like Karl, are victims of family discord and bureaucracy. They are never given a chance to work out the purpose of their being.

Therefore, let us recall the teaching of Christ and check our involvement in raising children: "Whoever receives one such child in my name receives me; but whoever causes one of these little ones who believe in me to sin, it would be better for him to have a great millstone fastened round his neck and to be drowned in the depth of the sea." (Matthew 18:5-6)

Severity of punishment for our failure to comply is implied in Christ's strong words of exhortation: "Woe to the world for temptation to sin! For it is necessary that temptations come, but woe to the man by whom the temptations come." (Matthew 18:7)

The family that follows the model of the godly
life has Christ as its center.

The family that follows the model of the godly life has Christ as its center. This family will withstand pressure and influence that could harm its relationship with God. It will survive despite the fact that worldly institutions are embroiled in its affairs and seemingly even wield power that dictates their authority over it.

And the family dedicated to God recognizes its obligation to draw on his power because it wants to do the will of God. When we see this happening, then Christianity is the living faith that God had ordained it to be.

When the purpose of God is fulfilled, the family then has rightfully assumed its core position within the church of Christ. And Christ, as the Lord of his church, will supply all of God's blessings so that it can properly and successfully reach out with the message of salvation that is the good news of the gospel of Christ.

Divisions in the family will be healed only when we prayerfully request God's intervention and prepare ourselves in a way so that God can act. God is the source of all power, as by God's power the family unit was created and sanctified.

Therefore, God alone is the power who can restore it when the difficulties of trials and temptations are overtaxing the family's ability to handle them. Because God established and ordained the family, we can rest assured that God will also sustain it through times of trouble.

Thus, the healing process of the family unit is a matter of divine power *and* our faith. But we must remember that God's healing process demands our commitment before it can start. The family that was created by God can only be healed and restored by God through Christ when a genuine effort is made to rebuild what was torn down and to mend what had been ripped apart.

This genuine effort is evident when contrite hearts seek forgiveness from God and through Christ seek forgiveness from one another. When this happens, then the Holy Spirit of God takes over as the mentor. We suddenly will experience the Spirit's work as the helper that Christ has provided for comfort and as guide in our short pilgrimage on Earth. The Holy Spirit supports our life on Earth.

It is not uncommon to find the family, which is the unit that God has ordained as his instrument for posterity, to be under constant attack from within as well as by Satan's external forces. Any family that is forced to live under internal duress becomes drained of its energy. It will have little strength left to withstand long periods of attacks unless it seeks the power of God and prepares itself for reconciliation if it is to survive.

If this is not done, then it will succumb to the forces of discord, and envy and greed will be substituted for the genuine love that family members once shared with one another.

Signs of discord are evident when we fail to respect the feelings of our spouses and neglect each other's needs; or when we fail to take seriously our obligation in raising children.

The story of Bill and Sue exemplifies this point. Like people in Christ's parable of the Sower (Luke 8:11-15), they also enjoyed the temporary bliss of something new. Both were full of starry-eyed admiration for each other during the festivities of their wedding ceremony. Their honeymoon in the Caribbean was equally rewarding. It was like a visit to paradise. They found all the trimmings in proper place: sandy beaches, blue sky, gentle breezes and, most importantly, the companionship of people in love.

They were happy with each other. Bill was a clever engineer and overflowing with confidence. He found satisfaction at work and enjoyed life at home. The dream house became complete with two beautiful children.

But difficulties in their relationship surfaced when Bill's interests became self-centered; because of it the husband-wife communication started to fall apart.

Sue was talking about Brownies and Boy Scouts. She recited the children's adventure stories, for she knew them so well. And she also talked about helping them unlock doors when they got stuck with problems and homework.

Bill used "equal time" to bore the family with shop language. His one-way conversation analyzed his expertise with computers and his acumen for business, and he also bragged about the future and growth of the family's investments. Sue couldn't have cared less. And to the children, these were fairy tales.

Sue was frustrated because of the lack of coherence within the family. And Bill harbored hurt feelings because no one really paid any attention to him.

Short moments of deadly silence started to grow longer as

mealtimes actually shortened. Only Sue's love and energy held the family together; Bill never wasted time in keeping current on bank balances, money market certificates, and stocks. A once happy family was courting disaster.

This was prevented from happening by a moment of truth, which confronted Bill and Sue with the demand of faithfulness and obedience to God. This came by means of a phone call from their mutual friend Jim. He was desperate and in need of money. He had been out of work for some time, his health insurance had lapsed, and now Bill and Sue's godson Scott needed surgery. Could they help?

No time was wasted. They helped. By giving of themselves they again found each other in the need of another person. Perhaps Bill's sudden embrace of Sue was sparked by God's love for a struggling human family. We can only speculate, but God knows.

The Christian family wields power—the power of love.

A strong family is like a healthy tree. When its roots are soundly anchored in fertile soil, this tree will draw from God's fountain all the nutrients that it will ever need for growth.

As individual branches draw on the central supply and leaves then display the sheen that indicates a healthy root system, so it is with the family when it builds its foundation on the Word of God.

The Christian family radiates happiness and peace as a shining light. Its intensity penetrates darkness. The Christian family knows that its light is shining brightly because its source of energy is the powerful Word of God.

Therefore, it reflects the stability of a system that is secured in the righteousness of God, the only source from which life-sustaining energy must be drawn. The stability of life, individual and family, truly comes from God through Christ, as Christ is both cornerstone and foundation of a secure and peaceful family life.

So that we fully understand our obligation and fulfill God's purpose in living as a family of God, we must put in proper perspective our relationship with one another and with God. Our examination must begin with the purpose of our creation.

We must correctly answer the question whose we truly are. The answer to this crucial question will reveal that the family is the most significant element in the fellowship of believers. The Christian family in a growing civilization then fulfills the purpose of giving praise, glory, and honor to God.

The family is the instrument of God. It must be keen on all matters concerning the Word of God. This is what the Holy Spirit will reveal to each family member individually when Jesus Christ is the center of family life.

Christ explained to the disciples that his death on the cross and our sharing in his resurrection will make possible the Spirit's work among us: "I tell you the truth: it is to your advantage that I go away, for if I do not go away, the Counselor will not come to you; but if I go, I will send him to you." (John 16:7)

Therefore, Christ says: "When the Spirit of truth comes, he will guide you into all the truth; for he will not speak on his own authority, but whatever he hears he will speak, and he will declare to you the things that are to come. He will glorify me, for he will take what is mine and declare it to you." (John 16:13-14)

The Christian family then will have more than sufficient strength to overcome trials and temptations. It knows security from its trust in God and expresses this trust in the belief that it exists only by the grace of God. It knows that the power of God is in this grace and through this grace it knows how to share the love of God.

It knows that the divine love that promised salvation and decreed redemption is at work within the family and unites it through love for one another. This type of family we find fully dedicated to God in faithful and obedient service. Its existence is the truth of the new life in the Spirit.

It is certain that the Christian family wields power—the power of love—which itself is being received by it as the constant out-pouring of God's abundant blessing. This Christian family knows God. Christ is in its midst.

Through this connection, the Christian family knows God's reservoir of wealth, and it is neither afraid nor ashamed to make use of it, as we indeed must if we are faithful to God and obedient to his will that commands us to reach out to all of God's people. Only then do we fulfill our mission as the beacon that radiates God's glory.

The Christian family knows laughter.

The Christian family knows laughter, because it shares the joy of the new life in the Spirit. It knows how to laugh at itself because it knows the true security that comes from being a disciple of Christ.

The medicine of happiness that is produced by a soul that is securely rested in Christ has greater healing power for body and mind than any artificial formulations. Laughter is medicine. It is the contentment that comes from the knowledge that the grace of God sustains our lives.

The Holy Spirit keeps the Christian family in a state of constant blessing by revealing to it the truth about God. The truth in God's word alone is the power that sustains the family until Christ comes and takes each individual family member unto himself. The security of the family is based on a complete trust in God. The basis for this trust is God's grace. The tool for implementing it is faith.

"For the love of money is the root of all evils."

Material riches do not indicate either true wealth or security of any family. Christ in the Parable of the Rich Fool showed this to us. Christ's directive comes as a warning: "Take heed, and beware of all covetousness; for a man's life does not consist in the abundance of his possessions." (Luke 12:15)

In continuation of Christ's teaching, Saint Paul instructs believers to place proper attention on their relationship with God. We must not let the world overtake us. Wealth gives apparent power. But this power is never real, because what God has designated as a vehicle has been wrongfully turned into an authority.

Saint Paul writes to Timothy: "For the love of money is the root of all evils; it is through this craving that some have wandered away from the faith and pierced their hearts with many pangs. But as for you, man of God, shun all this; aim at righteousness, godliness, faith, love, steadfastness, and gentleness.

"Fight the good fight of the faith; take hold of the eternal life to which you were called when you made the good confession in the presence of many witnesses. In the presence of God who gives life to all things, and of Christ Jesus who in his testimony before Pontius Pilate made the good confession, I charge you to keep the commandment unstained and free from reproach until the appearing of our Lord Jesus Christ; and this will be made manifest at the proper time by the blessed and only Sovereign, the King of kings and the Lord of lords, who alone has immortality and dwells in unapproachable light, whom no man has ever seen or can see. To him be honor and eternal dominion. Amen." (1 Timothy 6:10-16)

The human response to God's contributions

We have learned in the previous section that high on God's agenda for all people in the world is the family. God says:

"Accept my gifts of faith, hope, and love. My love builds and sustains families!" God applies the principle of love to put things in proper perspective. The Word of God is the world's source for love. Practicing love is a requirement for all families in the world. Working God's gift of love in everyday life is Christ's command. Love is essential for healthy family life.

The following directions are selections from God's ABC on family life. They are but a few of the guidelines for building and maintaining strong and healthy families.

Love. Love is the ultimate power in families. Love heals. Love creates family happiness. Love is laughter. True love is a life-long marriage vow between husband and wife. God made his commitment in loving his family, and so should we. Love for family, therefore, is the combination of God's love and a firm commitment of our love toward the happiness of each family member. "Additionally," God says, "show your love to your family by spending time with your children. I made Sundays your special days for worship, family pleasures, and rest from the harsh routines of daily life." The denial of Sabbath rest in God's family is the fastest growing evil in modern America. God ordained Sabbath rest for the spiritual health and wellbeing for all members in the family. God made Sunday the day of family love, a special day free from work, shopping, and professional sports. Sunday is God's day for sharing family love and laughter, and he wants us to spend this day with him loving our children as God loves each of us individually.

Commitments. Commitments are the heartbeats of family life in which truth is the breath of God in each life. God says: "The members of your family deserve firm commitments, and they need truth. Remember, your family is your best friend. Support your family, and your family will support and defend you when everybody else is deserting you in your time of greatest needs."

Trust. Trust is the nurturing environment for faith, hope, and love. Children need our trust as we all need to trust God. Whereas trust unites the family through love, distrust destroys love and family. As we trust each other, the temptations of distrust will never haunt us. Trust heals, but distrust destroys.

Respect. Respect is the outgrowth of love, trust, honor, hope, and commitment. God says: "Respect these as my gift to you, and your family will respect you as their champion of love, trust, honor, hope, and commitment." As God is working overtime to respect his family on Earth, so must we in respecting our family.

Love, commitment, trust, and respect reveal God's love; and by these manifestations we show the world what our soul is truly like!

Family and Work—the spiritual perspective
(Selection from *I.D. Crisis*)

Assessment of everyday situations

The relationship of family and work deals with all aspects of human behavior. It will require a lot of effort on our part to make this relationship successful and running smoothly. Our attitudes and views on life are very important elements for establishing the necessary stability that will help us to function properly at home and at work.

Even though we must strive to separate home and work, we find that this division is not easily achieved. Unresolved issues at home usually spill over into our work life. In like manner, unfinished business is carried home.

We find it very difficult to suddenly empty our minds from every burden of a tough day. There are always some remaining pressures within us.

But only when we are not preoccupied with other problems can we give our full attention to the matters at hand, whether at home or at work. Yet we must be fully aware of the interrelation of family and work. Our encounters in either have definite bearings on the other.

Happiness at home has an influence on our work performance. And we also know the robust impact that our job income has on our family. Our action and reaction in either situation contributes to the groundwork for building a well-rounded stability in the human family. This stability also implies that we dedicate our lives to discipleship in Christ.

Emotions have a significant influence on stability. But emotions are cyclical. We are not machines that can be turned on or off simply by the throw of a switch.

The only way that our emotions can be controlled is through total submission to Christ and by letting him be the master of our lives. Only then can we realize the joy of family life and receive satisfaction from doing our work. We will then also be in harmony with the objectives of God for our lives. This realization is but another form of blessing that we constantly receive from God.

We have plenty of reasons for not letting God be God. We are too stubborn to let our Creator work his will and purpose through us. In support of this stubbornness, we then build our defense through false belief systems. Abilities and strengths join forces with pride and complicate matters further through the whispering of self-assurance. This then prevents people from realizing that we have wandered from the narrow path prescribed by God.

In other words, we have chosen to forsake the secure environment provided by God for our temporary journey on Earth. We have sinfully created an existence outside the protective custody of God.

Even today we continue to fall into the trap of personal ambition despite the numerous accounts in history that tell us over and over again that the cost of this rebellion toward God is very high. The Word of God tells us that whoever falls into this trap is subject to condemnation, misery, despair, and ultimate death.

Our destiny then becomes sealed, because we rejected the grace of God, which could have led us into the presence of God and eternal life.

We are neither the first, nor are we alone in this rebellion against the purpose of our creation. For example, we see the Psalmist bemoaning the sins of past generations as he cites the rebellious behavior of the Israelites in their life's journey.

The account of their travel through the desert to the Promised Land is symbolic of our soul's pilgrimage on Earth. Like the Israelites, we are also quick to forget whose we truly are. Like them, we also are very eager to declare ourselves masters of our own destiny: "But they soon forgot his works; they did not wait for his counsel." (Psalm 106:13)

Because we also have rejected the evidence of what God has done for mankind and continue to act and not wait for his counsel, we are guilty of not trusting God. Because of this unbelief, we lose our usefulness to God. Instead of searching for truth, we become preoccupied with ourselves. Thus, we are looking for trouble as "the cares of the world and the delight in riches choke the word, and it proves unfruitful." (Matthew 13:22)

These words of Christ taken from the explanation of the Parable of the Sower (Matthew 13:18-23) illustrate what happens when the Word of God reaches people who have no faith.

Whenever people choose to live without faith, they do not believe that God will do all that he has promised. And we fail to wait for God's directions. As a result, we gradually drift away from God's presence and let family and work turn into unbearable burdens instead of developing them into the blessings that God had commanded us to do.

Therefore, since we have fallen short of our commitment to God and not properly fulfilled our responsibility because of personal excursions to explore self, we must treat the interrelation of family and work as a subject of grave importance. Through it we channel the results of our behavior from this world into eternity.

Spiritual blindness

Difficulties within some families can spill into other family units when poor attitudes toward job performance and lack of cooperation among workers affects the place of employment. Companies are in business to make money. People must work to earn a living. Any mismatch will prove chaotic to either side.

Cooperation and respect at the workplace may not always be mutual. This usually is also the case in family situations. It is proven that relationships thrive best when respect, feelings, and understanding are reciprocal.

Family life gives us an opportunity to practice our faith at home. We need not make a search to determine who our neighbor is when we are confronted with the needs of members in our own family.

But our human nature is at times vehemently opposed to helping our own flesh and blood. Instead, we prefer to go out of our way trying to find strangers who we are more ready and willing to help whether or not they really need it.

This peculiar characteristic is a curse in human nature that makes us shy away from helping those we should truly love. We misuse the grace of God and make it selective.

Let there be no doubt. We are spiritually blinded whenever we behave in this manner. God is being shoved out of our lives when we put our ideas in the forefront as to how people should live, especially the poor and distressed. People are more willing to judge than to help. But God's gift to mankind for living peaceably with each other is captured in our tolerance, compassion, and mercy.

Christ's parable about the Good Samaritan (Luke 10:25-37) is a good example.

God commands that we work to bring glory to him (Matthew 5:16). This also applies to the workplace, where we have the opportunity to ask whether we are helping or hindering those who are not quite as quick in doing their job as we are.

The workplace is God's laboratory for developing team effort in demonstration of successful balance of different talents. A floor sweeper whose concern is to do the best possible job is a better person than the gifted loudmouth who neglects craftsmanship.

Abilities and talents are our tools for doing this. Another vivid example of being helpful is words of encouragement to young people who are tense when learning a new job. The workplace has unlimited opportunities to transform prejudice and intolerance into leadership.

Therefore, let us not shy away from those who need support. We must become aware that we are part of God's solution to problems and handicaps—the handicaps we experience ourselves, and the problems that confront people around us.

Christ explained spiritual blindness in giving sight to the man born blind. In this miracle, Christ demonstrated the mighty power of God at work: "For judgment I came into this world, that those who do not see may see, and that those who see may become blind." (John 9:39)

We are thereby told that we must envision the work of God with the humble eyes of our soul and let the Holy Spirit of God reveal it to our spirit. We will never perceive the work of God in the arrogance of the flesh. It is only by the power of the Spirit of God living in us that we will ever be able to exercise the power of God while living in the flesh. Only then can we recognize

God's work as bringing light—that is, truth—into the world. Christ says your light, therefore, must "shine before men, that they may see your good works and give glory to your Father who is in Heaven." (Matthew 5:16)

Christ implies that the power of God is light. It dispels the darkness of evil as embodied in disbelief. Therefore, Christ says that "we must work the works of him who sent me, while it is day; night comes, when no one can work. As long as I am in the world, I am the light of the world." (John 9:4-5)

Priorities

The importance of the interrelation of family and work must not become neglected. We spend a significant amount of time and a good portion of our energy in these domains.

In our selection of priorities, whether at home or at work, we exercise the choice to either serve God or reject his authority over our lives.

But whatever choice is made will definitely determine our ultimate destiny. Therefore, let us beware!

If our intention is to excel through the merits of good works, we have already fallen into the trap of works righteousness. Only faith can secure God's blessing of eternal life. The judgment of God is rendered depending upon the priorities of our life on Earth.

The opportunity to choose is ours. But so is also the burden of our decision. Our rejection of God will definitely consume us. Only our confession as disciples of Christ will enhance our life in the Spirit for all eternity, for we will have been true to the Word of God and have picked up our cross and followed Christ.

Christ established our relationship with God and with one another by directing us into the path of God's righteousness: "You shall love the Lord your God with all your heart, and with all your soul, and with all your mind." (Matthew 22:37)

Likewise Jesus commands: "You shall love your neighbor as yourself." (Matthew 22:39)

Christ reminds us of our great efficiency in selfishness, greed, and lust for power and tells us to love our neighbor, and our family, with that very same efficiency! Our relationship with God and also with one another must become one of total involvement.

The first step in this total involvement is constantly praying for guidance from God's Holy Spirit. In his example of the godly life, Jesus drew life and strength from God the Father through prayer. Christ was showing us the way to the power of God. Let us pause for a moment and examine the question whether a servant can live differently from the lifestyle of the master and still claim that he follows the master in obedient service.

The answer to this question is David's prayer for guidance and protection: "Make me to know thy ways, O Lord; teach me thy paths. Lead me in thy truth, and teach me, for thou art the God of my salvation; for thee I wait all the day long." (Psalm 25:4-5)

David's prayer expresses his heart's desire for steadfastness in commitment.

"Give me understanding," the Psalmist says, "that I may keep thy law and observe it with my whole heart." (Psalm 119:34)

We are shown by this example the model and the true meaning of allegiance.

In our restored fellowship with God there are no provisions for us to sway back and forth like a blade of grass bending in the wind. In our new life in the Spirit, we accept the Word of God as the authority over our lives. This we learn also by revelation of the Holy Spirit. The Word of God is the eternal light to guide us in the darkness and confusion of a troubled world. We ask God to help us: "Thy word is a lamp to my feet and a light to my path." (Psalm 119:105)

Our life in service to God is a matter of faithfulness and obedience. God gives the opportunity, but our response of commitment and wholehearted involvement make it work: "I have laid up thy word in my heart, that I might not sin against thee." (Psalm 119:11)

Thus, we cannot be many things to different people, if our confession of discipleship in Jesus Christ is true and we consequently long to live the model of the godly life that Jesus Christ has demonstrated to us. If our confession and our commitment are sincere, then the only witness needed to confirm whether or not we are what we profess to be is our life itself.

Our life in Christ then is a matter of commitment, similar to the commitment that God had expected from the Israelites when he called on them to accept the conditions for restoration and blessing following repentance: "I call Heaven and Earth to witness against you this day, that I have set before you life and death, blessing and curse; therefore choose life, that you and your descendants may live, loving the Lord your God, obeying his voice, and cleaving to him; for that means life to you and length of days." (Deuteronomy 30:19-20)

Goals in life

We have gone at length through the discussion of commitment, faithfulness, and obedience to the Word of God to show that all successful relationships with God demand single-mindedness in purpose to reach the goal of spiritual fulfillment. The setting of the goal requires a commitment itself.

Any relationship will disintegrate if there is no unity in spirit. Good intentions do not make a relationship. But commitment does. And our dedication to this commitment makes relationships prosper and grow, as we put our interest into it to give it the necessary impetus for advancement.

We must work hard at relationships to make them work. Good intentions have no power and are not worth the breath of speech or the paper for recording.

Relationships succeed when promise and anticipation are matched by performance. To amplify this point, let us borrow an example from business. When negotiations are over and an order is received there is happiness over it but not yet satisfaction. Only after a delivery of quality goods is made can the supplier claim to have gained a satisfied customer. Business transactions are completed deals. We cannot enter promises and hopes on a profit-and-loss ledger.

Human nature is dualistic. This is shown in several conflicts we face in life:
– Spiritual being versus physical nature
– Immortality of the spirit versus mortality of the flesh
– Obedience and faithfulness versus rejection of God

These have been the plague of mankind since the days of the first sin of Adam and humanity's downfall and disgrace because of it.

The dualism expands into the realm of the cosmos, as we speak of the power of light and the power of darkness, the Kingdom of God—where grace creates and sustains life—and the world, where in the ideal democratic society government rules by justice for the purpose of order.

As human beings we are touched by this structure of good and evil. And we must choose in full knowledge that our choice will determine life or death. This conflict is bemoaned by Saint Paul. But Paul also preaches the solution: "I do not understand my own actions. For I do not do what I want, but I do the very thing I hate … Wretched man that I am! Who will deliver me from this body of death? Thanks be to God through Jesus Christ our Lord! So then, I of myself serve the law of God with my mind, but with my flesh I serve the law of sin. "(Romans 7:15, 24-25)

The interrelation of family and work takes on significance in the world as society places certain values on our performance in family relationship and achievement at work. This judgment by peers can be cruel at times, because on many occasions we find conclusions reached that are not entirely based on fact.

In other instances we find opinions formed without any appreciation of circumstances. Our human nature has great talent to condemn and ostracize. When we are wrong, we do not wish to be reminded that we have erred.

We often say that it takes a real man—i.e., a strong person— to apologize for a mistake. But more is at stake when feelings and integrity are injured. Many people have left behind a growing cancer. The healing words, "I am sorry," or "I forgive you" were never spoken.

As disciples of Christ, we must not lower ourselves in dignity by responding to, or even acknowledging, any false accusations. Christ will in due time speak through the Holy Spirit on our behalf and keep us safe from the Evil One.

Let us remember that we are not alone, even though the entire world may seem to be against us. Eternal life in the Spirit is more valuable than the temporary rectification of problems in a sinful world. We know the truth of the Word of God and through this truth we claim our freedom from any vile accusations. We can definitely afford to lose our life in the world.

Christ addresses this subject when speaking about his suffering and death: "For what will it profit a man, if he gains the whole world and forfeits his life? Or what shall a man give in return for his life?" (Matthew 16:26)

The price of humanity's salvation is Christ's suffering and death. The world may never know this, but Christians do (1 Corinthians 1:18-31). And we have become instruments of God's promise to advance the Kingdom of God on Earth. Our concern is Christ's work to bring God's message of salvation to all people—even to those who may have offended us.

God valued our life by reaching down into the pit of his adulterated creation and lifting us out of it.

So let us make it our task to work on behalf of the Kingdom of God, and bring to the people in the world the message of salvation that we ourselves have received as the good news of the gospel of Christ. In this light, then, our sacrifice is God's work, as the work of God is divine sacrifice that saves sinners.

Our concern for the other person overshadows the temporary loss of time we suffer because we do not look after ourselves. God will bless the person who through our work was brought to Christ. We automatically will share in this blessing, as we are all one in Christ. We are merely drawing on what God through Jesus Christ is providing.

Our goals in life are set by us in the world and confirmed by God as the work of God for eternity. We work for what we know and believe to be the work of God.

At the crossroads of life

The true meaning for all relationships is found in Jesus Christ, the living Word of God. The power of the Word of God is the message of life that yields fruit of faith for eternal life.

God used the words of promise for sealing the covenant with the Israelites. He called on them to be faithful and obedient: "Now therefore, if you will obey my voice and keep my covenant, you shall be my own possession among all peoples; for all the Earth is mine, and you shall be to me a kingdom of priests and a holy nation." (Exodus 19:5-6)

If the people's response of faithfulness and obedience and their acceptance of God's promise made the Israelites priests and servants, then how much more must we, as his disciples, serve Christ because "He saved us, not because of deeds done by us in righteousness, but in virtue of his own mercy, by the washing of regeneration and renewal in the Holy Spirit, which he poured out upon us richly through Jesus Christ our Savior, so that we might be justified by his grace and become heirs in hope of eternal life." (Titus 3:5-7)

Let us remember that our life in Jesus Christ is the fulfillment of God's promise. Christ "gave himself for us to redeem us from all iniquity and to purify for himself a people of his own who are zealous for good deeds." (Titus 2:14)

How, then, do we react to the gift of God?

Solomon's words of wisdom establish the boundary conditions for our behavior. Let their truth refresh the weary mind and guide the tired soul in mapping a treacherous journey: "Unless the Lord builds the house, those who build it labor in vain. Unless the Lord watches over the city, the watchman stays awake in vain. It is in vain that you rise up early and go late to rest, eating the bread of anxious toil, for he gives to his beloved sleep." (Psalm 127:1-2)

So let us seriously look at relationships with God and also with one another. Equally important is to examine our attitude toward the work of God for which we were created. If we proceed according to God's plan, then our labor will be productive because it was done in light of fulfilling the expectation of God.

We respond to God in love, because he first loved us. Our salvation through Jesus Christ is based on grace, that unmerited love of God for all humanity.

Our relationship with other people, as well as the interfacing of people and work, must reflect God's expectation and make our life a hymn of constant thanksgiving. The Psalmist rejoices as he sings praises to God: "O give thanks to the Lord, for he is good; for his steadfast love endures for ever!" (Psalm 107:1)

We perceive the eternal goodness of God with the eyes of our soul. Our response is that kind of appreciation which prompts us to prepare in our heart a dwelling place for the Holy Spirit. Since a relationship of love involves the whole person, our dedication of love to God and our neighbor is total commitment.

True love cannot be acquired through analysis. Nor can it be created through study. Love requires a commitment of our total being.

It has its origin in understanding whose we are. It is instrumental in helping believers fulfill their mission of life on Earth.

Human life draws its meaning from the Spirit. God has ordained equality for all people through this spiritual connection. This divine truth prevails despite the privileged claims of people arising from status and position in life.

Diversity because of status or achievement is real in the world. God has given each person different talents. Yet, let us all remember that these gifts come from the same Spirit. In the sight of God, this is complementary and not at all a discrepancy to be looked at with scorn.

Saint Paul explains: "Now there are varieties of gifts, but the same Spirit; and there are varieties of service, but the same Lord; and there are varieties of working, but it is the same God who inspires them all in every one. To each is given the manifestation of the Spirit for the common good." (1 Corinthians 12:4-7)

We are part of God's team as we work in faith with our brothers and sisters in Christ to bring glory to God. The restored fellowship of all believers is God's answer to waywardness and sin.

Our equality before God is crowned by the divine act of Grace. God made a sacrifice on behalf of sinners. Jesus Christ died for the forgiveness of all our sins. The word all extends to people everywhere. Saint John clearly states this fact in the opening words of his gospel, when he talks about John the Baptist being the messenger who "came for testimony, to bear witness to the light, that all might believe through him." (John 1:6)

Divine truth versus human ambition

We may blame our bad behavior on human nature. People are prone to defend any poor attitude toward life by saying that this is so because human nature is bad and makes it so.

This is not true!

When Saint Paul speaks about the conflict in people, he does not point the accusing finger at all aspects of human nature, but at the sin in human nature. God has given us human nature, but we are responsible for its sin, the throne of which we have built in our mind. And its evil empire we sustain within our hearts through lusts and greed.

These are manifestations of selfishness. They have grown out of our disobedience and faithlessness toward God. Saint Paul faced a similar problem. But he also says that we must properly recognize this as sin: "For I do not do the good I want, but the evil I do not want is what I do. Now if I do what I do not want, it is no longer I that do it, but sin which dwells within me." (Romans 7:19-20)

Let us now look more closely at the nature of our human character and trace it back to creation and then examine God's response to our wayward behavior. We will soon learn that we are not really as great as we think we are. The Psalmist has recorded the truth of the Word of God: "Hear, O my people, while I admonish you! O Israel, if you would but listen to me! There shall be no strange god among you; you shall not bow down to a foreign god. I am the Lord your God, who brought you up out of the land of Egypt. Open your mouth wide, and I will fill it. But my people did not listen to my voice; Israel would have none of me. So I gave them over to their stubborn hearts, to follow their own counsels. O that my people would listen to me, that Israel would walk in my ways! I would soon subdue their enemies, and turn my hand against their foes. (Psalm 81:8-14)

Only the Word of God can bridge the shortcoming created by the rebellion of people toward God. An outgrowth of our rejection of God is disrespect for human life. This evidence is commonly visible in dealing with less fortunate people and also those lower in status than ours. Such downgrading of people continues despite full knowledge that all humanity is God's creation. This perpetuation of the sin of discrimination is but a subtle form of an overall rebellion toward God.

The selection from the 81st Psalm discusses what human behavior is like. It also tells us what is being missed when people fall short of God's expectation of faithfulness and obedience.

God's address is a warning. But it definitely also contains the promise of hope. The Word of God assures us that when we worship God and with absolute reliance wait on him for all our needs, then we will enjoy God's blessing of restored fellowship. To have this come about, we are firmly reminded of God's declaration from Exodus concerning the meaning of a true relationship: "You shall have no other gods before me." (Exodus 20:3)

Behind the authority of the address in this Psalm again is God's own power. The power of the Word of God already has been demonstrated in history. Here again are the specifics: "I am the Lord your God, who brought you out of the land of Egypt, out of the house of bondage." (Exodus 20:2) In detailed language, God is letting people know whose they are. He traces relationships for a clearer understanding. Believers now can be free of doubts.

The specificity of the Word of God, as recorded by the Psalmist, has indeed been fulfilled. We read the promise, "Open your mouth wide, and I will fill it." (Psalm 81:10b)

As disciples of Christ we suddenly feel overtaken as we realize the power of the good news of the Gospel.

Christ took on human form for the sole purpose of saving sinners. Through God's act of grace, believers have the opportunity of receiving life and light. This is our redemption.

Jesus Christ dwelled among people. Christ is an event in human history: "In the beginning was the Word, and the Word was with God, and the Word was God. He was in the beginning with God; all things were made through him, and without him was not anything made that was made. In him was life, and the life was the light of men." (John 1:1-4)

As further evidence that the human race is really slow in learning, Saint John writes that Christ was in the world as the light that "enlightens every man … yet the world knew him not. He came to his own home, and his own people received him not." (John 1:9-11) Thus, people continue to live in disobedience toward God.

Consequently, we are given a foretaste of God's judgment: "So I gave them over to their stubborn hearts, to follow their own counsels." (Psalm 81:12)

When God abandons all intentions to discipline us further, let there not be any doubt that God's judgment is upon us.

Saint Paul wrote to the members of the church at Rome: "For the wrath of God is revealed from Heaven against all ungodliness and wickedness of men who by their wickedness suppress the truth. For what can be known about God is plain to them, because God has shown it to them." (Romans 1:18-19)

Human resourcefulness, with all its excuses, is now exposed. Christ has affirmed: "As long as I am in the world, I am the light of the world." (John 9:5)

Despite anger and judgment, God's overwhelming concern for humanity is visible. Threads of mercy hold together a statement of compassion that is designed to inspire hope in people: "O that my people would listen to me, that Israel would walk in my ways!" (Psalm 81:13)

Jesus gives the Christian community the opportunity to follow him as the light of the world. Christ has already paid the price for the forgiveness of sins. Now Christ illuminates this truth further. Salvation is a free gift from God: "I am the light of the world; he who follows me will not walk in darkness, but will have the light of life." (John 8:12)

To make sure that we grasp this fact of restored fellowship, we are told that the best way to show our new status as God's chosen people is by becoming what we continuously recite in the confessional creeds. Christ's reminder is additional help: "You are the light of the world ... Let your light so shine before men, that they may see your good works and give glory to your Father who is in Heaven." (Matthew 5:14-16)

Abraham was justified before God because of his trust in God's promise. How much more assurance then do we have in claiming our justification through God's act of righteousness, for which the death and the resurrection of Jesus Christ is the living example!

The desire to know truth transforms guilt into faith. Christ is there to help us cross the gulf of sin. As we recognize the Word of God, we will respect it as the only authority in our dealings during the soul's pilgrimage on Earth. The value of the Word of God is secured for us in divine promise.

Believers are assured that the righteousness of God, for even the worst of sinners, is all sufficient to find forgiveness and the return to God. All this has been made possible through Christ.

The grand finale: cosmic victory

The upholder of the universe loves each person so deeply that God personally supports every relationship with himself, family, friend, neighbor, and associate in the workplace. We are challenged in the workplace to copy the harmonious precision by which God operates the universe.

For this purpose God has blessed us with families. God is giving us work and a workplace to support our families. God has blessed us with talents to excel in all that we do. The challenge is now ours to love and support our families and children. Success in the interrelation of family and work is a definite part of God's blessing for people everywhere.

"For the love of God who made and sustains us, we thank you, Lord; we thank you for our families, and the opportunities of work to support them!"

Economics
(Selection from *I.D. Crisis*)

Preface

The economy is an integral part of God's domain. And economics is God's way of managing it. The spiritual treatment of the economy and economics, therefore, is essential for a clearer understanding about our involvement and is also critically important for the survival of humanity as spiritual beings in the image of God. The leitmotiv in this writing about the economy and economics is the spiritual connection.

There are six sections: (a) Preface, (b) The spiritual perspective on the economy and economics, (c) Modern economics (d) Global economics, (e) The human side of economics, and (f) The renaissance of manufacturing in America.

The spiritual perspective on the economy and economics details the spiritual connection. It sheds light on our responsibility as God's faithful stewards of his resources on Earth.

In *Modern economics* we look at the important three Ws central to all critical reviews: what, where, and when. What does the past tell us? Where do we stand in the present? When will we act to improve the human condition in the future?

In *Global economics* we take a critical look at this relatively new phenomenon. We will review economic justice in the context of helping underdeveloped countries secure their independence through economic freedom.

In *The human side of economics* we examine how the spiritual connection bears on modern economics in terms of the needs of the Kingdom of God on Earth. We will also review some of the major shortcomings in modern economics. We will focus on America. We will examine how political lobbyists influence the action of government and the creation of laws. We will further expose economic abuse by opportunists, manipulators, and self-styled "paper barons" who exploit the public trust for personal gain.

In *The renaissance of manufacturing in America* we see a concerned public rising up to regain control of jobs in manufacturing. This action "by the people for the people" asks for God's help to recover what has been squandered and lost.

The spiritual perspective on the economy and economics

The economy and economics is not a free-for-all the way greedy people in the secular world would like to have it. The economy and economics are of God, and God is in control. God has definite expectations of people. He expects top performance according to his will and purpose. Indeed, there are obligations in economics, similar to other obligations that we experience in our relationship with God.

Economics is stewardship of God's wealth to a predestined

end. God provides the means, and he defines the outcome. The means is the economy, and the predestined end is quality of life. Our performance, therefore, will determine our destinies. Ultimately we will be asked to give full account of our use of time, talents, and money.

As citizens of the world we have the obligation to use God's wealth in ways that agree with his purpose for our creation. If we want to realize our hope of eternal life in the presence of God in Heaven, we must comply with God's way on Earth. Our independence on Earth is contingent upon the quality of our spiritual connection with God in Heaven. We are his children in the world to do our father's bidding.

Our father in Heaven is a loving God. And God trusts us to be faithful in managing his wealth on Earth. Economics and the economy are servant functions. Therefore, the role of faithful stewards over God's vast economic domain is precisely doing what God wants to get done. God trusts us with his wealth on Earth, and we have no choice but to respond to this trust with a commitment that love of God alone affords.

In this understanding, trust and faithfulness are words of spiritual importance. As citizens of the world we compliment these spiritual components with civility, honor and respect; our behavior then identifies us as decent human beings in the secular world. As practitioners of the Golden Rule, therefore, we look to our partners in economic matters to have integrity, respect, honor, and commitments that are similar to what they expect of us.

Economics is faithful stewardship. We prioritize available resources to fulfill human needs in a fair, just, and equal manner. Faithful stewardship implies responsible management of God's resources. Responsible management means the preservation of materials and responsible maintenance of the quality of the environment for future generations. This is our obligation to our children.

The story of good economics in the Bible is the stewardship of Joseph at the court of the king of Egypt around 1600 B.C. (Genesis 41:25-47).

Bad economics, on the other hand, are multitudes of human aberrations of God's principles. Bad economics is driven by greed. Satan is the promoter of all kinds of greed.

The Bible indicts greed as the worst of human aberrations. God condemns the insatiable appetite of greedy people for the possessions of others. All types of greed are destructive. Greed kills relationships. Greed kills people in wars and in economic oppressions. Satanic greed will eventually consume the souls of greedy people. Wherever human aberrations of God's way promote greed, the consequences are chaos and human despair.

Singly against greed stands the Word of God. By the power of the Holy Spirit, God is telling us in plain language to shape up, change our evil ways, and accept his Word as the sole authority on economics.

Modern economics

America's current economic difficulties are self-inflicted by a service economy that had its start in the early 1970s.

Low-paying service jobs make it difficult for American families to make ends meet. Two incomes are now essential to support a family. Often parents are forced to work two jobs. The constant loss of manufacturing jobs is wiping out any hope in the future for decent wages with associated benefits.

Whereas manufacturing jobs have a ripple effect on the economy of nations, a lopsided service economy consumes the wealth of nations. A service economy does not contribute to the building of highways, bridges, and schools. A service economy offers little support to pay for police and fire protection. And deficit spending in a service economy squanders the future of children.

Today's service economy favors the rich in a two-tier society of the have and the have-not. Two-tier societies threaten community life.

Two-tier societies are impersonal and pose a threat to the survival of families and communities. Overworked parents have little time left to raise their children. Volunteer work in the community is almost nonexistent. And there is little time left to converse with a neighbor. Families in neighborhoods were once supportive of each other, and we could count on each other in times of need but this has now become a dream world for many people. The good times when we could call on our next-door neighbor and borrow a cup of sugar are gone.

The modern impersonal lifestyle created by the service economy has replaced relationships with concerns about money. Money wields power. Money now speaks.

The need for money is ever increasing to support the family. The cost of housing is alarmingly high. Health care consumes a major portion of the family's income. Everywhere we look in the service economy, people are driven by money needs. The modern service economy is a quagmire of debts. We need money—lots of money—to pay for the basic needs in life.

Compounding the problems of the flimsy service economy is the lack of hope for a better future. Job security has become a foreign concept, but families need a dependable income to prepare their children for the future.

America's economic situation has taken a turn for the worse. Huge corporations continue to wipe out the local manufacturing base that once provided reliable income for many families. In its place we now find these same large corporations peddling foreign-made goods at high profits. They charge the consumer whatever the traffic will bear. In this modern dilemma, trade deficits and foreign investments threaten the future freedom of

American children.

The well-being of individuals and families is at the mercy of corporate peddlers of foreign-made merchandise. The citizens of the once most prosperous nation in the world are now trapped in a silly numbers game played by financial manipulators. Financial gurus in control of huge corporations are mercenaries without mercy. Their sole compassion is money. "Paper barons" have replaced the visionary entrepreneur-managers.

"Paper barons" now run huge enterprises in insidiously hidden ways to make high profits for themselves at the expense of consumers. For example, while the contents of food packages are getting smaller, frequent increases in the price of these smaller-sized goods are quite common. While the weekly income of working families diminishes or remains flat, the salaries of "paper barons" are increasing at immoral rates.

The world revolves around economics. Therefore, we rightfully ask: "What is good economics? This is *the* key economic question for the modern world, as good economics is the criterion for quality of life. Good economics is our statement of faithful stewardship.

A good economy respects the life, liberty, and happiness of each individual in his or her search for the way of God. Good economics recognizes that all resources on Earth belong to God, and we are but stewards of his creation. We honor God as supreme reality. And we love him for what he is, and for what he is doing for us in our short pilgrimage on Earth. Good economics is synonymous with a prosperous life on Earth.

Political meddling in economic matters is just a license for greedy people to do as they please. In these aberrations of God's way, the rich get richer, and the poor are being pushed into the bottomless pit. The children of America must pay in the future for the folly in leadership now.

Unscrupulous operators, in America and throughout the world, manipulate supply and demand to their advantage. We see this especially in Third-World nations that depend on goods and services from their more highly developed neighbors. For the residents of Third-World countries, like those in Africa, economic fairness is a matter of life or death. We see death from starvation in many African countries where opportunists have unfairly exploited a nation's natural resources without fair compensation. On top of this evil are power-hungry tyrannical rulers in underdeveloped nations who are in collusion with ruthless global conglomerates and their political cohorts to fill their own pockets.

Therefore, God condemns the evil antics of economic manipulators. God says: "The world is mine, and all that is therein is mine. Belief and trust in me is all my people need." And God continues: "I will take care of you. I will provide for your spiritual needs. And once your spiritual needs are met, your physical needs will also be met. Life is more than food. And your body is more than clothing. I care about your life. My Word alone can satisfy the needs of your soul. And my blessings shall be food for your soul and clothing for your body."

Despite God's support for less fortunate people, the exploitations by large international corporations keep growing, and the conflict of spirit over flesh seems like a losing battle, for God and people. It appears that the modern economic conflict is more severe than the plagues of the Dark Ages in which scores of innocent people died.

Huge corporations have created woes for innocent people as never before. To correct this great evil of huge corporations taking advantage of poor people in the modern world, God is encouraging each person to become self-sufficient. And, by the grace of God, "individual economies" will take root and grow.

In this new approach to economics, the presence of God will help each person in sundry ways to nurture individually owned enterprises, while economies of scale are doomed to failure as a direct result of uncontrollable size. Though the evil may always try to gain the upper hand in controlling the lives of people through large-scale economic oppression, God as the champion of ethics, justice, and faith will bless individual entrepreneurs who operate their business according to the Golden Rule.

God assures quality of life for workers and owners of local enterprises. God says: "The world is mine, and all that is therein is mine. Persevere in my way of life, and I will give you the Crown of Life in eternity! My faithful people will do extremely well in my presence, and I will let them bask in my glory. Therefore, choose life. Nurture your spiritual connection with me, and I will help you make good economics your quality of life."

Some of the tactics of ruthless governments and large corporations are not always obvious. The unsuspecting minds of trusting citizens are too innocent, and a gentle citizenry may not immediately come to grips with the antics of economic greed by politicians and their financial backers. Even though we feel the pain of the injustice and inequality in the distribution of the national wealth, often they are so overwhelming that we seem helpless and give up. Economic evildoers and their lobbyists seem more powerful than all the citizens of many nations combined.

When the American public needs replacement parts to fix the flimsy products, there are no replacements parts to be found in the large stores. The common reply to the search for replacement parts is that the new items are bigger and better than what is broken. The bigger and better, of course, refers to the peddlers' profits; peddlers have little concern about the financial straits of their customers.

God expects us to clip the wings of powerful "paper barons" in the community, the nation, and the world. God sees our needs, and he wants us to bring about change and correct an evil situation. The masses of American consumers have greater power than all the powers of "paper barons" in the world combined.

Global economics

*God demands first-class stewardship
of time, talents, and money.*

In the modern concept of global economics, a few select nations control the rest of the world as a matter of greed. Global economics is colonization in disguise. The "paper barons" of international conglomerates and ruthless politicians may temporarily fool the public with their business glamour. In the Era of Faith, God is not interested in business glamour, but God expects our trust and faith through the spiritual connection with God in our consumption of his wealth on Earth.

*Hockey stick cowboys are the paper barons of global
economics. They talk fast. They talk smooth to gain control.*

More than in any other human discipline in the world, economics is full of wolves in sheep's clothing. Christ has warned us about greedy people whose *modus operandi* is the promotion of falsehoods through misleading statements or selfish business practices. Peers in commerce, industry, and financial institutions have coined the phrase "hockey stick cowboys" to identify co-workers whose ambition is rise to power through the promotion of falsehoods. Hockey stick cowboys are ruthless "paper barons." They talk fast. They talk smooth. They want full control of the global economy.

"Hockey stick cowboys" force themselves onto center stage

by criticizing conservative management as not aggressive enough for growth. Their growth charts always start out flat to criticize past performance. But once they are in charge, their hockey stick theories of growth opportunities turn into projections, and the exponential growth opportunities that a hockey stick implies never materialize. Hockey stick cowboys take advantage of style without substance. Style without substance has ruined many established businesses, and the employees of defunct enterprises suffer the consequences of folly in leadership when the business fails.

Christ tells us how to identify "paper barons." Christ says: "Look at the fruit of their labor. Evil cannot grow good fruit."

The evil in economics is commonly the fruit of indifferent business leaders, whose prime qualification for dealing with God's wealth is not rooted in the wisdom of God but is based on a piece of paper that bestows on them the secular title of master in business administration. "Paper barons" arrogantly believe that a master's degree from a business school entitles them to rule over God's wealth.

God says: "Wisdom comes with experience. Wisdom is not book knowledge. Wise business leaders are entrepreneurs with vision. They build on their vision, and they know how to correct evil situations. They maintain what they built. On the other hand, book-smart business leaders tear things down. And they flee the scene to pursue other opportunities when chaos confronts them."

Inspired stewards of God work responsibly the stewardship role and provide justly for their co-workers in commerce, industry, and financial institutions according to the precepts of ethics, justice, and faith. Inspired stewards supply the needs of employees and customers as a matter of public trust, where justice and equality are prime movers for economic stability and growth.

Whereas "paper barons" fight for their power, God honors his inspired stewards with dignity and respect, and common people also honor and respect faithful stewards as they have demonstrated responsible leadership in commerce and industry for the well being of all.

While the majorities of business leaders are faithful stewards of God's wealth and deal honestly with his people in economic matters, "paper barons" take advantage of doubts and then step in to commandeer a marginal economic situation to their personal advantage and gain. Their *modus operandi* are promises of unlimited growth and high profits. God calls it style without substance. They are the politicians who will promise anything that the public wants to hear. God has been impatiently watching how "paper barons" have bartered away a strong manufacturing base and subsequently eroded the quality of life for peaceable families and diligent workers in modern America.

The global economy is the supply engine for food and medicine in underdeveloped countries. The pressure is now on inspired leaders in successful economies to be compassionate and attend to the needs of starving and sick people. Any failure to meet the physical needs of suffering people spells disaster for the global economy—and the global supply engine will sputter or may even explode.

The mission of global economics is to fill physical needs.

The mission for the modern world is to fill needs—physical and spiritual. Economics is the business of filling physical needs. Life in the world revolves around basic needs. Global economics is a system driven by needs. Our way of filling these needs to God's satisfaction will determine destinies.

Selfish desires are as real as life itself. It is up to us to adjust our ambitions to God's satisfaction and his plan for creation. Any desires beyond the basics for quality of life are greed. Good economics is having enough resources for each day. Anything beyond that is evil. Therefore, we rely on God's wisdom to stop us when enough is enough.

As human beings in the modern world we desire spiritual satisfaction without having to give up physical pleasures. But this cannot be. We can't have both. It is now up to us to prioritize and find the high ground for quality of life. The choice is ours. But so are the consequences of our decision. While God carefully watches our actions in this conflict of spirit and flesh, he will not influence our decision.

The human side of economics

Cain's calculating view of his relationship with the living God had become formalized into a simple formula of economics.

We carry on as Adam did. He denied God's generosity of life in paradise. Adam rejected life in the presence of God. We too deny God in the modern world, though God made the world we live in. God beckons for an active role in our lives, but we refuse him entry.

Our failure to be grateful for the presence of God in daily life leads us astray. In the subsequent confusion, all uncommitted people, like Cain in Biblical times, are ideal candidates for God's concern.

Biblical literature has preserved divine truth to act as guidance and direction for life: "In the course of time Cain brought to the Lord an offering of the fruit of the ground, and Abel brought of the firstlings of his flock and of their fat portions. And the Lord had regard for Abel and his offering, but for Cain and his offering he had no regard. So Cain was very angry, and his countenance fell. The Lord said to Cain, 'Why are you angry, and why has your countenance fallen? If you do well, will you not be accepted? And if you do not do well, sin is couching at the door; its desire is for you, but you must master it.' Cain said to Abel his brother, 'Let us go out to the field.' And when they were in the field, Cain rose up against his brother Abel, and killed him." (Genesis 4:3-8)

In the Biblical legend, Cain had great ambition to prove his humanity. He wanted to make it on his own; his human aspirations overpowered his senses. Ambition and aspirations condemned Cain to commit murder.

In these modern times, we are even more blessed than Cain was. Yet many people reject God's offer of support. The Holy Spirit is our companion, counselor, and guide. By the power of the Holy Spirit, God is our friend. God in Christ is generous sharing his life with us. We are humbled to invite him into our hearts. In our relationship with God all other things are superfluous. We are indeed the choice of God's creation. Why, then, do many of God's people reject the presence of God in their lives?

Despite God's assessment of the evil in envy and greed, there are legions in the world today who scorn knowledge and enlightenment through the truth of Christ's teaching. They continue a way of life similar to Cain's. Cain had chosen a life in total ignorance of his spiritual identity.

Cain's calculating view of his relationship with the living God had become formalized into a simple formula of economics.

Whereas Abel dedicated himself to God when he brought the

first lamb born to one of his sheep, killed it, and gave the best parts of it as an offering, Cain considered some of his fruit harvest just fine for meeting the minimum requirement for assurance of God's blessing and favor.

But God found only Abel's offering acceptable. Abel had truly presented himself and committed his entire future into God's hands.

The evidence indicates that Abel knew God as a matter of trust. Abel relied on God to provide for all his future needs. But we also learn from the demise of Abel that faithful and obedient people face danger whenever they make known their commitment. History has proven over and over again that the world has never suffered from a shortage of Cains.

> *We find modern Cains exploiting family, friends,*
> *co-workers, the community, and the nation by working*
> *the rule of getting the most for the least.*

Greedy and envious people are in the world wherever we go. They are part of a Christian's challenge to make known the living God to all people in the world. This also includes bringing the witness of divine grace in equal measure even to the Cains of this world.

Thus, Christ is telling all followers to carry their own crosses when doing God's work in service to God and people. The instructions are clear: "Let your light so shine before men, that they may see your good works and give glory to your Father who is in Heaven." (Matthew 5:16)

Yet despite knowledge of Christ's commands to change the self-destructive ways of the past and believe in the Gospel, people continue to choose living in the curse of Cain. Selfishness is driving these possessed souls to the idol worship of accumulated wealth. In their self-assertion, people work themselves to death.

As a direct consequence of self-assertive obsession, greed makes people useless in doing the work of God, for there is not to be found among them even the slightest concern with the Kingdom of God and what he requires. In its stead we see ruthless wielding of power, whose foundation is not God but accumulated wealth.

We find these modern Cains exploiting family, friends, coworkers, and the community by working the rule of getting the most for the least. They will remind those associated with them that it is a privilege to be working together. They are generous with sweet talk. It does not cost them anything. Some even do it in full knowledge of any oppressive burdens they themselves have placed on others.

The poor and the destitute are relegated to subhuman levels of existence. There is little or no hope for the better way of life for the less fortunate simply because all opportunities for advancement are viciously guarded, even the ones that people of influence and power administer as a matter of public trust.

Yet, like Cain, these arrogant "benefactors" of society scowl whenever they see the grace of God uplifting downtrodden spirits. They are jealous of happiness in others whenever the power of God's love is seen active and real. The glow of genuine brotherhood among poor but inspired people is seen in their sharing and caring for each other.

As the love of God is real among the faithful and the obedient disciples of Christ, so is the anger of arrogant people, as they sense that their phony piety does not measure up to God's expectation that demands true love in return for Grace.

Christ's teaching is clear that only those who live in a true state of sincere humility of the spirit will be able to share the Kingdom of Heaven as rightful heirs together with Christ.

In the Sermon on the Mount, Christ promises true happiness. Christ's promise is universal truth. It requires that we fully know our identity. We must recognize that the status of restored fellowship with God is based on the righteousness of God alone and handed to believers in Christ as a gift of grace. This eternal truth must be clearly established in our mind even before we attempt to refresh our memories about whose we truly are.

Only when Christians see each other as children of the true and living God can Christianity be acclaimed as containing the principles of the one eternal truth and the one universal salvation. Its followers are like "light for the whole world."

People who live according to worldly standards will want to push spiritual involvement aside. So we hear the scornful, though seemingly logical question: "What does the spirit have to do with the price of bananas?"

But as quickly as green bananas ripen and spoil, so will the short human pilgrimage on Earth come to a sudden end.

This sad result will come about because people have failed to realize their spiritual identity. They have failed to recognize God's purpose for their lives. What must we do? This question implies desperation. Seekers of truth will have their answer in the spiritual connection with God.

To realize God's blessing we must humble ourselves and, in the humility of our spirit, desire to put our lives in harmony with the will and purpose of God.

Because despair is an ultimate consequence of faithlessness, all hope for a better future has vanished. In their hopelessness people will see eternity fleeting by right before their eyes.

There is no such thing as a second chance for recapturing time. Nor can the entries in the Book of Life be rewritten or amended by human effort.

Past experiences—good and bad alike—are history. Time is God's way of giving people a new beginning in preparation for meeting Christ on the Day of Judgment. Christians are told to let bygones be bygones: "No one who puts his hand to the plow and looks back is fit for the Kingdom of God." (Luke 9:62)

Some people are more interested in raising their self-esteem within the realm of worldly affairs than being concerned with the Kingdom of God and with what he requires. They will protest that words with spiritual connotations are meaningless to them.

People whose only intentions are worldly considerations want to see the power of the Word of God reduced to the level where it will serve them. This reasoning is the biggest excuse for not wanting to make a commitment of dedication to God through Christ.

Like all other self-serving approaches to life, so is this unwarranted demand to make religion understandable nothing more than a trick. It has been in existence ever since the church was formed; it wants to cheapen the grace of God by making religion worldlier. Yet there is no justification for lowering God's expectations of faithful witness to the Gospel. We must recognize that the Kingdom of God and the world are not meant to be reconciled and that the Spirit has authority and power over the physical and emotional being of man.

In the parable of the rich fool, Jesus warns that accumulated wealth cannot be transferred to Heaven (Luke 12:16-20). True wealth is the hope of eternal life. All faithful and obedient people will share with Christ in the glory of God.

If as Christians we fail to speak up and defend what is right, we are guilty of contributing to the tensions of others. For instance, this is the case when economic hardship is caused by deficit spending. We are involved and responsible when we approve the action of government to pay for any programs that may benefit us now but whose debentures have dire consequences on the livelihood of future generations.

We rob our children of their potential in the future by tapping this potential to pay our commitments. We are guilty of dragging future generations, not at all connected with our difficulties, into our predicaments.

Deficit spending and inflation are the two major economic burdens in modern times. Even when inflation is at a low level, it diminishes the value of fixed assets and set income.

People and institutions alike feel the effects of inflation. From 1953 to the 1970s people in America have seen the biggest inflation in its history. During this period creeping inflation of 1-6 percent per year—some years even higher—has raised havoc with the best of intentions in budgeting and planning. Grocery prices are constantly on the rise while the contents of packages are getting smaller. Families are hurting to keep up with the cost of living. The increasing cost of the market basket neutralizes raises in income, while those on fixed incomes see their purchasing power diminished.

How does the high cost of living create family problems? The issue goes beyond basic survival of the family.

We must look at the well being of children in households where both parents are forced to work in order to cover expenses. The immediate effect is a generation of youth that has to raise itself. Is it then any wonder that such children are full of frustration, because there is no family outlet for their adventures in life?

Even if children manage to keep their stories bottled up till evening, they seldom will be heard as exhausted parents return from a hard day's work—and even two jobs— and don't want to be bothered with matters so seemingly insignificant as a child's discovery.

We see the retired, whose savings have evaporated as inflation has reduced the value of money. We find homes being confiscated for taxes. People cannot afford to live in the residences they have legally paid for.

One of the greatest economic injustices occurs in industrialized society. It is not right to force a dedicated breadwinner in the prime of life into unemployment because reorganization has eliminated senior positions.

Why focus on hard-working individuals and families during times of economic hardships?

If we don't, no one else will. Hardworking individuals always are forced to carry the burden of bad decisions. In searching for causes of economic disasters we must always keep before us the tired faces of people who are hurting by the actions of "paper barons" or impulsive politicians and governments. Economics is not just a numbers game. The human side of economics is a story of the oppression of ordinary, hard- working people!

The renaissance of manufacturing in America

God looks with compassion at modern America, and he suffers with the victims of economic abuse. With scorn he addresses the arrogant and seemingly invincible "paper barons" and impulsive politicians: "You have become too big for your breeches. All the world's resources are mine. Your greedy appetite and lust for power is wasting what belongs to me and all my people!"

And God continues: "I have made America the bastion of free enterprise. You have eliminated your competitors by swallowing them up one by one, not with your own money but at the expense of my people. You have borrowed money and then passed on the cost of your insatiable growth to the consumers. They carry the burden of your grandiose schemes through higher costs of the market basket or smaller food packages. In your grandiose plots you start new ventures with borrowed money and then fold them up when things do not work out. Who do you think is absorbing the loss? Surely, it is not your financial backers. They are even greedier than you are. They are in business to make money no matter what. And look at your accounting schemes. Suddenly you play the fool, claiming that you do not know what is happening. You know how to give yourselves huge salaries, bonuses, and generous pensions. My people must pay for them by your denying jobs, health coverage, and pensions for my hard-working people."

God's voice now thunders: "By what rules do you gamble the hard-earned savings of my working people in 401(k) plans? Who decides that you have the right to declare a stock under value or encourage companies to dilute the number of shares? Who do you think is picking up the tab when your schemes fail? Unscrupulous institutional managers of the public trust are great evils in modern times. A lot of money is changing hands without control and without considerations of the needs of the owner."

God says: "You pay obnoxiously high salaries in professional sports. Whose money is it that you are wasting? You recover every penny through advertisements of the products my people must buy in order to live. But it is my people who must swallow with each spoon of food the bitterness of your schemes. I, the Lord, have spoken."

In the past, families envisioned great times as industries grew and so did employment, and the future was promising. Enlightened entrepreneurs looked protectively after workers; those leaders less inclined to share the wealth were obliged to sign labor contracts through unions. In either situation industry and the American workforce was a viable partnership, each partner benefiting through benevolent relationships. Even when work was slow during recessions or depressions, local employers cared for their struggling families.

Unfortunately, it took wars to perk up sagging economies. Two world wars lifted industry out of the doldrums. During each national crisis the American workers were ready to pitch in and do their part. They did not debate. They simply helped. A job needed to be done, and they were there to do it.

Enlightened entrepreneurs remembered that each worker had to support a family, so they compensated their workers fairly. Quality of life in the early period of America's industrialization consisted of family, the church, and an unyielding faith in God. As the family enjoyed income security, they had time to share. And they shared laughter, often in the company of friends and neighbors. Because the employers were benevolent, there was great respect for business leaders. Business ethics were crowned with an unwritten commitment to look out for each other at all times. Accounting was simple and free of tricks. Honesty and fairness fostered respect in the workplace. God was happy because his people were satisfied.

Industrialization was conceived to make life simpler, more abundant, and more secure. America was producing things in large volumes to make them affordable. America had a sound manufacturing base. And America was making money. Sunrise and sunset defined the day for work and shopping. Evenings were for the family, and Sundays were days of rest for fun and laughter. God was the center of family life.

Subtle changes gradually appeared on the horizon. "Efficiency experts" entered the scene. There were shifts away from the personal relationships workers enjoyed with entrepreneurs. Professional managers appeared to run the business on a new and impersonal platform. The new focus was on the bottom line. Ethics was put into the back seat, and the once-vital work ethic slowly faded into oblivion. The 1960s saw the beginning of the end of manufacturing in America.

This shift broke the backbone of the American economy. Cheap labor overseas overpowered the American workforce with the approval of management. The American workforce in textiles, shoes, and eventually high technology was hung out to dry by its business leadership. Besides the loss of jobs, America is losing all rights to genuine American technology. Business leaders claim to need the technology transfer to manufacture their products overseas. God is troubled.

God says: "My wealth in America belongs to the American people. It is my gift to them." God admonishes America's leadership—business leaders and politicians alike—concerning job losses: "When you scorn the American workforce as an expense that is prohibitive, you are attacking the foundation of the American dream that I put in place for a bright future of job stability and family income. You are attacking me when you take work away from my people. Your cheap labor tactics are now the cause of many social ills in America. Your greedy appetite is placing the American family in jeopardy. Your greed is a monster that gnaws at the hopes and dreams of my people. And that is not all. You now sell in America for dollars what you have manufactured offshore for cents. Your exploitation of cheap labor markets is slavery. Your greed is responsible for hatred and wars because exploited people feel the injustice done to them. You are fools if you think that I will let you get away with it. Beware of your greed. Greed is a killer. I will not stop your greed, for eventually your own greed will destroy you in due time. Repent therefore. I, the Lord, have spoken."

Education
(Selection from *I.D. Crisis*)

God's contributions to education are truth and spiritual values

Our happiness is complete;
the Holy Spirit is our guide and companion.
Christ tells us:
The Holy Spirit "dwells with you, and will be in you."
(John 14:17)

Education helps to strengthen faith, but it is faith that secures our unwavering confidence in God. Believers then practice God's will faithfully and obediently.

Knowledge dispels fears. This further strengthens faith. Christ expects us to search for the truth about God and know its value for the new life in the Spirit. This is a natural request for Christians so that we can share as Christ's disciples the fullness of God's grace through a life that is enveloped in divine wisdom.

The truth about God is the wisdom revealed by the Holy Spirit. We receive this wisdom whenever we become enlightened through knowledge about God.

Our happiness is complete, because the Holy Spirit is our guide and companion. Christ tells us: The Holy Spirit "dwells with you, and will be in you." (John 14:17)

Success in life on Earth is knowledge of God's presence. We will experience this assurance whenever we accept the Holy Spirit's guidance to lead us in a life pleasing to God. Our life is complete when we are found acceptable in God's sight.

With this knowledge before us, life on Earth can now rest in the peace that Christ has given believers as his blessing: "Peace I leave with you; my peace I give to you; not as the world gives do I give to you. Let not your hearts be troubled, neither let them be afraid." (John 14:27)

Through our study of the Scriptures, we see the mysticism of blind faith evaporate and sense it being replaced by God's power of truth. We now can give full glory to Christ. Henceforth our objectives in life are similar to what the Holy Spirit does at Christ's bidding: "He will glorify me, for he will take what is mine and declare it to you. All that the Father has is mine; therefore I said that he will take what is mine and declare it to you." (John 16:14-15)

The realization of God's presence is also the moment of deliverance from the power of evil and all its forces of darkness. When we learn to trust God, we will further appreciate the new confidence we gain from growth in faith.

This process eventually leads to a total dependence on God as the Holy Spirit "will guide you into all the truth; for he will not speak on his own authority, but whatever he hears he will speak, and he will declare to you the things that are to come." (John 16:13) This revelation by the Holy Spirit is God's special class in spiritual education.

Education is God's answer to mysticism and fear. Only when the eyes of the soul are opened can people give full praise to God. We then can indeed echo the words of Saint Paul: "O the depth of the riches and wisdom and knowledge of God! How unsearchable are his judgments and how inscrutable his ways! 'For who has known the mind of the Lord, or who has been his counselor? Or who has given a gift to him that he might be repaid?' For from him and through him and to him are all things. To him be glory forever. Amen." (Romans 11:33-36)

The confidence that we then have in our hearts is worth more than all the power on Earth. Earth is but a small part of God's creation. With the Psalmist we will then also repeat the praises of God. Thanksgiving is a daily confession: "God is our refuge and strength, a very present help in trouble. Therefore we will not fear though the Earth should change, though the mountains shake in the heart of the sea; though its waters roar and foam, though the mountains tremble with its tumult." (Psalm 46:1-3)

Through grace and faith, believers will now share divine wisdom. God's invitation to learn universal truth has been made available to all people: "Come, behold the works of the Lord, how he has wrought desolations in the Earth. He makes wars cease to the end of the Earth; he breaks the bow, and shatters the spear, he burns the chariots with fire! 'Be still, and know that I am God. I am exalted among the nations, I am exalted in the Earth!' " (Psalm 46:8-10)

We have looked at education as an obligation in our new life in the Spirit. The truth of the Word of God helps us to overcome barriers. It widens horizons for a deeper and more meaningful faith. Ignorance is a tool of Satan, but the Word of God is "the sword of the Sprit." (Ephesians 6:17)

Let us remember, therefore, "the Word of God is living and active, sharper than any two-edged sword, piercing to the division of soul and spirit, of joints and marrow, and discerning the thoughts and intentions of the heart." (Hebrews 4:12)

We have a common saying in the world that education is a life-long process. Indeed, education must never become neglected. A keen mind is a God-given talent to demonstrate God's glory on Earth.

With increased knowledge through learning we also gain in wisdom as we come to realize to how little we really know. Only a fool will display his knowledge arrogantly.

When we come to realize our obligation to gain knowledge for the good of our fellow men and us by making the world a better place to live, we then can truly say that our process of education has begun. Our education then is like a part of David's song of praise: "I delight to do thy will, O my God; thy law is within my heart." (Psalm 40:8)

The human response to God's contributions

God says: "Know that I am God!"

The Word of God is the source for truth. Truth alone can help us to put things in proper perspective. The person who understands truth also knows how to navigate the murky waters of a troubled world—a hopeless world that seems always ready to kill people and cause trouble among nations. Truth is a must for spiritual survival in these modern times. Truth is essential for quality of life.

God applies the principles of truth in securing education for all his children.

God says: "I have given you a sound mind to learn, think, and reason."

God wants our undivided attention in learning truth. He wants us to advance in the skills of knowledge. God says: "I have given you a sound mind to learn, think, and reason. Education is nourishment for the mind. Your mind needs education in the same way as your body needs food. If you starve the mind, you incapacitate both mind and body. Ultimately you will end up as a hopeless nomad in a desert of despair."

Christ says: "Learn! Learn to correct your attitudes. Learn to change your behavior toward God and people near you. Learn to align your objectives with the needs of God's Kingdom on Earth."

In a secular sense, education is the transmission of skills from previous generations to help us cope with man-made situations in modern times.

God's truth is a decisive element in this transmission of knowledge. Jesus Christ stressed truth in his teachings. "I am telling you the truth…" Other versions in biblical literature state it as "truly" or in the more emphatic form of "truly, truly."

Truth is important to God. Truth is the foundation of reality in the Era of Faith. The focus is now on America.

God is very disappointed with the education of American children. Children continue to struggle with the fundamentals of knowledge. Many American children lack the basic skills in reading, writing, and arithmetic. Also a great number of college educated adults lack the basic skills of intelligent communication. These basic skills are but stepping-stones for young people to become successful adults. Appreciation of truth, values, and creativity begins after the fundamentals are mastered.

God's universal axioms on education

Education is the backbone of civilizations. Civilizations survive when education is a continuous process of learning. Knowledge dispels fears. Education is the means to help nations prosper, grow, and secure the future.

Societies, communities, and families thrive when eagerness to learn is the foundation of education.

Education is crucial in God's plan for children. Children are the future. God wants children to become productive adults for doing his work in the world. Parents have a significant role in the growth process of children. God is the ultimate judge of parental performance in education.

The role of education. Education fosters the growth process in young people. We teach our children cultural values, skills, and religious beliefs. In classroom instructions, children learn about the humanities, the arts, sciences, applied technology, and sports. The proper blending of these disciplines helps children grow into productive human beings.

Religious education. Religion, i.e., education in matters of faith, is a gift from God, presided over by the Holy Spirit. Religion must be free of government interference.

Secular education. Society is responsible for providing the proper environment for education. This includes facilities, tools, and books. The principles in secular textbooks are just an extension of the Book in religion. Yet, in our eagerness to educate, we must separate the Book of the church from the textbooks of the state.

Discipline. Discipline in education—religious and secular—is a prerequisite for success. Discipline and respect for teachers and students is the core ingredient in education. It is the duty of society to enforce discipline in schools.

Drug abuse. All the above are wasted efforts when the delicate human mind—especially in the formative stages of children—is adulterated by drug abuse. The purity of the human mind is crucially important to the future of God's people. God speaks out against the disaster of drug abuse that has flourished for decades in the modern world. God says: "I have formed the human mind as my creative agent in the world. Do not destroy what is important to my children and me. Control the use of illegal drugs through education—don't waste money and time on stopping the supply. If there is no demand for drugs, the supply will automatically dry up!"

Diversity of talents. Education requires respect for the diversity of talents. Not every child in the world is an Einstein in physics. God says: "Be practical. Teach vocations when children want to learn a trade. Help them to apply the powerful human mind when children want to create with their hands. Remember, the trades and the arts have been honest professions since days of old. Tradespeople and artists are among my faithful people in the modern world."

Homework assignments. Homework assignments are an extension of classroom instructions. Parents are responsible to enforce time for homework assignments. Parents are responsible for a productive learning environment at home. Completing homework assignments is a definite part of the learning process. Proper supervision of children learning at home is the responsibility of parents.

Relationships

The Era of Faith proclaims the powerful Word of God on faith, hope, love, trust, and relationships. The Word of God on relationships applies to all members of the three major religions: Christians, Jews, and Muslims.

God's contributions to relationships are trust and respect
(Selection from *I.D. Crisis*)

> *God wants you! Not your things.*
> *Not your good works and accomplishments.*
> *God says: "I want you as a person."*

We have achieved our mission in life when we know, believe, act, and live according to whose we truly are.

When we realize that we are children of God and, as disciples of Christ, God's chosen people, then we know that we have a relationship of value.

Jesus said: "Not every one who says to me, 'Lord, Lord,' shall enter the kingdom of Heaven, but he who does the will of my Father who is in Heaven. On that day many will say to me, 'Lord, Lord, did we not prophesy in your name, and cast out demons in your name, and do many mighty works in your name?' And then will I declare to them, 'I never knew you; depart from me, you evildoers.' "

The phrase "true value" in the modern world is a contradictory expression.

"True" implies authenticity. It is something that is conforming to an established standard. Its nature depends on an authoritative standard. "Value," on the other hand, is relative. Value can be many things to different people. When something is of value, it then has some worth to the beholder, but not necessarily to all. Value is relative to time, place, and one's outlook on life.

The true value of the earthly life is our relationship with God.

Let us recall that the story of mankind is a drama of many tragedies. Its authenticity is attested by many saved or wrecked lives.

We are not the authors of life, but we are the authors of all our shortcomings. Through the frailty of human nature, people continually fail to measure up to the expectation of God. When we study the Scriptures, we can see all the gruesome results of sin and rebellion.

"Stop right there!" you may shout. "What gives you the right to call me a sinner? I am an upright citizen. I am a leader in the community. I do always what is right. I work hard earning a living for my family. I struggle not to rub anyone the wrong way. I try to make friends and keep peace. Even once in a while my family drags me to church, although I must admit that somehow I feel very uneasy when I am there! What more do you want? What else must I give?"

But God wants you! Not your things. Not your good works and accomplishments. God says: "I want you as a person." That is why God came down to Earth in the person of Jesus Christ to take you back to himself!

Jesus came for the benefit of people. Christ taught the truth of the Word of God so that everyone who believes in him can be freed from all the hang-ups of the world.

Therefore, Christ says, "If you continue in my word, you are truly my disciples, and you will know the truth, and the truth will make you free." (John 8:31-32)

Jesus did not leave us alone in the world. He asked God to give us a helper and guide. We have God's Holy Spirit among us and in each of us: "And I will pray the Father, and he will give you another Counselor, to be with you forever, even the Spirit of truth, whom the world cannot receive, because it neither sees him nor knows him; you know him, for he dwells with you, and will be in you." (John 14:16-17)

Only in this relationship has our earthly life true value!

The human response to God's contributions

Knowing God as Father is all that counts in the spiritual connection. All other relationships are secondary. As we focus on relationships and spiritual values, we share our faith with all of God's people.

Key word: RELATIONSHIPS. (1) Relationships are real-life dramas. (1a) Each relationship is a personal statement of belief and trust. (1b) Relationships are spiritual engagements and personal encounters in three dimensions: the believer's relation to God, the believer's relation to one another, and the believer's relation to the world. (2) In our spiritual relationship with God, we know God as Father, and God meets us face-to-face in our daily needs. In our relationship with nature, we are protective of God's creation, and nature makes our environment a mighty fortress. (3) In our relationships with family, friends, and neighbors our happiness is the happiness of the other person. (4) In our relationships with the community and the world, our helping hand satisfies the other person's needs. (5) Relationships are dynamic, creative, and subject to evolution and change. Wholesome attitudes and discerning behavior are fertile soil for growth in relationships. (6) Servants of God experience relationships as the stewardship of time, talents, and money. In every encounter, faithful stewards are responsible partners of the love of God.

Key word: FAITH. Faith is a timeless relationship of trust with the living God. The duly inspired confession of faith is the Lord's Prayer.

Key word: TRUST. Trust is the essence of relationships. Trust in God is the nucleus of faith. Trust builds bridges of friendships. Trust is the glue that connects people and God for a lasting and fruitful spiritual life in the world. Plain communication and clear understanding are paramount in maintaining trust. The time-honored adage "Mean what you say, and say what you mean" is key to trust and relationships. Mutual trust makes relationships a blessing.

God's priority in spiritual relationships is
submission to the Holy Spirit.

Relationships are the bonds that all creatures of God enjoy in their social lives. They are common in the human family.

In a gratifying spiritual life, we are filled with enthusiasm to tell others about our vibrant relationships with God.

In a satisfying social environment, we boast about rewarding family relationships. And our friends patiently listen to our long stories about children, brothers, sisters, parents, and pets.

Philosophers dating back to Socrates, Plato, and Aristotle have debated ethics and written volumes of books about justice. Jesus Christ taught ethics and justice in the Sermon on the Mount. In all this teaching, God is telling us over and over again to make ethics and justice the principle of good human conduct in daily life.

ACT III
AMERICA IS GOD'S COUNTRY

America and Americans
A modern phenomenon
Spiritual vs. secular conflicts
The ever-present God
God's faithful remnant
Unity through diversity II

Chapter 7

America And Americans

America is more than just a nation with defined boundaries. America is a diversity of people. America is the land of pilgrims. Americans make America God's fortress of faith, hope, and love in the modern world to demonstrate unity through diversity.

A modern phenomenon

Every time we say, "America is God's country," we acknowledge a free people spiritually connected with God. Americans are Christians, Jews, Muslims, and other people from the many different belief systems in the world. "America is God's country" is a faith statement of diverse people united for the common good to serve God and neighbor as brothers and sisters.

God has singled out America as the cultural and religious melting pot of the modern world. America is his contemporary model for faith. America is his country of choice to show the world the successful integration of diversities of faiths and cultures.

Immigrant pilgrims to America, like Abraham in ancient times, have heeded God's call and become spiritual pioneers in a land of unknowns. They have abandoned known comforts in the Old World, but they are never alone in the New World. God is always one step ahead of faithful immigrant-pilgrims. And by the examples of their lives, God is securing the future for every citizen of America. God says: "America is God's country."

"America is God's country" is God living with his people.

The Era of Faith is God's manifestation of the new world order in which he assures every faithful believer of his presence. We live in America by the power of the Holy Spirit to set the example for making the world a better place in the Era of Faith by improving the lives of all people.

Spiritual versus secular conflicts

In no other time in history has the demand been greater on Americans to declare what we believe and stand up for our beliefs.

In no other time in history has the demand been greater on faithful believers to practice the faith we confess.

Every American—Christian, Jew, Muslim, and members of diverse religions—must learn and understand the virtues of faith, hope, and love in the context of each faith.

Faith, hope, and love are universal spiritual values. They are instrumental in winning the conflict over ignorance, intolerance, indifference, injustice, and inequality. Faith, hope, and love are forces for advancing the Kingdom of God on Earth.

We must free ourselves from the insanity of man's inhumanity to man. We must stop religious intolerance. We must end killing in the name of God. We must stop religious fanaticism. God calls us to have respect for the Word of God as it applies to Christians, Jews, and Muslims!

The ever-present God

The ever-present God blesses us when we are his blessing to others. All too often, however, we feel helpless when helping others. And many times the recipients of God's blessings through us feel as inadequate as we are.

Often, for example, our senior citizens feel embarrassed to accept our help because they cannot reciprocate. We hear it said over and over again: "Thanks so much for helping. I am such a nuisance. I am such a bother. You are always here for me, and I cannot do anything for you."

These are the feelings all of us have when we experience the grace of God in our lives. God is there for us in big ways, but we are so helpless to accept his generosity. God listens to our prayers. He sees our needs. He answers our cries for help. God searches our souls to match his blessings with our needs. When he finds us wanting, he provides the right solution at the right time. In great compassion, then, he does for us what we never would be able to do ourselves: God makes sure that we are secure in his care! God's only expectation of us is a sincere "Thank you, Lord." God never embarrasses us with his blessings.

In all these experiences of blessings, God never takes us out of the world. We experience his loving presence as citizens of the secular world. In visions and dreams Christ leads us spiritually to mountaintop experiences. In the serenity of his abode high above the tops of mountains, God invites us to look down at the turbulent world we leave behind. His presence instills confidence. His smile is the smile of a loving father. Silently God is whispering: "You are my child. I love you!" God softly melts all our human desires into his Will. God loves to encourage the children he loves. The ever-present God is in the world of harsh realities to make us comfortable and spiritually whole.

God's faithful remnant

A majority of Americans makes up the faithful remnant that continues trusting God. God will bless America to honor and glorify this remnant of believers, even if the remnant is just 10 Americans or fewer who are faithful to God. God is using American saints to demonstrate to the world his rule on Earth.

Saints of God are experts in restoration. We restore broken lives and damaged relationships. By the power of the Holy Spirit we heal body, mind, and spirit. We heal what has been torn apart by an arrogant and brutal world. We are the remnant of faithful believers whom God considers worthy of saving the entire obstinate world. Our mission in life is to bring glory to God! We work toward this end by filling the spiritual needs of people.

What do we do as the faithful remnant of God in America?

We teach the Word of God. We demonstrate the Word of God by the example of our lives. Thus says the Lord: "America is God's country. Her pilgrims are children of God. But many of my people have rebelled against me. To these I say: Repent. Your claims of greatness are meaningless in my sight. Your boasts are empty. Correct your attitudes, and change your behavior out of respect for me. Come, let us reason together, and I will reveal your salvation. I desire justice and righteousness. Hear the Word of God, America, for the LORD has spoken."

What does God require of every American?

God requires a contrite heart, a receptive mind for learning to be just and kind, and faith to walk humbly with God and accept his Word in trust and hope. Everything else is in God's hands.

Unity Through Diversity Part II

The unity of God and people in the Era of Faith ensures a quality of life previously unknown in the history of mankind. Unfortunately America—and the rest of the world—has not yet reached this goal.

The Holy Spirit strengthens each of us to make sure that unity through diversity in America is the shining light for the rest of the world. The unity through diversity in the melting pot of diverse cultures in America is but one of many manifestations of God in the modern world.

How successful is unity through diversity in contemporary America?

Major adjustments in attitudes are needed to help people of the world become self-sufficient. We must deal with them justly and fairly as equal partners in trade. This is the foundation for unity through diversity.

God wants actions that align our performance with his objectives for harmony, economic justice, political savvy, and peace throughout the world. To be sure, God favors diversities of culture, and diversity of cultural values. But God is also looking for unity in the Spirit of God so that diversity can bear the fruit that God's righteousness alone affords.

All too often American ideals, opinions, and solutions to world problems prevent this from happening. All too often we do not meet the social needs of people with different outlooks on life from ours and whose cultural ideals do not match with our specific backgrounds. To be sure, unity through diversity is the American way of life. But what is good and practical for America may not always be applicable to the rest of the world.

ACT III
ILLUSTRATIONS OF SPIRITUAL REALITIES

God is out in the world
Pilgrim T. Homosapien
Trust
Inspiration
Chief doctrine of Christianity
Christian covenant of love
Fear and stress
Drug abuse
I.D. Crisis
Do we exist in an identity crisis?
War and peace

Chapter 8

God is out in the world

God is out in the world. By the power of
the Holy Spirit, we are his hands in the community
to strengthen troubled souls.

The Era of Faith is God's most recent creation and the second most important spiritual event in human history. Primary, of course, is God's self- revelation in Jesus Christ some 2,000 years ago.

God is out in the world to redeem even the worst among sinners. God uses his faithful people to help him in this immense undertaking of saving people in the Era of Faith.

Pilgrim T. Homosapien.

*God called Pilgrim T. Homosapien to be
his servant in America.*

Pilgrim Thanksgiving Homosapien has dedicated his life to serving God and people. God calls Pilgrim his friend.

Pilgrim salutes America.

THE AMERICAN PILGRIM SONG

I am a pilgrim.
I celebrate the years I have lived among you.
You accepted me from a distant land.

I adopted your ways to find golden opportunities.
Like you, I searched and searched.
This I found: America is full of pilgrims.

In our life of pilgrimage on Earth together therefore,
I share my faith, my hope, and my trust.
These are sources for life in God's plan of salvation.

I lift up my hands in praise and thanksgiving,
And greet you, Pilgrims of America,
My sisters and brothers,
In the name of God our Father:
Peace!
The LORD be with you.

In service to God and people

My name is Pilgrim T. Homosapien. My middle name is Thanksgiving. My Heavenly Father made my middle name special to keep me humble in speech and manner. I represent modern man.

My friends call me by my first name, Pilgrim. I share my Christian name Pilgrim with all of God's friends. My family is God, humanity, nature, and every living being on Earth. We are all sojourners on Earth. Therefore, relationships are vital to my health and happiness.

Pilgrim's mission to America

Our primary goal in the secular world is spiritual freedom.

Pilgrim's mission to America started as a vision at a very young age.

Pilgrim soon learned that visions—the highest order of dreams—succumb to the harshness of life in the physical world, unless we persevere in faith and follow through with our inspirations.

In our unity with God we are blessed with the joy of freedom. Christ continues to pray for us: "But now I am coming to thee; and these things I speak in the world, that they may have my joy fulfilled in themselves." (John 17:13) Christ summarizes God's support as our victory over evil: "I do not pray that thou shouldst take them out of the world, but that thou shouldst keep them from evil." (John 17:15)

Evil is the archenemy of God. In his prayer for the safekeeping of believers, Christ is assuring every disciple of deliverance from all conditions of evil in the world. Christ tells us that his victory over evil is also our victory!

Pilgrim says: "I experienced tragedy, pain, and suffering since my fourth birthday when the Second World War started. The burning wounds inflicted by seemingly good people during all my experiences were smothered by the love of God. The love of God was all that I ever wanted and needed. God was at my side. God embraced me. I felt at ease. Christ always whispered at the height of each stormy conflict: 'I am your friend.' My trials are now over. My spiritual fulfillment is now complete. The Holy Spirit continuously assures me that I am truly a friend of God.

"Nonetheless, I am troubled. I relentlessly search for answers to life's drama in America. My search gives me a clearer understanding about the nature of suffering. Why do Americans suffer? What went wrong with the model of my childhood dreams about America being God's country in war-torn Germany in 1945? I want answers to satisfy my personal agenda. I want to know so that I can better serve America and her people.

"To be sure, God has tempered my life well for this service. God was right with me in the horrors of war when death was all around me. God supported me in my homelessness. God went hungry to bed with me when there was not enough food to eat. By pain and suffering I am, indeed, a true suffering servant of God. The Holy Spirit works through me to bring relief to suffering Americans. I suffered. And now I can give the suffering people in the world the right kind of support. I understand God's agony and pain for his people. My mission in America is helping people find themselves in the presence of God. I want Americans to live by the Word of God in order to overcome suffering. I want to help Americans remove the self-imposed barriers of class division of race, gender, and economic injustice. I want every American to succeed in his or her relationship with God as well as their relationships with other people. I condemn adverse conditions in America that disrupt relationships. I saw

God cry over America in the terrible 1960s."

God declares: "All human plans that rebel against me will fail. The rejection of God is the most grievous sin. Sin against the Holy Spirit is unforgivable."

The Word of God in action

God expects us to excel in the wisdom and knowledge of him.

We know very little about creation and the universe. God asks us pointedly: "Where were you when I laid the foundation of the Earth? Tell me, if you have understanding. Who determined its measurements—surely you know! Or who stretched the line upon it? On what were its bases sunk, or who laid its cornerstone, when the morning stars sang together, and all the sons of God shouted for joy?" (Job 38:4-7) God expects us to excel in the wisdom and knowledge of him.

God told his servant Job about the falsehood of human wisdom some 3,500 years ago. In light of God's question-and-answer session with Job about the creation of the universe, Job subsequently used the same process on his contemporaries. Job was more aggressive with his friends than God was with Job. Job accused them as ruthless liars when it comes to their objection to the truth about God. God stood beside his servant Job in this confrontation.

Pilgrim now applies the Word of God as spoken by God's servant Job to the contemporary world. The Word of God today carries the same content of truth as it did over 3,500 years ago. The effect is the same: Human wisdom does not measure up to the wisdom of God. Job says: "You whitewash with lies; worthless physicians are you all. Oh, that you would keep silent, and it would be your wisdom! Hear now my reasoning, and listen to the pleading of my lips. Will you speak falsely for God, and speak deceitfully for him? Will you show partiality toward him, will you plead the case for God? Will it be well with you when he searches you out? Or can you deceive him, as one deceives a man? He will surely rebuke you if in secret you show partiality. Will not his majesty terrify you, and the dread of him fall upon you? Your maxims are proverbs of ashes, your defenses are defenses of clay." (Job 13:4-12)

The prophet Micah issued the divine reply to the age-old question as to what God requires of people. God's directive distinctively calls for holiness and justice: "He has showed you, O man, what is good; and what does the Lord require of you but to do justice, and to love kindness, and to walk humbly with your God?" (Micah 6:8) The direction is straightforward. There are no hidden meanings.

God inspires us to practice justice.

In the 47th year of his mission to America as Servant of God Pilgrim T. Homosapien now declares the Word of God concerning changes in America: "He who is greatest among you shall be your servant; whoever exalts himself will be humbled, and whoever humbles himself will be exalted." (Matthew 23:11-12) God expects us to serve him by the example of our lives. Our task is to prepare the Way of God in America and the world.

Some 2,700 years ago, the prophet Isaiah explained that our God is far away in the heavens, yet always nearby to support us. God is distant, but always near: "Build up, build up, prepare the way, remove every obstruction from my people's way. For thus says the high and lofty One who inhabits eternity, whose name is Holy: I dwell in the high and holy place, and also with him who is of a contrite and humble spirit, to revive the spirit of the humble, and to revive the heart of the contrite." (Isaiah 57:14-15)

God speaks in a commanding voice: "Let justice roll down like waters, and righteousness like an ever-flowing stream." (Amos 5:24) His voice emphatically thunders once more: "I, the Lord, love justice." (Isaiah 61:8)

Pilgrim consequently admonishes Americans in these modern times to change and correct their behavior: "Social and economic injustices in contemporary America strain relationships and threaten peace. Henceforth, work the principles of love and strive for justice and peace in America to show the world God's glory."

Man proposes—God disposes

The wisdom literature in Proverbs elaborated thousands of years ago eternal truth about proposing and disposing things in the world. It is written: "A man's mind plans his way, but the Lord directs his steps." (Proverbs 16:9)

Unknown authors have abridged the eternal truth recorded in Proverbs for easy human consumption as a very simple truism: "Man proposes—God disposes." Every language has its own version. In German, for example, the common dictum is "Mensch denkt—aber Gott lenkt."

This important truth requires total submission to the will and power of God to make it real in daily life. We must submerge all human desires in the purpose of God.

Publisher's tribute to Pilgrim T. Homosapien

I have known Pilgrim T. Homosapien all my life. Pilgrim is a reliable servant of God, and also his friend. He lives the Word of God. He teaches it by the authority of the Holy Spirit. Pilgrim knows God as One God: Father, Son, and Holy Spirit. His mission in life is to fill spiritual needs.

Pilgrim is an expert on the spiritual relationship of people and God. Pilgrim says: "The essence of quality of life on Earth is the spiritual connection. Knowing God as father is all that counts. All other relationships are secondary."

I watched Pilgrim moving around in my neighborhood. I have seen the effectiveness of his work in the community. He radiates confidence in the workplace. His positive outlook on life is contagious. His optimism is supportive. I have been infected by it.

I followed Pilgrim in one of his frequent trips to the mountain-top. It was a great experience. The wide-open sky was beckoning us to enter Heaven. Heaven was saying: "Enter! Widen your spiritual horizons!"

Pilgrim said: "Now close your eyes. Live the moment of vision. Picture yourself in Heaven." In the Kingdom of God, I saw harmony. I experienced peace. The Peace of God enveloped me. There was God. "Father, my Father," I said. My heart was weeping with joy.

Below us was the city. The streets were dirty with the grease and grime of selfishness and hatred. People were muddling around, each person doing his or her own thing. In my vision, I saw friend taking advantage of friend. People were fighting. It was a jungle. "Bricks and mortar do not a city make" is indeed truth. But the people in it do.

The world may never change, but I have changed. This writing is testimony to my change in attitudes and behavior toward God and people. I have always believed in the importance of relationships.

Relationships are the essence for the spiritual journey. Relationships provide limitless horizons. Relationships are roadmaps to harmonious living.

The Publisher

Trust

Trust in God is the nucleus of faith.

Trust is the essence of relationships. Trust in God is the nucleus of faith. Trust builds bridges of friendships. Trust is the bond that connects people and God for a lasting and fruitful spiritual life in the world. Plain communication and a clear understanding of each other's needs are paramount in maintaining trust. The time-honored adage "Mean what you say, and say what you mean" is key to trust and relationships.

We also experience trust in our relationships with our pets. Our animal friends are totally uninhibited in showing us how important trust is. They trust us for their care. In return they reward us with loyalty and love even beyond the most complex definition of trust.

Inspiration

Background

Key word INSPIRATIONS: Inspirations apply to life in the presence of God. Inspirations are means of Grace. The goal in inspirations is to advance the common good in the world.

Inspiration and quality of life

Inspirations are the working elements in the divine gift of grace. The worldly complement to inspirations is aspirations. Inspirations emanate from the wisdom of God. Christ says, "Wisdom is justified by her deeds." (Matthew 11:19) Inspirations work by the power of the Holy Spirit. Inspirations, like all other spiritual achievements, prove everlasting.

There are no models in the world for inspirations. God is the authority and sole source of inspirations and subsequent visions. The Holy Spirit helps us to understand all that is important in spiritual life. God speaks to each person by means of inspirations and, because of this, things truly happen in the world.

Inspired for service

The Holy Spirit inspires us to follow the model of the godly life as demonstrated by the life and teaching of Jesus Christ. Like Christ in his time, we are the teachers of the Word of God by the examples of our lives in our time. The Holy Spirit is our inspiring influence and guides us in the Way of God. He prompts us to do what is right and proper in accordance with God's plan for creation. Toward this end, God empowers us by means of inspirations.

The faith-trust cycle is a never-ending inspiration cycle. Trust is the human contribution that makes the inspiration cycle robust. Inspirations strengthen us to serve God, people, and nature. Our service is in the name of God. We do not act in our own name. As we live and work to bring glory to God through inspiration by the Holy Spirit, the universe sings praises to God for all that is being done by us in the name of God.

Food for thought

The human mind is the world's biggest reservoir of inspirational truth. The French philosopher Descartes once said, "Cogito, ergo sum," (I think, therefore I am), singling out the mind as a powerful resource for doing things in the world. God encourages us to use the human mind as his wellspring of power for the good of family, neighbor, nation, and the Kingdom of God on Earth.

If faith as small as a mustard seed can move mountains, let us envision for a brief moment all the good we can create from the combined divine and human energies stored in the minds of people as inspirations and aspirations.

Truly, every human being is a powerhouse of inspiration in the world. When all this potential energy is submerged in the will and purpose of God, then we are, indeed, the salt of the Earth, and the light of the world. Christ says, "Let your light so shine before men, that they may see your good works and give glory to your Father who is in Heaven." (Matthew 5:16) Christ tells us to put our minds to work for the common good of all; but most of all to advance God's Kingdom on Earth.

Chief doctrine of Christianity

The chief doctrine of Christianity is the divine declaration as recorded in Holy Writ: "He who has my commandments and keeps them, he it is who loves me; and he who loves me will be loved by my Father, and I will love him and manifest myself to him." (John 14:21) A successful relationship with the resurrected Christ is contingent on love. Divine love is Jesus Christ alive in believers: Love unites believers with God. Love keeps believers faithful; love has more power than any decree of law. Commitments based on love draw believers together in a permanent bond of unity. Love embraces; love forgives; love never threatens, denies, or rejects. The love of God for people is Christianity's chief doctrine.

Christian covenant of love

God made the Christian covenant of love supreme reality for modern man. God is the creating authority and the Word of God is sole source of power for maintaining it. The Christian covenant of love bonds God and people for eternity.

The Christian covenant of love governs the Era of Faith. The essence of the Christian covenant of love is total dependence on God. Child-like trust makes it work.

Fear and stress

Background

Human stress is an acute spiritual problem.

In the worldly domain, the force behind stress is Satan as the ancient enemy of God and the lord of evil. Human stress, therefore, is an acute spiritual problem.

God looks at modern America, and he sees a lot of people stressed out. The American family suffers, and some families suffer more than others.

Searching for answers

Knowledge dispels fear. Knowing our enemy is the first step toward victory in any battle. Knowledge is power. But knowledge requires details. Generalities will not do. Knowing the specifics about the adversary—identity, intent, and *modus operandi*—empowers us to expose fear and stress. But fighting fear and stress are more than fighting ordinary enemies. Our opponents are satanic principalities. And the battle against fear and stress is a cosmic war—at stake is the human soul. Therefore, we rely on God to help us fight fear and stress, as Christ already has won the victory over death for us. To overcome stress is applying his victory to individual life.

We must identify the following:

– Who are the forces of fear and stress?
– Why do these external forces go after believers in God?
– What are the methods evil forces use to seek victory over God?
– When will they strike?

Let us watch and see how the answers unfold.

Who are the forces of fear and stress?

A quick inspection will show that the modern world is like a giant reservoir of imperfection and discord. Humanly imposed limitations create fear and stress of the worst kind. Manipulative individuals work fear to keep people ignorant of truth. They purposely place barriers on other people; the foundations of these wicked barriers are envy and greed. Humanly induced stress to control the lives of people is killer stress. The modern world is full of horror stories about vicious people capturing and manipulating their weak and confused victims.

God says: "Fear and stress-inducing agents wielding control over my children are a variety of secular forces. Among them are sensations driven by the news media, business barons who worship the bottom line without regard for the wellbeing of workers or the community, political manipulators who want to be elected to office at any cost, and a huge entourage of smooth-talking opportunists. By the world's own standards, the common denominator of evil opponents to the way of God is lack of ethics and a lack of respect for God, and total disregard for my believers."

Why do these external forces go after believers in God?

Faithful believers in God are targeted because Satan hopes to win cosmic victory over God through his remnant of faithful people by severing the spiritual connection of people and God.

What are the methods evil forces use to win cosmic victory over God?

The "benefactors of society" come disguised as patron saints looking for people in despair. Once they have gained the confidence of less fortunate people, they put down, disgrace, ridicule, and then abuse their victims. Fear paralyzes the mind, and stress then comes in for the kill—be it people or relationships. Stress does not respect status or age, riches or poverty. The most common weapons of fear and stress are economic hardships. Satan's objective is to extinguish a flickering flame of hope and scare people into submission through fear. This type of fear is an acute spiritual problem, for it attacks human dignity. Stress then attacks faith, hope, and love to finish the kill. It follows up what fear has started and rips wide open the wounds of despair. Fear and stress are awful weapons. Stress is the most inhumane killer of people. It mercilessly attacks workers and their families.

When will the forces of evil strike?

Satan always works overtime to strike down the children of God. Satan will defeat people who stand by themselves, but he can never overpower the faithful who are united with God. The Holy Spirit defends with the Sword of the Spirit that is the living Word of God. Satan flees when we call on the Word of God in our defense.

Freedom from fear and stress

God empowers the faithful to overcome
fear, stress, and deceit.

The solutions for overcoming the great evils of fear and stress in modern America are changes in attitudes and behavior, and getting rid of unrealistic goals. Faith and trust in God are the only reliable weapons to fight this evil. Hope is God's shield of choice to keep his faithful children from harm in the battle against the forces of evil that aim to destroy us. We can change our behavior and make spiritual fulfillment the new goal in life by following Christ as the model of the godly life.

God's victory over fear and stress is our freedom in Christ

We join Saint Paul in prophetically proclaiming to the world the Gospel truth: "If God is with us, who is against us?" (Romans 8:31) Among the great acts of Christians in the modern world, then, is helping our neighbor become free from fear and killer stress.

Progress may be slow. We must patiently wait for God to complete his work in us. God works with us according to his plan, and the timetable for the world's restoration is his.

Spiritual freedom in the modern world may always appear to be a short distance away. For some people, spiritual fulfillment may be a breath away. Many unfortunate souls have given up hope for a better future and died. Others insist on their independence and continue to live in misery, and then they die.

Progress in spiritual wellbeing will always be too slow for the "sophisticated" achievers of the secular world. People living in the secular world demand of God to be a speed demon in blessing them with wine and roses on gold-paved streets, and then demand that God get out of their lives quickly so that they can carry on as they please, at a much faster speed.

But God says: "My grace is sufficient for you. I will act in due time and in due season. In the meantime, practice your faith. Do not question my love for you; all I am expecting of you is to practice your faith. Put all your trust in me, and believe!" And the resurrected Christ affirms eternal truth in the workings of grace, faith, and trust: "I am with you always, to the close of the age." (Matthew 28:20)

The Era of Faith provides the Way for faith, trust, and relationships. And where love prevails, stress is no more.

Drug abuse

Drug abuse in these modern times is rampant. Satan as the ancient enemy of God could not accomplish the permanent separation of God and people; he now has God's people doing his work with drug abuse. Illicit drugs kill. Illicit drugs tear families apart. Illicit drugs raise havoc with the economy. Ultimately, drug abuse will alter civilization beyond recognition.

For many young people, drug abuse appears like an appealing relief from the doldrums of a future without hope. Only when it is too late do young people and parents realize that drug abuse is a deadly journey.

Drug abuse is denial of the sacred in humans. At the end of each drug journey waits the bottomless pit.

I.D. Crisis.

(Excerpt from *Introduction to I.D. Crisis*)

> *People must learn to appreciate for themselves*
> *the way of truth.*

I.D. Crisis was written to alert all people everywhere about a better way of life, God's way. The purpose of the text is to help diligent readers get started on the road of discovery to eternal truth and universal salvation.

No writing, however eloquent, can prescribe a step-by-step procedure for this search. People must learn to appreciate for themselves the way of truth. Such is the beginning of an ever-lasting relationship.

And the authority for guidance belongs to God. In human ideas, what may be totally acceptable to some is highly objectionable to others.

Even though attitudes and behavior may vary from culture to culture, the essence of life, nonetheless, is changeless. The model of the godly life has been given to the world. The message about the Kingdom of God and the will of God is clear in Christ's teaching.

Much confusion is nourished by ignorance. And evil enters in when theories are declared as facts and dogmatic pronouncements attempt to protect doctrines and traditions. This is typical when ecclesiastical organizations feel threatened and try to perpetuate themselves. But such defensive moves are not always necessarily in the interest of truth.

There is no need to speculate concerning the truth about God. The teaching of Christ is God's summary. The message given explains the Kingdom of God and the Will of God. Nothing more is required for the short human pilgrimage on Earth of 70 years more or less.

> *"You shall love the Lord your God with all your heart,*
> *and with all your soul, and with all your mind."*

Christ affirmed God's expectations of faithfulness and obedience. The call to worship and service—the ancient Shema Yisrael—is confirmed for all people everywhere as a primary event in everyday life: "You shall love the Lord your God with all your heart, and with all your soul, and with all your mind." (Matthew 22:37)

No additional explanation is needed. The human race is the height of God's creation. And God has definite expectations of people.

Christ summarizing the historic Law of Holiness and Justice further enhances eternal truth. This divine command stands as the foundation of all human relationships: "You shall love your neighbor as yourself." (Matthew 22:39)

Prior to Christ's confirmation of these standards for human behavior, God's prophet Micah provided the divine reply to the age-old question as to what God requires of people. The subject again concerns holiness and justice: "He has showed you, O man, what is good; and what does the LORD require of you but to do justice, and to love kindness, and to walk humbly with your God?" (Micah 6:8)

The direction is straightforward. There are no hidden meanings.

Yet Abraham Lincoln, one of the greatest Americans, lamented about the sad condition of ecclesiastical religion. The prophet Micah's detailed summary to "walk humbly with your God" was compared by Lincoln to the workings of the institutional church.

This is how Lincoln saw the problem: "When any church will inscribe over its altar, as its sole qualification for membership, the Saviour's condensed statement of the substance of both Law and Gospel, 'Thou shalt love the Lord thy God with all thy heart, and with all thy soul, and with all thy mind, and thy neighbor, as thyself' that church will I join with all my heart and all my soul."

Faithful believers live in the world according to divine promise.

What otherwise may appear as sarcasm on the part of non-committed people are actually cries of desperation—sometimes even calls for reform. The vacuum within an empty soul is the greatest imaginable abyss. It is as consuming as the bottomless pit.

– Where is God in times of war?
– Why all the starvation in the world?
– Why do people suffer?

These outcries are real. Death and suffering are in the world. Where is God in all this trouble? Assuredly, with the faithful believer! God is right in the center of war, starvation, and suffering to support and uphold the faithful.

Faithful believers live in the world according to divine promise. What God ordains, God also sustains. This message of hope has been given many times. But it must be repeated again and again.

God has already demonstrated his perfect record of performance. He has proven to be faithful and steadfast. Therefore, any demands for new themes in the teaching of eternal truth are mere tactics of arrogant people. With their demands they wish God's creation to march to their tune. Anyone more concerned about the ways of the world than the Kingdom of God does not have a working relationship with the Living God at heart.

Biblical writings are sufficient evidence about the concerns of a righteous God for sinful people. The Bible, indeed, is a text on relationships. It is a true God-and-people book.

However, eternal truth is a matter of revelation by the Holy Spirit. The written word, indeed, is human, but its inspirational message is divine.

God inspires believers by means of divinely ordained channels. The Bible is the means by which the Holy Spirit makes known the truth about God.

Education is a continuous process of learning. But somehow people have conceived the unfortunate notion that formal education ends the learning process. Nothing is further from the truth.

A worse situation exists in religious education. It is truly sad to see children elated at having been freed from the burden of learning about God at the day of their confirmation. They have learned fast to follow the example of elders.

With the exception of some sporadic programs, teachers in religion have done little to advance learning the truth about God.

Good behavior is a matter of faithfulness and obedience to God. The quality of our response to God is not subject to human consideration, for the will of God is the purpose of our being. Christ taught and demonstrated God's intent for people. When people live and act accordingly, they have achieved true greatness. Then they also have something to boast about—because of what God through Christ has done—and not brag about worldly achievements.

The Word of God in Jeremiah encourages our concern for

the Kingdom of God. "Thus says the Lord: 'Let not the wise man glory in his wisdom, let not the mighty man glory in his might, let not the rich man glory in his riches; but let him who glories glory in this, that he understands and knows me, that I am the Lord who practice steadfast love, justice, and righteousness in the Earth; for in these things I delight, says the Lord.' " (Jeremiah 9:23-24)

Do we exist in an identity crisis?
(Excerpt from *I.D. Crisis*)

We are God's people!

We live by priorities.

The routine of daily life is subject to value judgments. Our decisions have far-reaching consequences on personal behavior and relationships. The quality of life on Earth depends upon a successful balancing of priorities—with God and with one another.

Choosing priorities requires people to exercise their God-given freedom. Any outcome will necessarily be influenced by personal convictions and views about life. People decide to make materialistic greed or spiritual hunger their priority. Blessing or curse of life on Earth depends upon a thorough appreciation of the purpose of our creation.

To help us live by the right decision requires that we become fully aware as to whose we truly are.

Therefore, in light of God's purpose for human creation, let us ask: "Do we have an identity problem?"

Because of its serious implications, this question certainly merits attention. So let us look at the problem with genuine concern and examine the quality of daily life. Let us expose all the consequences that result from spiritual neglect. Thus, we must make our review a matter of personal involvement.

As we commit ourselves to the search for truth, we seek to find answers to understand the secrets of life. And any truth uncovered will hopefully guide us back on the right path of faithfulness and obedience.

A potential crisis can be turned into the better way of life. Our quest for purpose and meaning on Earth will also lead to a deeper appreciation of the nature of our being. A dedicated search will lead us to fundamental truth and point the way to whose we truly are.

We are God's people!

God's mark of ownership is the divine act of our creation. And on the strength of God's righteousness alone, this claim on our lives was renewed. God made it permanent through the divine act of redemption.

God acted despite the sinfulness of people. Redemption—life in union with Christ as God's anointed Savior—offers all people the opportunity to live by grace in the newness of life. It further secures for the faithful and the obedient a place of restored fellowship in the presence of God. For as grace and faith combine, then all people who believe in God's plan of salvation will experience the oneness that identifies human beings as the image of God.

If our behavior in thought and deed is not in harmony with God's expectations for the purpose of our creation, then we are in the center of an identity crisis. Our behavior—together with the fruits of our labors—is all the evidence needed to indict us.

Whenever people as individuals, families, or societies that make up a nation continuously miss the mark of realizing the life-giving relationship ordained by God, God's expectations of faithfulness and obedience have become sidetracked. When this happens, devotion as well as service to God degenerates into a purposeless ritual. People will go to church once a week solely to satisfy the ego. The absence of any genuine sign of repentance will serve as additional proof that pride and arrogance have combined forces with selfishness and greed.

Neither families nor societies benefit from the spiritual decay of their members. Satan is the only one to gain from any degeneration of the human race. Therefore, Satan will offer help to the wayward in making the final break from knowing God by severing any remaining strains of conscience. Thereafter evil can claim victory over the conflict in man.

Sheer physical existence becomes the new order of the day. Without hope, life has already been shown to be very harsh. People compete for self-esteem, increase greed to remain above average, and excel in empire building to maintain an image.

For people who live without hope, the world is nothing more than a jungle. This type of world consumes energies and people. In it, people will fight and kill in order to survive.

Within it, people will tend to live in their own ocean of self-righteousness. Only the choking from the corrosive atmosphere of hate and greed will make them aware of spiritual blindness. Missed opportunities to overcome this way of life lead to deathbed despair in which the dying see the horizons closing in for the final curtain call.

People have created their own death trap when they make the world a place in which ruthless ambition is the order of the day. In it we will constantly see people working extra hard to outsmart and outdo their fellow men.

As people fight for supremacy, the tenderness of conscience becomes dulled in proportion to the fierceness of worldly struggles. Eventually the wayward will also become insensitive to the pain of slow spiritual death. As they compensate for this painless loss with overindulgence in the pleasures of materialistic gains, Satan waits prepared to reap the harvest in a field full of people who have lost all spiritual identity with God.

Because human beings were created to be dependent creatures of God, an identity crisis is really upon us. We simply have failed to appreciate divine truth as the message that alone can satisfy the hunger of starving souls.

What must we do?

This is not just a cry of desperation of the humanly frail and physically weak. There are moments of truth in all people— good and bad alike. These times of root awakening are opportunities to change. It can be the beginning of the better way of life.

Unfortunately, not all people will take advantage of the chance for a new beginning. We all know that the shedding of bad habits is good for us, and there is even some honesty to our hidden desire for change. Yet this is seldom pursued with sufficient impetus to make a new beginning in the new routine of daily life.

We are not alone in this tragic situation. We share this dilemma with multitudes of people around us.

Because pride makes us cry for even greater independence, we are slaves of our own pride. It makes us want to dictate the ground rules for communion and fellowship with God.

Thus, the sin of rebellion, defiance, and independence is compounded by the greater sin of pride. Even though this conflict is harsh, let us not become overwhelmed by the fierceness of our own problems. Nor must we let ourselves become intimidated by the evil around us. There is nothing in the world that can destroy what God has ordained.

At the same time let us also recognize that there are no alternate or substitute ways for God's plans for our spiritual well-being. For on the basis of God's righteousness alone, grace is the divine gift that secures salvation through Jesus Christ. Thus, the only proper reaction to God's offer of grace is to take refuge in God our Redeemer.

Life in today's world is a mixed blessing. Aimless drift and apathy is a predominant problem among the well-to-do.

Hunger, disease, and death darken all signs of hope for the less fortunate. Though present in different ways, despair can touch rich and poor alike. Nonetheless, life continues to run its course because God sustains it.

This world is the proving ground for Christian faith. The faithful and obedient are given the opportunity to live the faith that we as Christians have so readily professed. Life must be shared with zealots, opportunists, the confused, and even those who reject everything, including themselves.

Yet, the presence of God is evident. For from within this unlikely bundle of people, God continues to use individuals in many ways to accomplish divine purpose.

Through his grace, God is providing ample help. Christians can draw on the power of God to let the Holy Spirit work his will through them. Thus, we do not live for ourselves but to the glory of God.

Christ's prophetic words in the Sermon on the Mount serve to identify followers and their mission: "You are the light of the world … Let your light so shine before men that they may see your good works and give glory to your Father who is in Heaven." (Matthew 5:14-16)

For a better understanding of "good works," let us keep in mind the story of the Good Samaritan (Luke 10:25-37). God is glorified when we recognize the other person also as a child of God and give of ourselves.

If Christians—as the body of Christ—are really concerned about their mission and work, they need not defend or be apologetic about their witness to the good news of the Gospel: Jesus Christ came, died, and was raised back to life for the forgiveness of sins—for even the worst of sinners.

To end the identity crisis, we must yield to the Holy Spirit, who alone will reveal the truth about God.

The flourishing of falsehoods—such as religious cults—during an identity crisis is alarming but should not come as a surprise. Whenever people feel spiritually destitute, they will accept even their own manipulation for the sake of temporary relief.

But false teaching will go on. Saint Paul mentioned that this will continue as long as there are people who like to promote human ideas: "For the time is coming when people will not endure sound teaching, but having itching ears they will accumulate for themselves teachers to suit their own likings, and will turn away from listening to the truth and wander into myths." (2 Timothy 4:3-4)

As people of God—our true identity through creation and redemption—we live in the world by the grace of God.

This rules out all clever manipulation by the human mind to become giants in intellect and develop our own methods of pleasing God. God provided restored fellowship 2,000 years ago—despite sin—as a gift of grace.

God has acted. We now must respond, faithfully and obediently, and live out God's plan of salvation.

War And Peace.
(Excerpt from *I.D. Crisis*)

The crucial issue

War is utter futility.

This statement is a summary of experiences by innocent victims of war—soldiers and civilians alike. The world is not big enough to contain the necessary comfort in support of people for the upset caused by suffering and death.

Irony crowns all assumptions that there is glory in war. After any conflict, people of ordinary walks of life on either side pick up the broken pieces and work together to heal the wounds of battles. The humble and meek mend what was torn apart by the proud and the strong.

Throughout the ages, as in the present time, politicians and warlords have been defending their innocence as causal agents of war. Eventually, however, national leaders will modify their position and concede prior activities before wars explode. But the modifications in their position come with a qualifier. The qualifier throughout the ages is calling war a necessary evil, and politicians and warlords suddenly speak in terms of just war.

What is a just war? Are wars just?

While politicians and warlords demand a workable definition for a just war so they look good when asked to give account for their involvements in the killing of people, God is not responding. God says: "Look within yourselves and see what you were doing before war explodes. Your evil thoughts select the enemy. You then collude with other nations by forming alliances to antagonize your selected enemy. To make matters worse, you then manipulate your formal alliance partners and plot against them with other secret alliances. You create chaos. And chaos creates war. You scheme these evil situations and call them plans to protect your national interests at home and abroad. All wars are human creations, and now you dare ask me to sanctify your evil actions by having me declare it a just war. You create monsters and monstrous situations, and then you ask me to help you destroy the monsters you created."

The Bible indicts human involvement in war as our inability to get along with one another. For the purpose of clarification, Christ repeated the laws of holiness and justice when giving us the second most important commandment—to love our neighbors as we love ourselves: "You shall not hate your brother in your heart, but you shall reason with your neighbor, lest you bear sin because of him. You shall not take vengeance or bear any grudge against the sons of your own people, but you shall love your neighbor as yourself: I am the Lord." (Leviticus 19:17-

18) The law in Leviticus applies to strife within a nation. Many modern wars are civil wars caused by ethnic strife. This we have seen in the Balkans. This we currently see in Africa.

In war, people glorify destruction and killing for the sake of it. Futility abounds when greed and lust for power motivate the ambition of individuals and nations. Jeremiah's prophecy concerning Moab is God's universal warning to all proud, arrogant, and conceited people: "I know his insolence, says the Lord; his boasts are false, his deeds are false." (Jeremiah 48:30)

Over the past 3,000 years, history has witnessed the rise and fall of Egypt, Assyria, Babylonia, the Persian Empire, Alexander's conquests and the spreading of Greek influence, and the Roman Empire.

From 500 A.D. to 1500 A.D. the world experienced the meddling in political affairs by the popes in Rome. No nation in the Western World exercised authority without ecclesiastical consent.

Modern history contains its share of conflicts and ruthless settlements of people by princes and kings. More recently, World War I—"the war to end all wars"—precipitated World War II and brought on many horrors and merciless suffering. Today's jungle warfare in Africa adds to this sad and futile record. Legions of innocent people have suffered and died because of the attempt by a few individuals to satisfy their greed and lust for power.

Battles may be won, but only Satan benefits from any victories when people attempt to destroy each other. No one will ever realize full satisfaction out of winning a conflict or war, because the greed of human nature is like a bottomless pit.

Yet, we try to fill it! We justify our attempts to satisfy this pit through a neatly compiled summary of reasons. However logical these may sound to us is of no consequence. Any reasoning to justify war will never prove true on the Day of Judgment. Only when we are called to defend the glory of God is our involvement in war truly justified.

When that conflict ends, then Christ will victoriously raise the banner of salvation high on the cross. And all creation will see that the Day of Judgment has been set for the world (John 16:25-33). This alone can be rightfully called the war to end all wars.

When that time comes, believers will know eternal peace. The hatchet of hate, as an instrument of greed, will be relegated to the eternal fire of hell. And hate will have no more substance left to feed its destructive appetite.

People will give glory to God in constant praise and adoration. Fiery discord will not be kindled anymore. Peace will be realized through complete harmony of our being with God (Isaiah 2:4).

The heart of man will become like a fountain of love from which will flow forth the life-giving water of regeneration. No longer will the heart of man be the breeding ground for future evil (Isaiah 12:1-6).

We are in the world (John 17:15). But we have overcome the world by victoriously rising above it through our life of union with Christ (John 17:21).

Our strength, as well as our true source of peace, is God. God manifested his strength in the person of Jesus Christ. *Christ came declaring war on the evil in our hearts*: "Do not think that I have come to bring peace on Earth; I have not come to bring peace, but a sword." (Matthew 10:34)

When all was said and done, Christ left *us* in peace: "Peace I leave with you; my peace I give to you; not as the world gives do I give to you. Let not your hearts be troubled, neither let them be afraid." (John 14:27)

Christ talks about a type of peace that heretofore has not been given. Christ's peace (John 14:27) is the divine gift that is prompted by our proclamation of Christ as Lord and made perfect in God's blessing of restored fellowship. At that moment of spiritual salvation, sin and evil have no more power over believers.

The conflict in man as the source of war

War and killing is not an evolutionary development.

In total disobedience, Adam rejected the will and purpose of God the Creator. With the disobedience of the man Adam, humanity was condemned to share the punishment of missing God's objective in life. Adam and all of humanity after him was banished from the presence of God. Human life was limited by God's sentence of judgment.

And ever since then, the downslide of humanity has continued. Cain permanently punctured the protective umbrella of the peace of God with the murder of his brother, Abel.

Peace had been ordained by God as a blessing in a life of devotion to worship and service. But now it was lost.

War and killing is not an evolutionary development. It was in the first generation of humanity that Cain killed Abel. This act of selfishness and human greed devoured the innocent blood of Abel, who knew how to be faithful to God and live up to God's expectations.

The blood of Christ is given to believers as the seal of a new covenant with God. In this divine sacrifice, the blood of Christ fulfills God's promise of life. The grace of God assures our restored fellowship. Salvation in Christ frees believers from all past sins. The Good News of the Gospel is God's message of hope: "You have come to Mount Zion and to the city of the living God, the heavenly Jerusalem, and to innumerable angels in festal gathering, and to the assembly of the first-born who are enrolled in Heaven, and to a judge who is God of all, and to the spirits of just men made perfect, and to Jesus, the mediator of a new covenant, and to the sprinkled blood that speaks more graciously than the blood of Abel." (Hebrews 12:22-24)

Christ, as the redeemer of people everywhere, is God's answer to making us perfect again. This provision comes to us through divine grace and is given as an opportunity. But it demands our decision and our faith.

God does not force himself on people. God looks for a response and commitment of faithfulness and obedience. Yet humanity roams the Earth according to its own desires. People forcefully exert their influence over God's creation.

We must be aware of circumstances that will demand that we do the work of God in stopping evil. This point is demonstrated in God's charge to King Saul. When the prophet Samuel anointed Saul, he specifically instructed him to protect God's people "from the hand of their enemies." (1 Samuel 10:1)

But we must realize that any involvement in the fight against Satan and all the forces of darkness is not our battle but the Lord's. We are only instruments to do God's will. Faithfulness to God will bring about God's purpose according to divine plan.

Such obedience Saul had failed to acknowledge. Consequently, the traps of Satan proved his downfall. And God executed the sentence of divine judgment on Saul at Mount Gilboa (1 Samuel 31:8).

Despite knowledge that God demands obedience, people today continue to act like Saul in their deliberations about future events. Saul reacted to threats instead of acting on the instruction of God.

The prophet Samuel had specifically told Saul to wait for him at Gilgal (1 Samuel 10:8). Samuel was concerned that proper sacrifices be offered to God to show the people that God was leading them into battle.

But Saul was spiritually blinded through his disobedience. He failed to recognize the importance of putting God first. Self-esteem and popularity were of greater value to Saul than the will of God. Satan's diversion of unrest among the people was not a sufficient reason for Saul to abandon trust in God.

Satan's trap closed permanently on Saul as God pronounced judgment. Through Samuel God wielded the "double-edged sword": "You have done foolishly; you have not kept the commandment of the Lord your God, which he commanded you; for now the Lord would have established your kingdom over Israel for ever. But now your kingdom shall not continue; the Lord has sought out a man after his own heart, and the Lord has appointed him to be prince over his people, because you have not kept what the Lord commanded you." (1 Samuel 13:13-14)

The choice at the crossroads of life to either go their own way or consult God in prayer is given entirely to people. Human beings can either act on the Word of God or react to the circumstances around them. Like Saul had done at Gilgal and repeatedly thereafter: "There's no time to consult the Lord!" This expression was like second nature to Saul.

The command to Saul, "Now go and smite Am'alek, and utterly destroy all that they have; do not spare them, but kill both man and woman, infant and suckling, ox and sheep, camel and ass," (1 Samuel 15:3) was God's renewed test of obedience.

We again see that Saul succeeded in battle. But Saul miserably failed in faithfulness to God: "But Saul and the people spared Agag, and the best of the sheep and of the oxen and of the fatlings, and the lambs, and all that was good, and would not utterly destroy them; all that was despised and worthless they utterly destroyed." (1 Samuel 15:9)

Any rejection of the will of God will bring ultimate judgment. Saint Paul tells the church at Rome that God will eventually give up on us: "And since they did not see fit to acknowledge God, God gave them up to a base mind and to improper conduct." (Romans 1:28)

Finally, God sealed Saul's judgment. The prophet Samuel

pronounced the truth of the Word of God: "Has the Lord as great delight in burnt offerings and sacrifices as in obeying the voice of the Lord? Behold, to obey is better than sacrifice, and to hearken than the fat of rams. For rebellion is as the sin of divination, and stubbornness is as iniquity and idolatry. Because you have rejected the word of the Lord, he has also rejected you from being king." (1 Samuel 15:22-23)

Ever since the day of God's judgment, Saul lived in obsession to kill God's newly anointed shepherd-king David. Arrogant pride and compromise for the sake of popularity had destroyed Saul's faithfulness and obedience to God. He was useless for doing God's work.

As happened with Saul, we also can make our life unbearable with opposing views about the glory of the Kingdom of God instead of trying to live up to God's expectations. All attempts to outsmart God are futile. Nor can we be all things to all people. Saul tried, and he failed.

Human life is created for the single purpose of being faithful to God. Christ confirmed this point by living, suffering, and dying in obedience to the Father. In the parable about the shrewd manager, Christ stressed single-mindedness of purpose: "No servant can serve two masters; for either he will hate the one and love the other, or he will be devoted to the one and despise the other. You cannot serve God and mammon." (Luke 16:13)

Compromise played a role leading up to World War II. The British prime minister accommodated the idiosyncrasies of a madman as the rest of the world stood idly by. Accommodation is like a cancer that grows at the expense of truth and principle.

When politics explode, war is inevitable because emotions are out of control. Participants and onlookers alike then defend their decisions to go into battle because honor and morality demand that all good people fight a just war.

King David, as successor to the unfaithful and disobedient

Saul, fought many conflicts. But he was battling the forces of evil around him in the name of God.

His faithfulness and obedience to God led to victories. They proved that David was involved in God's cause. David knew many sorrows, but he also acknowledged God in thanksgiving. The Psalms, as the prayer book of the Bible, is the record of David's songs of praise.

The shepherd-king knew war. But he also experienced God's blessing of peace on every occasion when he let his life and spirit become engulfed by the love of God.

Whenever Christians are the instruments of God against evil, they can be assured of receiving God's subsequent blessing of peace.

Although David was influenced by human nature and its animal instinct, he never fought battles to subdue other people to get their blessings.

Before any encounter in battle, David always acknowledged his dependence and trust in God. In his determination to do the will of God, David searched actively for God's purpose in his life.

Throughout David's early reign, conflict was God's tool to strengthen his faithfulness and obedience. But it took the story of the lamb to return David to his proper place of relationship with God after his adultery with Bathsheba and the subsequent premeditated murder of Uriah.

David's contrite heart in the prose of the 51st Psalm satisfied the requirement of repentance as God declared through his prophet: "The Lord also has put away your sin; you shall not die." (2 Samuel 12:13)

Thus, we can readily see that the conflict within man is the source of many troubles, with one another and with other nations. Wars do not just happen. They are created by the devilish schemes of the human mind. Human nature longs for getting by force what God otherwise has chosen to withhold.

Theology of the sword

Observation throughout the ages has revealed
human character as quick for action, slow in learning,
and arrogant to see the other point of view—
even God's will in Christ's teaching.

Whenever there is coercion in the teaching of the Word of God, the Gospel of Christ is misused. The meaning is changed from hope to a satanic instrument of fear. Such practices must be condemned vehemently.

To invoke divine authority is a natural desire of many people. James and John were drawn into this trap when the Samaritan village refused to receive Jesus. They felt tempted to destroy the inhabitants by calling fire down from Heaven. Christ's rescue is implied in the statement that Jesus "turned and rebuked them." (Luke 9:51-56)

Some modern preaching delivers an ideology of hell-fire and brimstone. "Doomsday artists" falsely project their own environment of darkness and misery as theology and as the truth about God. They roam the Earth on the strength of personal ambition and charisma in hopes of finding a following that, like them, subscribe to the theme "let's return to the basics" with regard to everyday life. The "new" spirituality they are promoting is founded on human ideas of piety and morality—self-justification's favorites, but also the last remaining vestiges of sin.

We are confronted by sectarian groups who deal in ideas about how life ought to be lived even though such notions are outside the will and purpose of God. They promote views that satisfaction and happiness can be achieved by reverting to the ways of the past because in the fiction of their own minds they remember how life "used to be" better.

One must know God through a living relationship in order to teach about faith. Truth must flow like streams of life-giving water out of a believer's heart (John 7:37-38).

The responsibility to properly witness to the Christian faith is part of our call to discipleship. The cost of being a disciple of Christ is to deny oneself. One cannot be a true disciple of Christ unless he gives up everything he has.

To empty our hearts is to make room for Christ. Only then can the Holy Spirit of God rule our minds for bringing to all people the Good News of the Gospel.

Our teaching, therefore, is witnessing to what God has done through Christ. It is not a detailed agenda to regiment people.

Believers teach by witnessing to their relationship with God. The example of their own lives must proclaim lives in union with Christ. Christian witness is to the glory of God in believers. This must become visible like a beacon if others are to be led to Christ so that they also may see, believe, and become saved.

Only the zealot, whose behavior fringes on fanaticism, wants to see things differently. Because of limited vision, zealous people know no other way but a brute force approach of flesh and muscle for witnessing to the glory of God. These false teachers are so opinionated that they fail to realize that brute force is a technique used to enslave people, whereas the Gospel of Christ is God's message of hope to set people free in the spirit. The task of preaching and witnessing to the Gospel of Christ is an appeal to the spirit that brings people the truth about God so that all people in the world may become faithful workers on Earth on behalf of the Kingdom of God.

We cannot teach faith with an approach of "mind over matter." The power of positive thinking is but another diversion that leads people away from knowing God. Like all other teaching that is not based on the authority of Christ and the inspiration of the Holy Spirit, "positive thinking" also lacks the authority of the Word of God.

Theology by the sword extended its millennium of power into the 21st century. People today are more sophisticated than those involved in the religious wars that lasted for 30 years (1618-1648) and spread blood all over continental Europe. It is truly an irony that people engage in armed conflict to bring the love of God to others as servants of the Gospel.

Despite warnings from Christ (Matthew 7:21-23), people continue dealing in a conceptual approach to religion instead of witnessing to the truth of the Gospel. Substance is not enhanced by any acquired expertise in teaching.

Evil surfaces when indoctrination tactics fail because of falsehood. For example, Martin Luther was branded a heretic and condemned to die because he dared to correct falsehood and stood by God's plan that salvation is by grace through faith. The best that church doctrine can do is producing "a most likely story," whereas Christ's teaching is eternal truth that sets people free (John 8:31-32).

Improvements in attitudes are noticeable in the recent past. The Roman Catholic Second Vatican Council (1962-1965) has made room for dialogues. And Christians throughout the world hail religious tolerance because of it. Ecumenism on local levels has become central in witnessing to Christ today. But let us remember that our obligation to God has as its foundation Christ and eternal truth.

Worldly councils can only point to God as the true authority to restore order in human lives. Therefore, Christians must celebrate ecumenism today because the Body of Christ recognizes the need for united fellowship in God's presence and acknowledges the guidance of the Holy Spirit in everyday activities. These objectives must not be confused with the commendable achievements by which people practice religious tolerance.

Observation throughout the ages has revealed human character as quick for action, slow in learning, and arrogant to see the other point of view—even God's will in Christ's teaching. It was as recently as 1984 that theologians from the Roman

Catholic Church in the United States openly acknowledged God's plan of salvation by Grace through faith. Saint Paul's tutorial in Romans 8 is indeed appropriate to help Christians today prepare themselves for making God known to all peoples everywhere.

Despite some progress, the body of Christ remains polarized. The church has really never suffered from any lack of personal opinions about truth. Nor has there been a shortage of statements. The influential bishops' letters from the Roman Catholic Church in the late 1980s on peace and economics are among the more recent examples. Remnants of earlier attempts to integrate religion and worldly affairs—like the religious activities at the beginning of the industrial revolution during the latter half of the 19th century—are with us still in the classification scheme that labels Protestantism (because of belief in work ethic) as being close to capitalism, whereas Roman Catholicism (because of its constant appeals to share wealth with the poor) is linked to socialism.

And there are other influences. Special-interest groups formed by fundamentalists from the Southern Baptist Convention have created a national forum for debating prayers in public schools. The politically active Moral Majority is a sectarian group that is not at all hesitant to impress upon the general public its idiosyncrasies. Therefore, in all this worldly confusion Christians must remember their obligation for the glory of God on Earth while at the same time living out God's expectations as a matter of personal commitment. The United States Constitution grants religious and political freedom to all citizens.

While secular law protects religious freedom, ecclesiastical law is known to control spiritual behavior. For example, members of the Roman Catholic Church who have remarried without having their previous marriage annulled by the church—even though such annulments have no legal status in the secular world—cannot participate in Holy Communion.

The modern world is further overburdened with violence. Religious fanatics will use the "sword" in its physical sense to demonstrate "true religion" according to the definition of their warped thinking. For example, fringe elements of Islam control the inhabitants of Iran. Lebanon's people must live in daily fear of terrorism that is sparked by religious insanity among Muslims and Christians alike. Intolerance in India is subduing masses of people with its outmoded caste system. The largest democracy in the world experienced Theology of the Sword in the murder of its prime minister.

The Western world is not immune to religious intolerance and its manifestation in terrorism. What many people would prefer to describe as a political struggle in the fighting among Protestants and Roman Catholics in Northern Ireland is a religious issue. It has become Christianity's shame.

To make satanic acts palatable for public acceptance, individuals are quick to invent labels and phrases to justify these activities. The rest of civilization stands by and washes its hands from guilt as long as "the other people's problems" are a safe distance away.

Instead of fulfilling our responsibility as disciples of Christ by speaking out against wrongs in the world, people are silently watching—secretly wishing that the party they are rooting for will win.

As these struggles go on, followers of the Theology of the Sword and by the sword gather in sacred assemblies to unify "religion." Conclaves and councils are formed to iron out little differences in philosophy. Experts compromise a little here and there. But they totally neglect to seek guidance from the Holy Spirit for knowing the truth about God, God's will, and the purpose for our lives as the only thing that must matter.

The Holy Spirit of God will expose any false teaching and coercion in light of truth and reveal truth to believers. Christ says: "When the Spirit of truth comes, he will guide you into all the truth; for he will not speak on his own authority, but whatever he hears he will speak, and he will declare to you the things that are to come. He will glorify me, for he will take what is mine and declare it to you. All that the Father has is mine; therefore, I said that he will take what is mine and declare it to you." (John 16:13-15)

One cannot instill hope in people with a weapon of destruction, which either sword or coercion represents.

The horror of war

War, with its many byproducts of horror,
is the fruit of faithlessness and disobedience.

Through the rejection of God, people deny themselves the opportunity of letting God work his will to accomplish divine purpose. As long as the sin in human nature is allowed to run rampant, people are proud, arrogant, conceited, selfish, and full of empty boasts.

We find this in Biblical history. The prophet Isaiah quoted the people of Judah as he describes the attitude of the people of Moab: "We have heard of the pride of Moab, how proud he was; of his arrogance, his pride, and his insolence—his boasts are false." (Isaiah 16:6)

Consequently Jeremiah prophesied that Moab would be humbled: "We have heard of the pride of Moab—he is very proud—of his loftiness, his pride, and his arrogance, and the haughtiness of his heart. I know his insolence, says the Lord; his boasts are false, his deeds are false ... and I will bring to an end in Moab, says the Lord, him who offers sacrifice in the high place and burns incense to his god." (Jeremiah 48:29-30, 35)

And the Biblical record shows God's judgment on Moab: "On all the housetops of Moab and in the squares there is nothing but lamentation; for I have broken Moab like a vessel for which no one cares, says the Lord. How it is broken! How they wail! How Moab has turned his back in shame! So Moab has become a derision and a horror to all that are round about him." (Jeremiah 48:38-39)

As the judgment is executed, a greater horror is experienced by those forced to witness the atrocities of war: "When the king of Moab saw that the battle was going against him, he took with him seven hundred swordsmen to break through, opposite the king of Edom; but they could not. Then he took his eldest son, who was to reign in his stead, and offered him for a burnt offering upon the wall. And there came great wrath upon Israel; and they withdrew from him and returned to their own land." (2 Kings 3:26-27)

Let us briefly examine the history of the Moabites. The Moabites and the Ammonites were the descendants of Lot, born by his daughters, after God had destroyed Sodom and Gomorrah.

Moses refers to the Moabites as he contrasts the nature of true power and human arrogance: "The Lord is my strength and my song, and he has become my salvation; this is my God, and I will praise him, my father's God, and I will exalt him ... Thy right hand, O Lord, glorious in power, thy right hand, O Lord, shatters the enemy ... Thou didst stretch out thy right hand, the Earth swallowed them." (Exodus 15:2, 6, 12)

But concerning the strength of the nations, Moses writes: "Now are the chiefs of Edom dismayed; the leaders of Moab, trembling seizes them; all the inhabitants of Canaan have melted away." (Exodus 15:15)

Lot's descendants are part of our Christian heritage. It was in Moabite territory that Moses explained God's laws to the Israelites. And atop Mount Nebo, high above the plains of Moab, God showed Moses the Promised Land, thereby establishing prophetically the destiny of the Israelites to live secured and in service to God.

But the record also shows the external influence on the faithfulness of the chosen people of God. For despite God's obvious presence for guidance and protection (Exodus 23:20-21), Balaam succeeded in making Israel turn away from God.

Because the Israelites disobeyed God, the king of Moab conquered them—not with might or sorcery, but with gifts of pleasure. Through them the Israelites became unfaithful to God: "While Israel dwelt in Shittim the people began to play the harlot with the daughters of Moab. These invited the people to the sacrifices of their gods, and the people ate and bowed down to their gods. So Israel yoked himself to Baal of Peor. And the anger of the Lord was kindled against Israel." (Numbers 25:1-3)

War, with its many byproducts of horror, is the fruit of faithlessness and disobedience.

Whenever the sin in human nature tries to satisfy greed, man strikes out to get by force what others have received as a blessing from God. Any subsequent war and its accompanying terror inflicts horrors more deadly than the most potent poison on Earth. Fear claims victory over body and soul.

Because scar tissues of war are a constant reminder of humanity's failure to get along with one another, future generations are forced to live in continuous threats of life. Even peaceful people will be pressured to respond to tools of an aggressor nation with an even greater appropriation of resources for their own defense to maintain peace. Satan desires people to live in fear. Fear is among the sly serpent's methods by which he tries to keep us away from the presence of God.

Additional trauma increases the fear about wars even further. Technological advances in warfare have raised the level of destructive power to the potential of total annihilation. Wipeouts of entire civilizations are highly probable.

Fears about war, therefore, are not wild imaginations. They

are real threats to spiritual well-being in all situations where the love of God does not control people's destiny.

Even faithful believers feel the pressure of horrors. The moment of truth demands that we demonstrate trust in God. Because faithfulness alone secures spiritual rest amidst all the turmoil in the world, obedience to the will of God separates Christ's followers.

We live according to God's promise. And we hold firm to the hope that God will look after us and provide for our safety. Christ, indeed, has promised to be with us "always, to the close of the age." (Matthew 28:20)

This hope is part of God's universal truth in the Gospel. There is no power on Earth that can separate believers from the love of God through Christ Jesus. Additionally, since our life is in God's service, we are sustained by the power of God's Holy Spirit for witnessing to God's grace in and around us.

Saint Paul describes the grace of God in his letter to the church at Rome as the steadfastness of God's love. In a way that affirms his own belief in the love of God, Saint Paul poses the question: "If God is for us, who is against us?" (Romans 8:31)

And Saint Paul continues: "Who shall separate us from the love of Christ? Shall tribulation, or distress, or persecution, or famine, or nakedness, or peril, or sword? ... No, in all these things we are more than conquerors through him who loved us." (Romans 8:35,37)

With these words, Saint Paul is refreshing the memory of believers with the teaching of Christ that restored fellowship with God in the way of obedience to Christ's leadership, whose obedience to God secured a relationship for believers that is best summarized in a shepherd's concern for his flock: "I am the good shepherd; I know my own and my own know me, as the Father knows me and I know the Father; and I lay down my life for the sheep." (John 10:14-15)

Therefore, the answer to the question, "Where is God?" is hidden in faith and trust in God. Faithfulness and obedience to God are the visible signs of Christ's followers.

The faithful believer in Christ knows the presence of God! In the noise of violent conflict, God calms the soul so that we can truly appreciate the serenity of God's presence.

We have peace, because we believe in God's promise. Our faithfulness is the key to God's assurance of peace. The Book of Revelation has recorded the foretaste of Christ's promise in eternity. This visionary text addresses the Church in Smyrna: "Be faithful unto death, and I will give you the crown of life." (Revelation 2:10)

But why does God tolerate war?

God does not tolerate war!

God does not incite war. People do!

War is a desire of human nature. Speaking on behalf of God, Moses lectured the Israelites on freedom of choice as they journeyed to the promised land: "I call Heaven and Earth to witness against you this day, that I have set before you life and death, blessing and curse; therefore choose life, that you and your descendants may live, loving the Lord your God, obeying his voice, and cleaving to him; for that means life to you and length of days." (Deuteronomy 30:19-20)

Christ has summarized God's challenge in the two Great Commandments as a guide for all believers (Matthew 22:37-39). The viewpoint is different, but the message is the same.

So, let us not act surprised that the burden of responsibility for making war rests with people.

The only surprise that should make us shudder is the irony that turns out to be the real horror of all times: Warring nations pray to the same God for victory.

Despite this being so, we must not become disheartened because of confusion. Neither should we let ourselves be fooled. What may appear as sincere prayers to God for deliverance are many times just ramblings of pious words.

The evil in human nature tries to justify its rebellion toward God through its own system of piety. The difference between the true disciples of Christ and those who consider themselves followers is catastrophic. One can usually notice this difference in the lifestyle of people. It commonly shows up as a distinguishable contrast of life and death: salvation in God's presence or condemnation to hell (Luke 13:22-30).

It is clear that only the true disciples of Christ will search for the will of God when praying for deliverance. Dedicated followers express their trust in God to safely carry them through hardships and horrors, similar to the protection envisioned by the Psalmist when he declared God as the protector of all faithful people: "A thousand may fall at your side, ten thousand at your right hand; but it will not come near you. You will only look with your eyes and see the recompense of the wicked." (Psalm 91:7-8)

Sometimes, horrors can be so overwhelming that many people will lose faith because of them. When this happens, let us not blame such incidents on a righteous and faithful God whose promise of salvation is secured in steadfastness.

It is certain that God will help faithful believers during moments of death and destruction when faith is put to the test, like that of Job was. Such trials establish the worthiness of our spiritual being, for in the flesh we are made to realize the futility of our human nature. Our spirit alone can be renewed only with strength from God.

Horrors of war are threatening to people when they lose faith and put their own ambitions ahead of a firm commitment of faithfulness to God. Therefore, let us always remember that God created the human race to be faithful.

Let there not be any doubt—some fears have substance. Man has advanced to the frightful state of existence where "bigger is better" borders on insanity. By relying totally on human intelligence, limited as it is, we have constructed weapons of mass destruction without really having a true understanding of how to harness their power, take care of their effect on anything living, or even dispose of them responsibly when not wanted or needed.

We seem to be more concerned about the immediacy of economic gain in weapon development than any ultimate effects on people or nature. If all these resources of God that are being wasted on tools of destruction were to be used to the glory of God, the way God had intended them to be used, then peace would be the assurance by divine decree.

As long as mankind concentrates resources, energies, and talents on weapons of destruction, then these very same weapons in which people place their security become a horror to future generations. And the threat of annihilation is indeed real.

The threat is real, because we have created not knowing what we are actually doing, despite the fact that well-educated experts claim to be in control. This will always be the case whenever people shut God out of their lives.

A great many fears nurture on past wounds. Hurt and resentment burden the souls of people because the scar tissue from past conflicts has inadequately healed. There are constant reminders of people killed, bodies maimed, and property destroyed through families who suffered the consequences of folly in leadership.

The shepherd-king David, despite his shortcomings of human nature, had as his most outstanding feature a deep faith and devotion to God. David knew how to rule because of his intimate relationship with God. But he also knew how to accept the punishment that God sent because of his shortcomings.

God can only heal the scars of any past wounds of war when a faith-trust-love relationship is the basis for life. Total dependence on God is the only way that will prevent future wounds from being inflicted. And our reliance on God will further quench any fear. Threats that otherwise might overpower the new existence in the Spirit will then have no power over believers.

Thus we profess Christ. As Christians we claim peace through promise. The truth of the Word of God is authority and promise.

The authority is clearly defined. Christ affirms: "All authority in Heaven and on Earth has been given to me." (Matthew 28:18)

And the promise is precisely given. Christ assures: "I am with you always, to the close of the age." (Matthew 28:20)

ACT III
THE HISTORIC 'FROM' IN "FROM/TO"

Source for reflections
Springboard for meditations
Baseline for change
Illustrations of "from" scenes
History tells us

Chapter 9

Self-examination establishes the historic "from" in From/to and triggers the process of change. God routinely makes changes. For example, God uses From/to to make adjustments to the environment, the climate, and our specific surroundings. But God also uses From/to in the transformation of human lives from chaos to order. In all situations of change, God always finishes the From/to process with his unyielding commitment to spiritual connection. He wants to make sure that his children will not have to wander in the hopeless desert of sin again.

We remember what we once were and where we came from. The historic "from" in From/to reveals detailed accounts by the Holy Spirit of Christ's transformation miracles of healing, redemption, and newness of life. The Bible has numerous teachings and illustrations about the work of Christ, and we acknowledge these spiritual encounters as sacred history.

Source for reflections

In transforming human lives, God asks us to reflect on the past, but he does not want us to dwell on it. He wants us to fully comprehend our involvement in the process for improving the human condition in the world, especially the quality of life.

Reflections lead to repentance. Repentance satisfies all essential divine requirements for change. And the ensuing new life in the Spirit is God's way for a new beginning that is absolutely free of the past. God wants us to move on in the newness of spiritual life by the power of the Holy Spirit.

"Fine and good," we say, "we all appreciate a fresh start, and we thank God for it." But what about our past? What do we do with it? Hence the obvious question: Is looking into the past a healthy thing to do?

God's answer is free of doubt and confusion. Thus says the Lord: "Reflections are part of my healing process. Once I hear a confessional prayer, the sin of my children is now my business. By the power of the Holy Spirit I forgive sins, as Christ has shown in healing the paralytic young man. My grace is appropriate for every child of God. Your ways are inappropriate because you let guilt interfere with your new life in the Spirit; furthermore, your ways are inappropriate because often you want to transfer guilt from parent to child. Once your sins are left at the Cross of Jesus Christ, spiritual freedom is my way of restoring you. Henceforth all my children are free from guilt, and I bless them with a new life in the Spirit. The spiritual connection is my new creation in you. I, the Lord, have spoken!"

We can readily see that reflections have an important role in the healing process. These introspective journeys into the innermost chambers of the soul are guided and controlled by the Holy Spirit, for the reasons previously mentioned. Under the leadership of the Holy Spirit, reflections are healthy excursions into the past for getting a clearer picture about the present and then planning for a better future

God wipes clean the slate of past sins to make us better servants in the future. People consumed by guilt are useless in the

Kingdom of God on Earth; therefore, God totally cleanses us to make us invincible beacons of the divine light in a troubled world. We are in the world, but we are not part of the world. However, sin is part of the world. God does not want the sinful world to influence the new life in the Spirit or, worse yet, force us to submit to its power through guilt.

Reflections and healing

The soul tells the whole story.

We talk a lot about soul-searching. What does soul-searching mean?

The soul is the bastion of truth. We look into the wide-open window of the soul, and what we see is what we truly are. Our soul-searching journey leads us into the innermost chambers of the soul where truth resides. And as we concentrate on truth with an inquisitive and open mind, we too will see what God sees in us. Since truth is free of pretense and imagination, the truth we see in our soul is reality in its purest state. The soul tells the whole story.

What we see is what we truly are. The soul lays bare hidden attitudes, and the divine light of Christ exposes the innermost miserable conditions of our thoughts.

But there are problems of perception. All too often we interpret the truth. When we look into the mirror of our soul, we may see something that is not to our liking. Then we add to it our human expertise to make it look better. But making such adjustments only fools us, for God is not impressed with human imaginations.

Therefore, applying reflections to current needs is not always simple. Although the mirror of the soul reflects the absolute truth, our perception of absolute truth is problematical. The world is driven by personal ambition. Too often our ego interferes with the search for truth in harmful ways. Many times we are reluctant to air our shortcomings. We tarnish the absolute value of truth through deceptions. We put pictures in front of our mind's eye of something that we are not. We suppress truth in ways that are self-serving because we want to impress the world.

Such shortsighted behavior is detrimental to the From/to process of healing and change. Ultimately God will overrule us, for he wants us spiritually in tune with his way for our spiritual well-being. The healing rays of God's light will always penetrate the shell of falsehood and get to the core of our problems.

The prime function of the historic "from" in From/to, therefore, is to lay bare the past. Once the past lies open before God, God will act and heal us by the power of the Holy Spirit. Then we are free in the Spirit to enjoy life that is solely based on the righteousness of God, and God turns his righteousness into our own righteousness. Henceforth we are spiritually connected with God. We are spiritually free to do his bidding in the world!

Springboard for meditations

The "from" in the From/to process further encourages us to seek God's help in prayer. Reflections without contemplation are exercises in futility. We know that we must change our attitudes and behavior to realize improvements in the quality of life. So we reach beyond our miserable selves and cry out to God for help. God then does the rest. His solutions are now our blessings.

Meditations build bridges

God holds our future in his hands.

People who choose not to accept God's way of revelation and inspiration are left to theorize. But theories are as numerous as the stars in the sky, and they are not always reality.

Theories are subject to re-interpretations. What was plausible in the Renaissance, for example, needed to be revised in the Age of Reason, and so on. Our horizons are widened as new advances in science and technology shed additional light on truth. Only the Holy Spirit can guide faithful believers into God's eternal truth.

Baseline for change

*God looks into our souls to fix the starting
point for change and transformation.*

From/to is a correction process. When God looks into the wide-open window of our soul, he focuses on poor attitudes and evil behavior. God is a God of perfection, and he wants us to be as perfect as he is; God especially wants perfection in our use of his gift of love. The Holy Spirit has the dominant role in the search for truth, for the Holy Spirit alone can discern the truth.

The quagmire of doubt and confusion

In the quagmire of doubt and confusion in the modern world, God looks closely at our response to his gifts of faith, hope, and love. Our indifference to his love is truly heartbreaking to him. He sees mind-destroying drug abuse. He sees brutal murder. He sees mean-spirited economic oppression. And he sees senseless wars.

Claims of human greatness are nothing new. They have burdened the relationship of people and God since God blessed
Abraham with faith some 3,900 years ago. We insist of having
the divine right to act the way we do because spiritually we are,
after all, the image of God.

Yet despite all human shortcomings, and in spite of ego and
self-righteousness, the human drama always ends up to God's
satisfaction and in accordance with the divine plan. God inter-
venes. He turns things upside down and inside out in our lives
to make us a better people. He puts us back on the high road
of his righteousness and faithfulness is the new reality. After all,
we are his dependent children.

Often it may appear that the flame of divine righteousness is
just barely flickering, but even in the faintest of human perception, the flame of God's righteousness continues to have very
potent powers. God keeps it going, for God wants us to change
by the power of the Holy Spirit. The divine flame now burning in
our hearts prompts us to reform attitudes and behavior.

By the power of the Holy Spirit, Pilgrim T. Homosapien,
Servant of God, concludes his lesson about the "from" in the
From/to process: "In our reflections about the past the mirror of
our souls tells the whole story *from* spiritual neglect *to* quality of
life in God's presence. We see how God is transforming our
lives. Our soul rejoices because of what God is doing in his miracles of spiritual renewal and blessings. Our trust in God is
more powerful than all the forces of evil in a consuming world.
The 'from' is the past; it becomes the future 'to' where we are
going. The processes for sorting things out are moments of
reflections and meditations initiated and guided by the Holy

Spirit. The baseline in reflections is God's starting point for our healing and transformation. Our new life is life by the power of the Holy Spirit, who leads us in ceaseless prayers."

Illustrations of *"From"* scenes

Transformation Scene 1:
From spiritual neglect *to* quality of life

God looks at his people in these modern times, and he sees many of them drifting aimlessly in a devouring world. He identifies spiritual neglect as the root cause in past human failures, and he confirms spiritual neglect as the root cause of current failures. The disease-causing agent in spiritual neglect is lack of love of God and neighbor. And the missing link in quality of life also is love. Hence God is out in the modern world to transform spiritual neglect into quality of life. He graciously showers his love on all.

God had great compassion for the people of Israel about 2,700 years ago. The prophet Micah pronounced the Word of God as a promise for transformation of life with hope for a new beginning. As spiritual neglect was rampant in Israel around 700 B.C., spiritual neglect is rampant in the world today. God uses historical events to demonstrate the "from" in the From/to process for healing and restoration. The prophet Micah proclaimed the Word of God to the people of Israel around 700 B.C.: "He has showed you, O man, what is good; and what does the Lord require of you but to do justice, and to love kindness, and to walk humbly with your God?" (Micah 6:8) The Word of God spoken by Micah rebounds in the world today and details the ethical and spiritual nature of quality of life in these modern times.

God calls us to promote justice in the world and advance his love in these troubled times. As God was adamant about changes in human behavior in 700 B.C., he is equally determined in the Era of Faith to transform desolate lives.

We cannot survive a breakup of the human spirit,
which is certain when we stop loving God,
neighbor, and ourself.

Spiritual neglect is a sickness unto death. We cannot survive the breakup of the human spirit, which is certain when we stop loving God, neighbor, and ourself.

God alone can undo the bumps and pits in life caused by spiritual neglect. Faith is God's way to transform life from spiritual neglect to quality of life.

Faith works miracles in the spiritual domain, yet the results are highly visible. We see wasted lives transformed from withered to healthy in the presence of God. Faith appreciates God's way for enjoying life in the present and building a better future because the Holy Spirit is with us in everything that we do.

As the Holy Spirit works with us by means of the From/to process to restore quality of life, the human spirit needs love. Lots of love is needed to uplift distraught souls. Quality of life depends on love. Where love is missing, quality of life has no voice, for spiritual neglect is a denial of the Word of God.

Transformation Scene 2:
From arrogance *to* friend of God

In our arrogance we have abandoned the
high road of God's righteousness.

The world is all about people. People are the foremost concern of a righteous God. The word "people" is mentioned in the Bible over 2,000 times—it is among the most commonly used words in the Bible. The Bible is a true God-and-people book. The central theme in the Bible is relationships.

We are free to live in the presence of God when we are free of arrogance. Therefore, we should not keep pushing our personal ambitions into the forefront. Let us bring our personal problems to God and pray for change.

The relationship of people and God in the last century has been anything but upbeat. The Holy Spirit is rejected. Jesus Christ is scoffed at and scorned, and his name is used in vain.

History keeps repeating itself every time we scorn God in Christ. We are without hope when we deny the Holy Spirit absolute control over our lives. We deny Jesus Christ and his message of hope when we take life into our own hands.

Every time we ignore the noble sacrifice of Jesus Christ, and the valiant sacrifices of martyrs and saints throughout human history, we crucify Christ over and over again. Belief in Jesus Christ opens the eyes of the blind and gives light to the world. Jesus says: "I came into this world that those who do not see may see and that those who see may become blind." (John 9:39)

We are now friends of God!

The Holy Spirit is God's prime mover in the spiritual transformation of human lives. God is blessing us with life in his presence with no strings attached. Our spiritual life is complete as soon as we open our hearts and joyfully welcome the One God of Father, Son, and Holy Spirit into our hearts. We are now friends of God!

We rely on the Gospel in our search for the true meaning of life in the modern world. We study the Word of God in earnest and then heed Christ's call to follow him. Consequently, we make the necessary commitment as the true friends of God and bring the very same Gospel to people whose spiritual needs have to be filled. Everything else is in God's hands.

History warns us about pitfalls. As thousands fall by the wayside, history cautions us to keep our eyes fixed on the high road of God's righteousness.

As friends of God we are now his pilgrims on God's high road of righteousness traveling with the Holy Spirit at a secure pace to be with Christ in Heaven. On the high road of God's righteousness all signs point to eternity. Eternity is where Christians are headed. Christ has already prepared our resting place in Heaven. Friends of God are assured a setting at God's table of grace in Heaven, where God is now celebrating our life in his life!

Transformation Scene 3:
From greed *to* spiritual wholeness

Relationships falter when money is king.

People who rely on aspirations without inspiration believe that getting rich is the only meaningful objective in life. Hoarding wealth becomes the primary goal in their short pilgrimage on Earth. But relationships falter when money is king.

Despite knowing that we cannot take things with us when we die, some individuals continue to accumulate wealth to influence and control people and nations. Excess money stored away is the modern idol in the secular world. Money is worshipped because money has the mirage of power. But money loses its power when we die. A friend once made an interesting point about hoarding money. It was at the burial of a very rich man. As he watched the casket being lowered into the ground, he offered his observation: "I have never seen a U-Haul at the cemetery."

In God's spiritual realm money has neither substance nor power. Opportunists and manipulators cling to the falsehood that wealth is power. They appreciate the temporary privilege of lording it over their fellow man.

Jesus invites us to study the story earnestly and apply the message in everyday life: "A man ran up and knelt before him (Jesus), and asked him, 'Good Teacher, what must I do to inherit eternal life?' And Jesus said to him, 'Why do you call me good? No one is good but God alone. You know the commandments: 'Do not kill, Do not commit adultery, Do not steal, Do not bear false witness, Do not defraud, Honor your father and mother.' And he (the man) said to him, 'Teacher, all these I have observed from my youth.' And Jesus looking upon him loved him, and said to him, 'You lack one thing; go, sell what you have, and give to the poor, and you will have treasure in Heaven; and come, follow me.' At that saying his countenance fell, and he went away sorrowful; for he had great possessions. And Jesus looked around and said to his disciples, 'How hard it will be for those who have riches to enter the Kingdom of God!' And the disciples were amazed at his words. But Jesus said to them again, 'Children, how hard it is to enter the Kingdom of God! It is easier for a camel to go through the eye of a needle than for a rich man to enter the Kingdom of God.' And they were astonished, and said to him, 'Then who can be saved?' Jesus looked at them and said, 'With men it is impossible, but not with God; for all things are possible with God.' Peter began to say to him, 'Lo, we have left everything and followed you.' Jesus said, 'Truly, I say to you, there is no one who has left house or brothers or sisters or mother or father or children or lands, for my sake and for the gospel, who will not receive a hundredfold in this time, houses and brothers and sisters and mothers and children and lands, with persecutions, and in the age to come eternal life. But many that are first will be last, and the last first." (Mark 10:17-31)

Christ is telling us to seek true riches in Heaven, where God's blessing are secured for eternity.

What history tells us

History tells us how the doors of the Dark Ages closed. The shackles of barbarity and intellectual darkness lost effectiveness in controlling the lives of people. Reform entered the world on angels' wings by divine decree.

Rays of hope and freedom appeared on the horizon and lifted up downtrodden hearts and minds. Hope and freedom questioned aggressive behavior. But change was slow, for hope needs deep roots to grow and flourish. Hope brings with it intellectual prowess, and intellectual prowess is a slow process.

The Renaissance provided the productive ground for the seedlings of intellectual growth. This further improved the human condition. A greater number of people than ever before, from diverse walks of life, now participated in the intellectual growth process. The Renaissance provided the springboard for the human mind to venture into previously forbidden territories of the unknown. This period was filled with enthusiasm for exploring new ideas.

Courage blossomed in the Age of Reason. Intellectual freedom gained ground and was taking on substance. What previ-

ously was declared taboo was now openly challenged and discussed. Unfortunately, many of the growth opportunities in the
Age of Reason turned out to be lopsided as reason gained the
upper hand. The new focus was on reason at the expense of
faith.

The newly thinkers sidelined faith. They failed to synthesize
faith and reason into a powerful and progressive partnership in
the search for truth. Intellectual proposals about life and human
behavior prospered at the expense of faith. Faith became the
innocent victim of the times.

As the dominance of reason increased with each new discovery, science and technology expanded. This offered the
promise for transforming visions into reality. Science and technology were favored over faith and inspiration in this new age
of discoveries. Faith and reason have continued in a state of
tension ever since.

History has many answers in our search for truth, if we but
listen. Let us strive, therefore, to change and integrate our
world into the harmony and peace that God anticipates. We are
the children of God to make the things happen on Earth that he
ordains in Heaven.

EPILOGUE
FROM EDEN TO ETERNITY VIA THE SERENE EXPANSE

Chapter 10

Islands of hope

God is now giving us again unparalleled opportunities in the Era of Faith to live by the power of the Holy Spirit and to enjoy the abundant life in the glory of God. The Christian covenant of love wipes clean old failures.

In the Era of Faith God provides islands of hope for his people.

The serene expanse at the Marginal Way in Ogunquit, Maine, is typical of an "island of hope" in a heavenly setting of peace and tranquility. Islands of hope are offered to pilgrims throughout the world. *The serene expanse* is a close replica of paradise—the permanent resting place in Heaven for the souls of the faithful. The roads leading to *the serene expanse* still take us through the wilderness of ordinary life; but once we are there, *the serene expanse* is real and inspirational.

Blessed are all modern pilgrims who find refuge and full appreciation of the spiritual life in these fortresses of nature as gifts of God for peace, tranquility, and inspiration.

POETRY ADDENDUM

The Celebration of Life

A good poem is like good music; both are uplifting.

May the pages in this section of poetry widen your horizons.

Era of Faith

We are the light of Christ:
Our faith lights up the world.
God nurtures the faithful with faith,
And each person is a child of God!

We are the life of God:
Our life proclaims his Gospel.
By the power of the Holy Spirit,
We live his Word, we bless, and we heal.

We are the truth of God:
Our truth is his power on Earth.
God blesses the faithful with love,
And we live in his presence.

Light, life, and truth:
All three are Christ in us!
We live in the glory of God,
And we are his friends forever!

Truth

Truth is a mighty fortress,
Truth is the armor of God,
Truth is a real friend in an uncertain world.
In the quagmire of human insolence,
Truth is the Sword of the Spirit.

Oftentimes truth seems elusive,
Yet truth is ever present,
Truth prevails when all is said and done.
God is Truth,
And Truth secures abundant life.

God says:
"You shall know Truth,
And I will set you free."
As children of God in truth,
We now live in peace!

Reality

Reality is truly puzzling:
People swear, pollute, threaten, and destroy,
But they cannot make it rain.

The sun shines and the rains come
On good and evil people alike.
And God wills life to go on.

Reality is life in the presence of God:
His love is real,
His gift of faith is real.

By the Power of the Holy Spirit

Life once again is a new creation:
God speaks and life is serene.
Entrenched traditions are no more,
Doctrines and dogmas sound full retreat,
Myth and legend depart the scene.
We are free in the Spirit.
We are free in the glory of God.

By the power of the Holy Spirit,
We are God's light of life and truth!
By the power of the Holy Spirit,
The Word of God is our Crown of Life!
On the righteousness of God alone,
We are free in the Spirit.
We are free indeed!

293

The Call

Do you want to be a healer of mankind?
Then heed the call of God,
And answer him with certainty:
"Here I am, LORD,
Use me in your work."

I am prepared, my LORD,
To help you bear the agony and pain
When a selfish world denies you,
And when your people suffer needlessly,
Through lack of vision, faith, and hope.

And God replies: "The world but loves its own.
Into this world I let you be born,
But you are not alone.
Child of God, I am your Father.
I let you be whatever you want to be."

Thus says the LORD:
"You are my servant, I so declare.
Wait! There is more:
You are my friend; I will not let you go alone.
You speak the word and I will do the healing."

Faith in Action

God blesses the faithful with faith,
And our lives are blessings to others.
God blesses the faithful with courage,
And we tell the world about hope and love.

Our faith is trust in God,
And we make the world a better place.
By the power of the Holy Spirit,
We pray for the blessing of faith for all!

Grace

Grace is descending,
And faith is bestowed.
Spirits are mending,
And life is restored.

Thanks be to God
For his love and his care.
Thanks be to God
For the life that we share!

Trust in God

I sing about faith,
I sing about love,
I praise God, for he cares for me.
The melody of life in my heart
Is my trust in God!

In deep distress I cried to God:
"Father, I need you!"
And God rushed to my aid,
His healing hands upon me laid,
And he set my spirit free—and more.

God and Christ made me their home,
And he crowned my life as holy!
What blessed joy,
My God, my Christ, the Holy Spirit
Is God in my heart!

True Happiness

Great is your righteousness, LORD:
But greater is my need.
LORD, on your mercy seat,
Bless as I plead.

Bless me with your presence, LORD:
It is all I'll ever need.
Bless us with your presence, LORD:
It is all we'll ever need.

Stress

Stress lurks for victims,
Only faith and hope can shield us.
Faith has the power to heal,
And where hope is, stress is no more.

Hope laughs at stress,
And stress flees the scene.
God laughs with us,
For hope is of God and so is laughter.

We speak the Word,
And stress is no more.
Great is the victory,
For stress fears the Word of God.

God is With Us

We are one with Christ,
Christ lives in us!
Christ is our salvation,
We are his light in the world!
By the power of the Holy Spirit,
God says:
"You are my child!"

Wholeness of Life

God loves the pure in heart:
He speaks to us face to face.
God loves the poor in spirit:
He shares Heaven with us.
God loves people:
He calls us his children,
And he blesses us for holiness.

Christ is our life.
With contrite hearts,
And humble spirits
We praise God:
"Hallowed by thy name!
Thy Kingdom come;
Thy Will be done!"

Miracles

"Ask and you shall receive."
We ask in faith,
And we wait in hope.
Faith is of God and so is hope.
God will provide, for we are his.

When in distress,
God answers our prayers.
Our prayers prompt miracles:
God speaks, and life quickens.
His Word is all we need!

We ask for little things,
And God provides in big ways.
He frees us from anxiety,
And our life improves with each breath of God.
God loves us more and more with each miracle.

God cares for us,
And miracles are his ways of love.
The Holy Spirit sustains us,
And faith grows more and more.
God wants us perfect, as he is perfect!

Family

We are children of God!
He inspires us to speak his Word,
And do his work in the world.
God assures us that we are never alone:
"I am your faith, and your hope, and I love you!"

We are his sons and daughters,
We are brothers and sisters,
We are parents and grandparents.
We all belong to God,
Our Heavenly Father is Father of us all!

We share his life,
We share his love,
We are his happiness!
Our life is full of laughter;
Our Heavenly Father gives us joy!

As God is happy,
We too are happy.
As God helps us,
We help each other.
Our Heavenly Father is Father of us all!

We are strong,
The Word of God is our fortress.
We pray together,
We worship God together,
Our Heavenly Father is Father of us all!

As we care for each other,
God cares for us.

As we laugh together,
God laughs with us.
In the end God affirms: "All is well!"

Bridges

We build bridges of peace in the world.
But God transforms the world,
And our bridges are relationships,
Blessed with bonds of love.

God builds bridges
To link Heaven and Earth.
At the rainbow bridge of grace
God welcomes home his faithful pilgrims.

God is Calling for Change

Creation mourns;
The universe suffers the pains of human rebellion!
God says:
"I have given you freedom to care for nature,
To accept the beauty of majestic mountains,
And the teasing of playful ocean waves,
To join their game plan with sun and moon.

"Where are the streams of pristine running water?
They labored so hard to be pure,
As they support life in lakes and seas.
It was I,
I placed them in deep forests and wide-open spaces,
As the habitats for wild creatures,
But also as places of rest for weary souls.

"Behold the birds of the air,
Consider the lilies of the field.
They know how to proclaim my glory.
With all things living they indict human ambition.
Defoliated trees cry out,
And poisoned creatures of land, air, and sea
Witness against the greed of mankind."

Where is this God of creation, justice, and peace?
We must diligently search and find him,
Let us then worship the God who is One.

Thus says the LORD:
"Stop your pretense and cleanse your minds.
For once in your life, look within yourself,
The place where I AM."

Assurance

I look to God in all of my needs;
I know that I can trust him.
Every time my troubled soul pleads,
He makes sure I am secure in his care.

Unity

Praise the Lord. Praise the Lord, people of God.
Nations of the world,
Proclaim the Word:
The Lord is God! The Lord is One.

By water and the Spirit, this union makes us free.
Our message is salvation,
For God in Christ is near.
We are one with the Lord in freedom,
We are one with the Lord in truth.

Rights and obligations define equality.
But Christians live by grace and faith
And work the will of God.
We are one with the Lord in justice,
We are one with the Lord in peace.

Christ is our salvation,
He blesses us with hope and trust.
For this the Church of Christ gives thanks.
We are one with the Lord in the Gospel,
We are one with the Lord through faith.

America

God speaks—let every pilgrim listen:
"America is God's country,
You are diverse as the grains of sand by the sea.
I bless you with faith,
And truth will always be yours."

God speaks—let every pilgrim listen:
"My blessing of faith will keep your diversity precious,
For I will keep you free.
Freedom shall be your national treasure,
And my blessing of faith will always be yours."

Come, Holy Spirit

Come, Holy Spirit into my heart,
And make my soul your home.
All that I am is now your own,
My faith, my hope, my love, my all!

Be my life, O Holy Spirit,
Let my soul be your enduring place.
As I breathe the love of God,
In you I see God's face!

Seeds of Faith

The tiniest seed in all creation,
Faith is God's most powerful gift on Earth.
By the power of the Holy Spirit,
Faith transforms the human spirit,
And energizes the soul for service to God.
Faith is the author of change.

When arrogance in her pride scorns faith,
God draws unto himself people of faith.
By the power of the Holy Spirit,
He gathers his children in need,
And he showers on them blessings of love.
Faith is the foundation of spiritual life.

God says, "Look at the birds of the air.
Consider the lilies of the field, how they grow;
They neither toil nor spin but live in my glory.
Put your trust in me and I will care for you.
Do not be anxious about tomorrow."
Faith is the crown of spiritual character.

God speaks, and by the power of faith,
Great things suddenly happen.
The once tiny but invincible seeds of faith
Are shelter, hope, and assurance for all
Who live in the presence of God.
Faith is eternal power at work in the world.

Sunday

Each day God puts up with me,
Each seventh day I go to his house.
I praise God, I listen, and I pray:
"Thank you, Father,
For sharing your life with me!"

Faith and Reason

Faith without reason is helpless,
Reason without faith is hopeless.

Melody of Life

We are one with the Lord in the Spirit,
We are one with the Lord in truth.

We are one with the Lord in freedom,
We are one with the Lord in love.

We are one with the Lord in justice,
We are one with the Lord in peace.

We are one with the Lord in the Gospel,
We are one with the Lord through faith!

A Ceaseless Prayer

Welcome home, my Heavenly Father!
Welcome home, Lord Jesus Christ!
Welcome home, God's Holy Spirit!
Welcome home, welcome home,
Welcome home into my heart!

Quality of Life

I pray for faith,
I pray for hope,
I pray for love:
My trust is God.

God is my life,
God is my liberty,
God is my happiness:
My trust is God.

God says:
"You are my friend,
I'll never leave you!"
God is my Quality of Life.

A Hobo With Class

There was a hobo,
Walking the breakdown lane on I-495 North.
His pace was very slow.
The trimmings were all in place:
The dilapidated hat drooped over his forehead,
The torn jacket was neatly buttoned,
Two bright eyes
Peaked through the soot of a dirty face.

The man could easily pass
As a character come to life
Out of a classical novel.
He would qualify as the central theme
In a Currier and Ives landscape.
He was a hobo with class.

His shoes did not look comfortable,
Though the man walked a steady gait.
Carrying his worldly possessions
In a tiny sack tied to a stick,
All his wealth dangled over his left shoulder.

The morning commuter traffic passed him.
The majority of drivers were breaking the law,
Driving over seventy-five miles per hour,
With an Interstate speed limit of sixty-five.
These upright citizens are America's work force,
Trying hard to earn a living.
They are caught in deadly rat races to outdo each other,
Though evil competition only proves human folly.

Who in this contrast is the fool?
Is it the hobo or the neatly dressed driver breaking the law?
Alas, behind the façade of proper business attire
Are calculating minds
Scheming to outsmart their fellow men,
And win the competition in an economy in decline.
The faces of success drivers hustling to work show stress,
The hobo is at peace.

My soul was troubled that morning,
Not about speeding and breaking the law.
My concern was attitudes in the workplace:
Is my contribution to a ruthless society—
Where the drive to succeed at any cost is the rule—
Making hobos out of meek and innocent people?
Was the hobo with class on I-495 North Jesus Christ?

Paradise

We greet the sunrise,
And God says: "Good morning!"
We smile at the other person,
And our happiness is now complete.
We say "goodbye" to friends at eventide,
Yet God never leaves us, for we live in paradise.

Paradise on Earth is good and beautiful!
The little things in our life make God happy,
And God is blessing us more and more to love him!
The presence of God is assurance,
And spiritual fulfillment is Quality of Life:
God is our life!

The Serene Expanse

Everybody owns a serene expanse!
It is our gift from God for peace and tranquility.
Peace and tranquility are important as life itself;
They are essential for a healthy body, mind, and spirit.
The serene expanse serves as a refuge for spiritual renewal.
Against the stress and pressures of an uncertain world,
God is overly generous with gifts of the serene expanse.

Every person needs shelter for sorting out issues and facts:
Oceans, lakes, mountains—nature caters to human needs.
Oftentimes nature is our friend at the fish hole:
Nature is a mighty fortress for reflective meditations.
All people are offered this haven of security,
It is our birthplace of oneness with God.
The serene expanse is a birthright!

Places of beauty on Earth qualify as the serene expanse,
The Marginal Way and the rocky coast of Maine are among them.
Here the God of creation, evolution, creed, and enlightenment found me.
Centuries of human wisdom and controversy melted before my eyes:
I came to realize that strength is in diversity and tolerance.
The background of ocean and sky
Was the majestic splendor in this moment of truth.

I saw God in the ocean, the moonlight, and the coastline.
I saw God in the faces of pilgrims walking the Marginal Way.
But I also witnessed how God on stormy days
Was mercilessly pounding the coast:
Violent waters are brutally dissolving the earth,
And boulders are Ping Pong balls in the hands of the Almighty.
In this panorama of revelation and truth the beautiful prospers.

The Marginal Way provides more than an experience in time:
This earthly replica of a perfect form in Heaven
Is a unique environment for inspiration.
I witnessed the moon—in naked splendor—
Accept the invitation of teasing waves for a swim.
Then in its reflected light the moon naughtily dared
Steal kisses from virgin ocean waves.

Praise God for the security of the serene expanse!
Thank God for the beauty of the rocky coast of Maine!
Thank God for all his earthly sanctums sanctorum:
Where God inspires the faithful with faith,
Where grace and truth are divine revelations,
Where life, liberty, and happiness are spiritual freedoms.
At the serene expanse God meets his pilgrims face to face.

Eternal Value

No other person can chart the destiny
Of son, daughter, brother, sister, friend, or stranger.
Each soul is responsible and accountable
For all actions and reaction in life.

God says:
"I want you!
Not your good works or accomplishments,
I want you as a person."

In the domain of eternal values on Earth,
The Peace of God is supreme.
The Holy Spirit is authority and guide,
And Jesus Christ prevails when all else fails.

311

Freedom of the Press

"You will know the truth,
And the truth will make you free."
These eloquent words of promise are eternal truth:
The Word of God exceeds all conventional wisdom.

The Word of God is a portrait of a righteous God;
He inspires visions abundant with faith, hope, and love.
The scene is the mature state in individuals and nations
Where truth prevails as light over darkness and evil.

Truth is God's lens for a righteous world,
Truth is robust and always will be.
God is championing his faithful people:
"Know that I am God and live by truth!"

Journalism is a powerful force for truth.
But when journalism is interpreted reality
Then people and nations must arm for war
And fight for truth in the freedom of the press.

Freedom of the press has many privileges
And will yield great honors in proper use.
Evil enters in when editors select news solely
To control the people they are expected to serve.

Journalism is truth in black and white!
Truth speaks for itself.
Truth dictates content, substance, and style.
Truth stands tall when the going is rough.

My Tribute To God

Dear God and Father:
"Hallowed be your name.
Your kingdom come,
Your will be done."

I rejoice in your sunshine, Lord.
I love the cloudless blue sky at high noon.
I thank you for giving me joy and laughter.
I praise you, my Lord and my God!

A Silly Numbers Game

Pythagoras proposed in the sixth century B.C.
That numbers are ultimate reality.
In the 1960s America's MBAs started a campaign—
With no signs of compassion—
The Bottom Line, The Bottom Line,
The Bottom Line is the Bottom Line.

There is more to life than numbers.
Visions among creative people are myriad,
And dreams are far beyond the limits of numbers.
The advances of civilization are great in substance,
And the ones with value defined
Are really not worthy of consideration.

A lifetime of seventy years—more or less—
Is pointing to the uncertainty of numbers.
The belief in numbers is false prophecy;
It has enslaved the greatest nation on Earth.
In the years of America's darkness in the last forty years,
Wealth is eroding and plastic has replaced gold.

The Bottom Line Experts went into the bottomless pit
To complete the conversion,
And new slogans and acronyms came into being.
America shifted gears from personal commitment—
Loyalty, hard work, quality, and the desire to excel—
Now lifeless numbers rule commerce and industry.

Gone are the personal involvements and the thank you.
Appreciation in the workplace is rules and regulations,
All are based on the Bottom Line.
To show improvements in profits,

Senior positions are being cut.
There is no regard for continuity and the future.

Lifeless numbers of a Bottom Line are not creative.
Grapes are not gathered from thorns,
And figs cannot be gotten from thistles.
Likewise visions need hope,
And future plans need dreams.
Continuity in the workplace needs hopes and dreams.

Puppy

Puppies are little furry balls overflowing with love.
You came to us as a bouncy ball of fur,
You were barely eight weeks old.
There you stood.
You were a pilgrim in the wide-open unknown.

With haste you started your mission,
Giving lessons about love by way of puppy love.
You were full of love,
And your tongue went a mile a minute,
Sending your love from person to person.

Your big brown eyes were spilling a beautiful story of love:
"Accept my love but also accept me,
Be part of my pilgrimage and my mission."
Life has not been the same at the house—
Puppies surely have ways to deliver the love of God with love.

These words are in tribute to your mission and work:
We can say only good things about you.
We watched you grow and are truly amazed:
It took but a year to transform a furry bundle of love,
And soon you were a gracious German Shepherd lady.

You are smart and cute.
Your posture and those pointed ears alone afford protection.
Taking nothing for granted,
You leap with joy
For even the smallest happiness that comes your way.

You molded a family around you,
You are cheerful without reservation.

You wait impatiently for the door to open,
You want to make sure that everyone is safely home.
Your name is Cyna, and you are family.

Rays of Hope and Freedom

My life was in chaos.
Darkness clouded my senses,
My heart trembled in fear.

I prayed to God:
"Father, help me!"
And God transformed my life.

The world is still the same.
But I am now secure:
Christ is my Savior!

His love fills my heart,
His faith is my faith.
Rays of hope now light up my soul.

Rays of hope and freedom
Show me the way to God,
And where Christ lives I too will live!

A National Prayer

Dear God and Father:

Jesus commanded us to pray in his name. Let your Holy Spirit guide us in everything you want done. Help us with confession and commitment, strengthen our faith and keep us united.

You have made us a nation of peers, rich in resources, and overflowing with talent. We decided to change all that.

And now many unresolved ills are tearing us apart, straining the social fabric. We have acted willfully and tarnished our opportunities to excel in service to you. At times we are even harsh toward ourselves. You have given us humanity, yet we manage to treat family and strangers less than humanely.

While you expect of us faithfulness and obedience to your will and the purpose of our creation, we have been busily building our own empires in a society of institutions. On these we depend to take care of us.

We have exchanged the attributes of equality for all human beings—individual rights and personal obligations—in favor of a system of collective agents in our institutions. They are no substitutes, even though we believed these to be better qualified to handle our relationship with you and the relationships with one another.

We let ourselves become saturated with information based on the bottom line of selling papers and air time, and we have neglected searching and listening to your Word.

We have become complacent when financial opportunists deal away our economic independence.

We export manufacturing and import investments. We do nothing to prevent the prospects of our children from becoming servants of foreign masters in their own land.

We have relegated trust in you to a meaningless imprint on

money, but as money decays, so will we, unless we change and return to you.

These are crucial times. We cry out to you to awaken a slumbering giant. Renew our spirit and help us to seek the only peace of value, your peace, where the human spirit is at peace with you and one another in a world of uncharted space to allow for the expansion of tolerance, compassion, and the blessing of your promise to take care of us.

O LORD, our God, act with haste and save us. Be once again our refuge and strength, for you are our God, and we are your people. Prepare for us your way to transform challenges into opportunities so that toward the end your name will be glorified in a new era in America, the Era of Faith.

In Jesus' name we pray: Your kingdom come. Your will be done. Amen.

Index to Scripture Passages

Genesis

2:24	157
4:3-8	200

Exodus

15:2,6,12	267
15:15	267
19:5-6	181
20:2	185
20:3	185

Leviticus

19:17-18	253

Numbers

25:1-3	268

Deuteronomy

30:19-20	178, 270

1 Samuel

10:1	257
13:13-14	258
15:22-23	259
15:3	258
15:9	258

2 Samuel

12:13	260

2 Kings

3:26-27	267

Job

12:13	110
13:4-12	232
38:4-7	231
42:5	xii

Psalms

25:4-5	177
40:8	212
46:1-3	212
46:8-10	212
81:8-14	185
81:10	185
81:12	186
81:13	187
91:7-8	271
106:13	173
107:1	182
119:11	178
119:34	177
119:105	177
127:1-2	182
145:18	58

Proverbs

16:9	233

Isaiah

11:2-5	38
16:6	266
57:14-15	232
61:8	233

Jeremiah

7:5-7	120
9:23-24	247
31:31-34	39
48:29-30, 35	266
48:30	254
48:38-39	267

Amos

5:24	233

Micah

6:8	232, 244, 281

Matthew

5:14	7
3:7	55
5:14-16	187, 251
5:16	xii, 20, 161, 176, 201, 237
5:48	134
6:3-4	109
7:12	120
7:15-20	69
7:21-23	217
10:34	255

Index to Scripture Passages

11:4-5 119
11:19 235
13:22 173
16:26 180
18:3-4 120
18:5-6 163
18:7 163
19:4-6 158
22:37 .... 177, 244
22:39 .... 177, 244
23:11-12 232
28:18 273
28:19-20 151
28:20 29,
48,119, 242,
269, 273

Mark

1:15 112
7:21 29
10:15 16
10:17-31 286

Luke

4:18 67
8:21 161
9:35 12
9:51-56 261
9:62 204
10:3-5, 9 114
10:10-12 114
10:20 114
12:15 169
15:20 72
16:13 259

John

1:1-4 186
1:1-5 3
1:6 184
1:9-11 186
1:10-13 102
1:11-13 37
1:12-13 6
1:14 .... 76, 102
1:39 xi

3:8 134
3:16 111
4:24 .... xi, 61,
135
6:63 82
8:12 187
8:31 112
8:31-32 .... 116, 218
8:58 .... 11, 31
9:39 .... 175, 283
9:4-5 176
9:5 186
10:14-15 269
14:6 .... 37, 58,77
14:12-14 95
14:13 73
14:15 73
14:15-17 99
14:16-17 73,
96,218
14:17 210
14:18-20 103
14:20 83
14:21 .... xxxi, 103,
237
14:23 .... 83, 103
14:24 .... 58, 101
14:26 .... 47, 95
14:26-27 95
14:27 .... 211, 255
15:16 109
15:26-27 77
16:13 .... 78, 211
16:13-14 167
16:13-15 .... 99, 266
16:14 82
16:14-15 211
16:7 167
17:13 229
17:15 229

Acts

1:5 94
9:20 49
13:9 49

Romans

1:18-19 186

Index to Scripture Passages

1:28 258
5:1-5 94
7:15, 24-25 180
7:19-20 184
8:26-27 63
8:31 .... 241, 269
8:35-37 269
11:33-36 211
12:4-8 150

1 Corinthians
12:3 48
12:4-7 183

Galatians
5:22 29
5:22-23 101
5:25 101

Ephesians
5:21 158
6:17 212

1 Timothy
6:10-16 169

2 Timothy
4:3-4 252

Titus
2:14 182
3:5-7 182

Hebrews
4:11-13 79
4:12 212
12:22-24 257

Revelation
2:10 270

Subject Index

Abel .... xxxi, 65,
200, 201, 256, 257

Abraham 9, 11, 13, 31, 32, 3
3, 34 35, 36, 37, 53, 54, 56, 58, 67,
113, 115, 131, 149, 155, 187,
222, 244, 280

Abundant life 44, 83, 84, 112,
131, 139, 289, 292

Act(s) of God .... xxxii, 1, 3, 55, 124,
128, 132

America .... xxxi, 32, 45, 68,
75, 144, 149, 150, 153, 155, 170, 188,
189, 193, 194, 198, 205, 206, 208, 209,
214, 221, 222, 223, 224, 225, 226, 228,
229, 230, 231, 232, 233, 238,
241, 304, 314, 319

Aspiration(s) .... xxxi, xxxiii, 13, 42,
70, 79, 82, 138, 139, 140, 200, 235,
237, 284

Attitude(s) .... xvii, xxxv, 12, 15,
23, 25, 53, 54, 62, 64, 68, 69, 73, 78,
80, 95, 105, 109, 112, 113, 117, 120,
121, 122, 123, 143, 148, 149, 162, 171,
174, 182, 184, 213, 219, 224, 225, 234,
241, 243, 263, 266, 277, 278, 279, 280,
309

Behavior .... xi, xvii, xxxi, xxxv,
12, 15, 21, 24, 25, 49, 53, 54, 62, 66,
67, 68, 73, 78, 80, 81, 105, 113, 114,
117, 121, 122, 123, 130, 133, 162, 171,
173, 174, 182, 184, 185, 190, 213, 219,
224, 233, 234, 241, 243, 244, 246, 247,
248, 262, 264, 278, 279, 280, 282, 286,
287

Bible .... xxxiii, 46, 111, 114,
127, 130, 191, 246, 253,
260, 275, 283

Bridges .... xxxvi, 12, 77, 78,
83, 105, 121, 142, 191, 219,
235, 278, 301

By the power of the
Holy Spirit .... iii, xi, xii, xv, xvii,
xxix, xxxi, xxxiv, xxxvi, 1, 2, 3, 12, 15,
17, 18, 25, 27, 28, 38, 39, 40, 41, 42,
43, 45, 46, 47, 50, 51, 56, 57, 58, 59,
62, 63, 64, 66, 68, 69, 70, 71, 72, 76,
77, 80, 81, 82, 83, 84, 90, 91, 94, 95,
96, 98, 100, 101, 102, 103, 104, 105,
108, 109, 111, 116, 117, 121, 123, 125,
128, 134, 137, 138, 150, 151, 154, 191,
200, 222, 224, 227, 236, 276, 278, 280,
281, 289, 291, 293, 295, 297, 305

Cain .... xxxi, 65, 199, 200, 201,
202, 256

Change(s) .... xiii, xvii, xxxv, 2, 10,
14, 15, 21, 25, 26, 43, 53, 54, 55, 56,
67, 68, 70, 80, 81, 110, 112, 113, 119,
120, 121, 122, 123, 124, 132, 134, 135,
137, 138, 139, 142, 145, 191, 196, 201,
208, 212, 213, 219, 224, 232, 233, 234,
241, 250, 275, 276, 278, 279, 280, 282,
283, 286, 287, 302, 305, 318, 319

Chief Doctrine of
Christianity .... xxxi, 103, 227, 237

Child-like trust 14, 16, 18, 238

Christian Covenant of
Love .... xxxii, 12, 13, 16,
17, 18, 19, 28, 35, 38, 40, 41, 49, 50,
56, 58, 89, 93, 94, 104, 108, 114, 116,
123, 129, 133, 134, 149, 227, 238, 289

Copernicus 115

Covenant(s) .... xvii, xxxii, 10, 11,
12, 13, 16, 17, 18, 19, 28, 31, 35, 36,
36, 38, 39, 40, 41, 49, 50, 55, 56, 88,
89, 90, 93, 94, 104, 108, 114, 116, 123,

Subject Index

129, 133, 134, 149, 181, 227, 238, 256, 257, 289

Cross............15, 57, 83, 90, 97, 105, 167, 176, 187, 255, 275

Day of judgment............133, 203, 254, 255

Divine calls............35, 106

Divine command............244

Doctrine(s)............xxxi, xxxii, 16, 70, 103, 104, 152, 160, 227, 237, 243, 263, 293

Drug abuse............125, 215, 227, 242, 243, 279

Easter message............124

Economics............xxxiii, 66, 127, 157, 188, 189, 190, 191, 193, 194, 195, 196, 197, 198, 199, 200, 201, 203, 205, 206, 207, 209, 264

Education............3, 118, 132, 157, 210, 211, 212, 213, 214, 215, 246

Environment............xxxv, xxxvii, 20, 23, 83, 115, 117, 118, 126, 136, 145, 147, 159, 162, 171, 172, 190, 215, 216, 218, 219, 261, 275, 311

Era of Faith............xi, xii, xv, xvii, xviii, xix, xxix, xxxii, 3, 19, 20, 21, 22, 23, 24, 25, 26, 27, 28, 30, 45, 59, 61, 62, 68, 70, 84, 93, 94, 96, 98, 119, 121, 122, 125, 126, 127, 128, 129, 131, 132, 133, 134, 144, 151, 155, 196, 214, 216, 222, 225, 227, 238, 242, 282, 289, 291, 319

Essence of life............7, 19, 77, 96, 112, 243

Eternal life............19, 46, 58, 81, 89,

103, 111, 124, 125, 130, 148, 169, 173, 176, 180, 181, 182, 190, 204, 285, 286

Eternity............xxxii, 3, 50, 51, 68, 86, 104, 117, 119, 129, 139, 174, 176, 181, 195, 203, 232, 238, 270, 284, 286, 289

Faith............iii, xi, xii, xv, xvii, xviii, xix, xxxiii, xxxv, xxxvi, 1, 2, 3, 8, 9, 13, 16, 17, 18, 19, 20, 21, 22, 23, 24, 25, 26, 27, 28, 29, 30, 31, 32, 33, 34, 35, 36, 37, 39, 40, 41, 42, 43, 44, 45, 46, 48, 49, 50, 51, 53, 54, 55, 56, 57, 58, 61, 62, 64, 65, 66, 67, 68, 70, 71, 72, 73, 76, 77, 78, 80, 83, 84, 87, 88, 90, 91, 92, 93, 94, 96, 97, 98, 101, 102, 103, 104, 105, 106, 108, 109, 111, 113, 115, 117, 118, 119, 120, 121, 122, 123, 124, 125, 126, 127, 128, 129, 132, 133, 134, 135, 136, 137, 141, 143, 144, 147, 148, 149, 150, 151, 152, 154, 155, 157, 158, 159, 160, 163, 164, 168, 169, 170, 171, 173, 174, 176, 181, 183, 187, 195, 196, 197, 208, 210, 211, 212, 214, 215, 216, 218, 219, 221, 222, 225, 227, 228, 229, 235, 236, 237, 238, 240, 241, 242, 248, 251, 257, 261, 262, 263, 264, 270, 271, 272, 279, 280, 282, 287, 289, 291, 293, 294, 295, 296, 297, 299, 300, 303, 304, 305, 306, 307, 311, 312, 317, 318, 319

Faith trees............44

Faithfulness............11, 20, 29, 38, 61, 64, 70, 101, 111, 112, 115, 121, 122, 127, 131, 160, 166, 178, 179, 181, 185, 190, 244, 246, 248, 257, 258, 259, 260, 268, 269, 270, 271, 280, 318

Family............xviii, xix, xxxi, xxxv, xxxvii, 3, 8, 9, 18, 22, 27, 28, 32, 33, 35, 37, 65, 66, 81, 84, 85, 87, 88, 92, 104, 110, 112, 113, 125, 127, 132, 140, 147, 148, 153, 154, 155, 157,

Subject Index

158, 159, 160, 161, 162, 163, 164, 165, 166, 167, 168, 169, 170, 171, 172, 173, 174, 175, 176, 177, 180, 188, 191, 192, 201, 202, 205, 208, 209, 217, 218, 219, 229, 237, 238, 300, 316, 317, 318

Freedom ———— v, xxx, 20, 38, 40, 62, 66, 75, 77, 83, 84, 89, 94, 101, 102, 109, 113, 123, 130, 137, 138, 140, 143, 144, 152, 161, 180, 189, 192, 229, 241, 242, 247, 264, 270, 276, 286, 302, 303, 304, 306, 312, 317

Friend(s) ———— xv, xviii, xxxi, xxxiv, xxxv, xxxvi, xxxvii, 1, 2, 3, 12, 15, 45, 53, 60, 62, 63, 65, 70, 72, 79, 89, 93, 99, 100, 101, 103, 106, 107, 109, 110, 112, 113, 118, 119, 121, 143, 166, 188, 200, 201, 202, 208, 217, 218, 219, 228, 229, 230, 231, 233, 234, 235, 282, 283, 284, 285, 291, 292, 293, 294, 295, 307, 309, 310, 311

From/to method for
spiritual fulfillment ——— 61, 123, 132, 135, 136, 137, 145

Goal(s) ———— xi, xxxi, xxxiv, 29, 32, 52, 53, 67, 84, 86, 90, 97, 105, 107, 110, 111, 115, 118, 131, 133, 135, 139, 140, 141, 149, 152, 161, 178, 181, 225, 229, 235, 241, 284

God's Plan ———— xi, 6, 21, 27, 84, 117, 153, 158, 159, 182, 214, 228, 236, 248, 252, 263, 264

God's Will ———— 20, 27, 100, 210, 257, 261, 263, 265

Golden Rule ———— 45, 120, 130, 1 90, 195

Gospel ———— 4, 5, 6, 7, 14, 15, 17, 25, 35, 37, 47, 49, 50, 54, 55, 57, 72, 77, 84, 87, 98, 104,

105, 106, 107, 109, 110, 112, 113, 114, 115, 121, 122, 128, 133, 138, 150, 151, 154, 158, 159, 164, 181, 183, 186, 201, 204, 241, 245, 251, 256, 261, 262, 263, 269, 284, 286, 291, 303, 306

Grace ———— xii, xxix, xxxiv, 1, 6, 11, 13, 14, 19, 24, 25, 27, 28, 29, 30, 46, 48, 49, 50, 68, 70, 76, 90, 91, 93, 97, 98, 100, 102, 106, 109, 110, 113, 117, 118, 121, 126, 127, 136, 140, 150, 157, 158, 161, 167, 168, 173, 174, 179, 182, 183, 186, 194, 201, 202, 203, 204, 210, 212, 223, 235, 242, 248, 250, 251, 252, 256, 257, 263, 264, 269, 276, 284, 295, 301, 303, 311

Great
Commandments ———— xxxii, xxxvi, 104, 129, 270

Harmony ———— xxxiv, xxxvi, xxxvii, 17, 21, 41, 42, 76, 80, 81, 88, 110, 111, 117, 121, 122, 125, 132, 135, 137, 139, 141, 149, 150, 153, 155, 157, 158, 172, 203, 225, 234, 248, 255, 287

Heaven ———— xi, xii, xxxiii, 2, 6, 8, 10, 12, 18, 19, 20, 24, 41, 46, 57, 64, 72, 87, 89, 90, 96, 100, 103, 112, 114, 120, 123, 130, 132, 136, 139, 148, 151, 160, 161, 176, 178, 186, 187, 190, 201, 202, 204, 216, 234, 237, 251, 256, 261, 270, 273, 284, 285, 286, 287, 289, 298, 301, 311

High Road of God's
Righteousness ———— 118, 121, 282, 284

Holy Spirit ———— iii, xi, xii, xv, xvii, xix, 1, 2, 3, 4, 7, 11, 12, 15, 16, 17, 18, 19, 25, 27, 28, 32, 37, 38, 39, 40, 41, 42, 43, 44, 45, 46, 47, 48, 49, 50, 51, 54, 56, 57, 58, 59, 61,

Subject Index

62, 63, 64, 66, 68, 69, 70, 71, 72, 73,
74, 76, 77, 78, 79, 80, 81, 82, 83, 84,
85, 86, 87, 88, 89, 90, 91, 92, 93, 94,
95, 96, 97, 98, 99, 100, 101, 102, 103,
104, 105, 108, 109, 110, 111, 116, 117,
121, 122, 123, 124, 125, 128, 134, 135,
137, 138, 141, 150, 151, 154, 164, 167,
168, 175, 177, 180, 182, 183, 191, 200,
210, 211, 215, 218, 219, 222, 224, 225,
227, 230, 231, 233, 236, 241, 246, 251,
262, 263, 265, 269, 275, 276, 278, 279,
280, 281, 282, 283, 284, 289, 291, 293,
295, 296, 297, 299, 304, 305, 307, 311,
318

Hope(s) .... iii, xi, xii, xv, xviii,
xix, xxx, xxxi, xxxii, xxxiii,
xxxvi, 2, 8, 13, 14, 19, 25, 26, 27, 32,
37, 44, 47, 50, 57, 66, 70, 83, 84, 87,
91, 93, 94, 95, 96, 97, 98, 99, 100, 103,
106, 107, 110, 112, 113, 114, 117, 118,
119, 121, 122, 123, 128, 129, 132, 144,
147, 148, 149, 150, 151, 154, 155, 157,
162, 170, 171, 179, 182, 185, 186, 190,
191, 192, 202, 203, 204, 209, 213, 216,
221, 222, 225, 228, 240, 241, 242, 245,
249, 251, 256, 261, 262, 266, 269, 278,
279, 281, 283, 286, 289, 294, 295, 296,
297, 299, 300, 303, 304, 305, 307, 310,
312, 315, 317

Human nature 24, 64, 75, 88,
96, 123, 129, 131, 160,
174, 179, 180, 184, 217, 254, 260, 266,
268, 270, 271, 272

Humanity .... xii, xix, xxxii, xxxiii,
xxxvi, xxxvii, 4, 8, 18,
22, 28, 35, 37, 113, 115, 126, 127, 129,
140, 147, 148, 149, 155, 182, 185, 186,
188, 200, 229, 256, 257, 318

I.D. Crisis .... xii, xix, xxxii, xxxiii, xxxvi,
xxxvii, 157, 171, 188, 210,
216, 227, 243, 247, 252

Image of God .... xxxii, 78, 80, 93,
129, 141, 149, 1
88, 248, 280

In God we trust 144

Inspiration(s) .... xxxiii, xxxiv, 13, 43,
49, 62, 64, 83, 88, 95,
113, 138, 139, 140, 144, 227, 229, 235,
236, 237, 262, 279, 284, 289, 287, 311

Judgment(s) 29, 74, 75, 88, 132,
133, 175, 176, 180, 186,
203, 211, 247, 254, 255, 256, 257, 258,
259, 266, 267

Justice .... v, xxxi, xxxii, xxxvi,
xxxvii, 15, 23, 67, 69, 84,
110, 116, 120, 122, 127, 129, 133, 137,
153, 154, 179, 189, 195, 197, 198, 220,
224, 225, 232, 233, 244, 247, 253, 281,
282, 302, 303, 306

Kingdom of God 16, 20, 30,
63, 68, 83, 105, 107,
112, 114, 115, 116, 122, 123, 135, 152,
158, 159, 179, 180, 181, 189, 202, 204,
222, 234, 237, 243, 244, 246, 247, 259,
262, 277, 285

Knowledge .... xxxiv, xxxvi, 2, 4,
37, 38, 49, 74, 76,
78, 127, 130, 135, 136, 137, 145, 168,
179, 185, 197, 200, 201, 202, 210, 211,
212, 213, 214, 231, 238, 257

Love .... iii, ix, xi, xii, xv,
xvii, xxxi, xxxii, xxxv,
xxxvi, 1, 2, 3, 5, 6, 7, 8, 9, 10, 12,
13, 14, 15, 16, 17, 18, 19, 22, 24, 25,
26, 27, 28, 29, 34, 35, 37, 38, 40, 41,
42, 44, 45, 46, 49, 50, 53, 56, 57, 58,
64, 66, 68, 69, 71, 72, 73, 82, 83, 84,
87, 88, 89, 90, 92, 93, 94, 98, 99, 100,
101, 103, 104, 105, 108, 113, 114, 116,
117, 120, 123, 126, 128, 129, 130, 132,

Subject Index

133, 134, 135, 140, 141, 147, 148, 149, 150, 153, 154, 155, 157, 158, 159, 162, 165, 166, 167, 168, 169, 170, 171, 174, 176, 177, 182, 183, 188, 190, 193, 202, 216, 219, 221, 222, 224, 227, 230, 232, 233, 235, 237, 238, 240, 242, 244, 245, 247, 253, 255, 259, 260, 263, 269, 272, 279, 281, 282, 289, 291, 295, 296, 299, 300, 301, 304, 305, 306, 307, 309, 312, 313, 316, 317

Mind ———————— xxxi, xxxvii, 1, 43, 4 4, 63, 68, 72, 75, 76, 80, 88, 112, 123, 127, 136, 138, 140, 143, 168, 177, 180, 182, 184, 203, 211, 212, 213, 215, 224, 225, 233, 236, 237, 240, 244, 245, 251, 252, 258, 260, 262, 277, 279, 286, 310

Miracle(s) ———————— xxix, 1, 8, 14, 71, 81, 97, 113, 136, 154, 175, 275, 280, 282, 299

Model of the
Godly Life ———————15, 24, 55, 61, 62, 96, 108, 115, 160, 163, 178, 236, 241, 243

Mystery(ies) ———————5, 6, 8, 10, 13, 14, 17, 18, 19, 136

Nature ———————— xiii, xxxiii, xxxv, xxxvi, xxxvii, 1, 2, 6, 16, 19, 21, 22, 23, 24, 28, 31, 40, 61, 66, 75, 80, 88, 95, 96, 109, 117, 123, 126, 129, 131, 139, 160, 174, 179, 180, 184, 217, 218, 229, 230, 236, 248, 254, 258, 260, 266, 271, 272, 281, 289, 302, 310

Obedience ———————— 11, 20, 49, 64, 70, 111, 112, 115, 121, 122, 127, 131, 160, 166, 178, 179, 181, 185, 244, 246, 248, 257, 258, 259, 260, 269, 270, 318

Peace of God ———————xxxiv, 8, 23, 29, 51, 58, 64, 94, 127, 130, 137, 138, 154, 234, 256, 311

Quality of life———————iii, xxix, xxxiii, xxxiv, 82, 86, 115, 124, 138, 139, 190, 193, 195, 198, 199, 208, 213, 225, 234, 235, 247, 275, 278, 280, 281, 282, 307, 309

Reason ———————— xxix, 35, 53, 78, 83, 91, 114, 121, 135, 136, 137, 143, 158, 213, 224, 253, 258, 279, 286, 287, 306

Relationship(s) ———————— xi, xii, xiii, xv, xviii, xxxi, xxxii, xxxiii, xxxiv, xxxv, xxxvi, xxxvii, 7, 8, 9, 10, 11, 12, 18, 29, 34, 35, 37, 38, 40, 42, 43, 44, 45, 56, 57, 58, 62, 63, 69, 70, 71, 72, 73, 75, 88, 93, 94, 100, 101, 103, 104, 107, 112, 116, 121, 122, 123, 124, 128,129, 130, 131, 132, 133, 137, 139, 142, 143, 152, 154, 157, 161, 163, 165, 167, 169, 171, 174, 176, 177, 178, 179, 180, 181, 182, 183, 185,187, 189, 191, 192, 199, 200, 208, 216, 217, 218, 219, 224, 229, 230, 233, 234, 235, 237, 240, 242, 243, 244, 246, 247, 248, 260, 261, 262, 269, 272, 280, 283, 284, 301, 318

Resurrection———————47, 90, 115, 167, 187

Revelation(s)———————2, 4, 6, 11, 13, 16, 20, 22, 28, 37, 42, 43, 53, 57, 58, 61, 62, 78, 79, 138, 139, 177, 211, 227, 246, 270, 310, 311

Righteousness ————————12, 16, 20, 23, 38, 44, 62, 64, 68, 70, 71, 73, 84, 90, 94, 118, 121, 130, 133, 135, 140, 166, 169, 176, 182, 187, 203, 226, 233, 247, 248, 250, 278, 280, 282, 284, 293, 296

Subject Index

Salvation ————— 6, 16, 42, 46, 47,
48, 49, 50, 51, 58, 64,
67, 82, 84, 88, 93, 97, 98, 100, 102,
107, 112, 113, 118, 119, 125, 157, 159,
161, 164, 167, 177, 180, 181, 182, 187,
203, 224, 228, 243, 248, 250, 252, 255,
256, 263, 264, 267, 271, 297, 303

Serene Expanse ———— xxx, 139, 289, 310,
311

Servant of God———— 61, 68, 106, 109,
110, 111, 230, 232,
233, 280

Spiritual character ————— 71, 74, 305

Spiritual connection ———— xi, xxxi, 8,
25, 29, 31, 35, 38, 39,
45, 46, 47, 48, 50, 51, 56, 57, 61, 62,
64, 66, 67, 69, 70, 71, 72, 91, 92, 93,
100, 104, 136, 137, 183, 188, 189, 190,
195, 196, 203, 218, 234, 240, 274, 275,
276

Spiritual freedom———— 77, 94, 101, 138,
152, 229, 242, 276

Spiritual fulfillment——— 20, 39, 61, 66, 70,
100, 119, 123, 132,
135, 136, 137, 139, 141, 143,
145, 178, 230, 241, 242, 309

Spiritual life ————— xii, xv, xxxiii, xxxiv,
8, 19, 38, 40, 41, 64,
72, 79, 80, 87, 118, 137, 149, 152, 219,
235, 236, 276, 283, 289, 305

Spiritual renewal ————45, 86, 280, 310

Sundays——— 62, 85, 86, 87, 88, 92, 141,
170, 208

Trials————45, 48, 127, 164, 167, 230,
271

Trust ————————— xii, xv, xxix, xxxii,
xxxv, xxxvi, xxxvii, 6, 8,
9, 11, 14, 16, 17, 18, 29, 35, 37, 44, 45,
71, 76, 91, 93, 97, 101, 105, 118, 120,
123, 128, 129, 133, 134, 142, 144, 148,
152, 167, 168, 171, 187, 189, 190, 194,
196, 198, 201, 202, 207, 211, 216, 218,
219, 225, 227, 228, 235, 236, 238, 241,
242, 258, 260, 269, 270, 271, 272, 280,
295, 296, 298, 303, 305, 307, 318

Truth————————— v, xi, xii, xiii, xxix,
xxxi, xxxii, xxxiv, 2, 3, 4,
5, 11, 14, 15, 16, 18, 27, 29, 31, 35, 36,
37, 42, 43, 47, 49, 58, 61, 62, 64, 70,
71, 73, 74, 75, 76, 77, 78, 79, 81, 82,
84, 95, 96, 98, 99, 100, 101, 102, 104,
105, 106, 108, 112, 113, 115, 116, 118,
124, 125, 127, 128, 129, 130, 134, 135,
141, 143, 144, 148, 150, 154, 158, 161,
166, 167, 168, 170, 173, 176, 177, 180,
182, 183, 184, 186, 187, 199, 200, 202,
203, 210, 211, 212, 213, 214, 217, 218,
231, 233, 234, 237, 239, 241, 242, 243,
244, 245, 246, 248, 250, 251, 252, 259,
261, 262, 263, 264, 265, 266, 269, 273,
277, 278, 279, 287, 291, 292, 293, 303,
304, 306, 310, 311, 312

Union with God ———— xii, 6, 16, 44, 46,
58, 62, 63, 64, 71,
82, 84, 89, 105, 137, 148

Unity————v, xxix, xxxi, 29, 32, 83, 87,
90, 100, 102, 125, 133,
139, 141, 147, 148, 149, 154, 155, 157,
158, 178, 221, 225, 226, 229, 237, 303

Whole Being ———— xxxiii, xxxvii, 139,
141

Will of God ———— xii, 29, 49, 62, 63,
105, 111, 112, 120, 127,
133, 159, 160, 163, 243, 244, 246, 258,
260, 269, 271, 303

Subject Index

Word of God .... xii, xvii, xxxii, xxxv,
1, 2, 3, 4, 5, 7, 8, 9,
10, 11, 13, 15, 16, 19, 20, 23, 25, 27,
29, 31, 35, 37, 42, 43, 44, 46, 47, 48,
49, 50, 51, 55, 57, 58, 62, 63, 66, 68,
76, 79, 81, 82, 84, 87, 88, 95, 98, 99,
100, 101, 104, 111, 112, 113, 116, 118,
121, 124, 127, 128, 129, 131, 132, 135,
140, 141, 148, 150, 151, 155, 160, 161,
166, 167, 170, 173, 176, 177, 178, 180,
181, 184, 185, 187, 191, 204, 212, 213,
216, 218, 223, 224, 225, 230, 231, 232,
233, 236, 238, 241, 246, 258, 259, 261,
262, 273, 281, 282, 284, 293, 297, 312